Hello, My Name Is Ice Cream

CLARKSON POTTER/PUBLISHERS
NEW YORK

Hello, My Name Is Ice Cream

The Art and Science of the Scoop

DANA CREE

Photographs by
Andrea D'Agosto

Illustrations by
Anna Posey

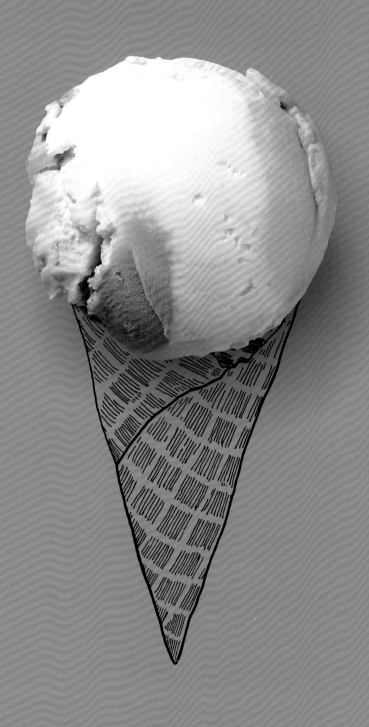

CONTENTS

INTRODUCTION

Like most of you, my relationship with ice cream started so young, there isn't a time I can remember without ice cream. As I grew up, my favorite flavor changed over and over—and at some point I became militant about my ice cream *not* touching my cake—but cold, creamy, lickable scoops of ice cream were always there. When I was an adult and went to pastry school, and I learned how to *make* ice cream, it seemed nothing short of a magic trick.

In the sixteen years since, my career has taken me into fancy restaurants, where I was afforded great room for creativity, advancing both my skills and my catalog of outlandish flavors. (Burnt artichoke ice cream, anyone?) I carried stunning composed desserts into the dining rooms of these restaurants and set them before guests, thrilled to share these unexpected flavors and textures with them. But, at some point, it felt disjointed, pouring my soul into desserts that I could only share with a handful of fortunate folks, in places where often even I couldn't afford to eat.

It was then that ice cream *really* became my favorite thing to make. Ice cream is accessible to everyone, everywhere. Any person I meet, of any age, can tell me what their favorite flavor is, and it almost always brings a smile to their face. Like me, hardly anyone can remember their first bite of ice cream. It's just always been there, sitting next to our birthday cakes, scooped into cones handed to us by our parents, presented at school parties, and served on a weeknight for no reason other than a treat. Here was a dessert I could pour myself into, and share with everyone, because they were already sharing it with each other.

When I moved from my hometown of Seattle to work in Chicago, I started packing pints of my ice cream for sale in a butcher shop called Publican Quality Meats, labeled with brightly colored "Hello My Name Is" stickers. It was then that I had a chance to reconnect with the kinds of ice creams people want to eat as a scoop. I mean, ice cream flavored with masa—the dough you make tortillas from—was delicious as a part of my butterscotch, corn, and cape gooseberry dessert, but you probably wouldn't sit with a big ol' cone of it. So, I jumped back into the world of beloved flavors like salted caramel, and I dove deeper and deeper into the world of add-ins, and started composing scoops of ice creams as I would a dessert—with sauces, chunks, and chewy bits strewn throughout. (You'll find some of these pint-worthy combinations in the "Composed Scoops" chapter.)

When I grew past the "how's" and started asking about the "why's" of ice cream making, I fell into a serious rabbit hole of scientific knowledge that's taken me ten years to hoist myself out of. I wanted to learn why the amount of butterfat in a recipe matters, what various sugars do to the texture, how the speed of churning ice cream makes a difference. I wanted to understand these and a thousand other things so I could know how to make my ice creams smoother or chewier or richer or brighter or more flavorful. I collected as much information as I could from the internet and textbooks, and I had a lot of help from a chef I met when I cooked at The Fat Duck, Chris Young, who co-authored the massive bible of modern cooking, *Modernist Cuisine*. And then I literally went to Ice Cream College, a.k.a. the Penn State Ice Cream Short Course.

By now, I've filled my head with ice cream, as an art and as a science, and I finally feel I can teach what I've learned along the way and help guide others in their ice cream journeys. It goes back to why I started to pack pints in the first place—to share the joy of ice cream with everyone. I hope this book inspires ice cream lovers not only to re-create the recipes I've included here but also to take the knowledge I'm sharing and create whatever your heart—or inner kid—desires.

How to Use This Book

This book is designed for ice cream makers at every level. You can use it to guide you through your first batch of ice cream, to help you understand how to combine the ingredients, and how to use your ice cream machine. If you've already mastered that, you can explore the recipes for different styles of ice creams and discover different ways of flavoring them. When you're ready to mix-and-match, this book is here to help you create scoop-shop-style ice creams of your own design, filled with homemade chunks, ribbons, cookies, and chewy doodads. And finally, if you are ready to really invent, you can use the scientific breakdowns to help you achieve textural and flavor mastery of your own ice creams. It's designed to be what you need, when you need it, and to be there for you as you grow as an ice cream maker. I only wish there were a way for us to share a taste of what you create!

This book is written in three primary sections: "The Knowledge," "The Recipes," and "Composed Scoops."

This is your ice cream hows-and-whys reference manual. In this section you'll find all the information you've ever wanted to know about ice cream, and a few things you probably never imagined you could know, like an in-depth look at the five components of ice cream and their physical properties. You'll meet the agents of texture—ingredients that stabilize water and lock ice into place—and learn when to employ them.

In this section, you'll find recipes for custard ice creams, Philadelphia-style ice creams, sherbets, and frozen yogurts. Each chapter opens with a basic recipe, a blank slate designed for you to adapt to make any flavor you like, and then follow some of my favorite flavors for that style.

You'll notice the ingredient quantities in each ice cream recipe are given in three measurements: percentages, grams, and standard cups and spoons. The percentages represent the working ratio of each recipe (see Appendix, beginning on page 221). Grams are the most precise, and my favorite, way to work. But there was a long period of my ice-cream-making life when I still used a set of measuring cups and spoons, so I've included those, too.

Note that in these recipes, the two styles of measurement are not direct conversions of each other; it didn't make sense to end up with wonky things like "1 cup minus a tablespoon plus a quarter teaspoon." I balanced each recipe within its own discipline—the metric measurements yield 1000 grams (1 liter), and the standard measurements yield 5 cups. The metric measurements also correlate directly to the working ratio (see page 223).

For each recipe, I considered 100 grams | ½ cup equal to 1 part, which makes the 1000 gram | 5 cup yield of each recipe, in turn, 10 parts. If you want the nuanced textures as I designed them, use a scale and measure your ingredients in grams. Otherwise, stick with cups and spoons, which are a little more approximate. The ice cream will be no less delicious, just a touch less perfectly textured. Once churned, the standard measurements will yield a little less than 1½ quarts of ice cream, while the metric measurements will be a little over 1 liter.

This section also includes recipes for add-ins. You'll find traditional ones like caramel ribbons, chocolate chunks, and marshmallows, as well as whimsical ones like a marzipan cake, passion fruit caramel, or cookie butter. Each recipe was designed to be the right texture when frozen, so soft things stay soft in the freezer, and crisp things crackle between your teeth.

Finally, tucked in the back of this book, you'll find a section called "Fruit Purees and Other Recipes." It contains all the information you need to make the exact quantity of fruit purees called for in many of the ice cream, sherbet, and add-in recipes, as well as recipes for homemade Greek yogurt and crème fraîche.

COMPOSED SCOOPS

Here, you'll find some of my favorite composed ice creams, as you'd find in a fancy scoop shop, carefully constructed from the different ice cream and add-in recipes. You'll learn how to "swirl" two or more flavors together, how to layer different add-ins, and, I hope, become inspired to make your own combinations.

In this section you'll discover everything, from the science behind the recipes to the chemistry and physics of how ice cream is made, even how to color your ice creams to match their flavors and why this is so important. With this knowledge, your ice creams will taste better, look brighter, and last longer, and you'll be a wonder to talk to at any ice cream social! Read it through in one sitting, or visit this section as your questions arise, collecting knowledge as you master ice cream making.

THE
KNOWLEDGE

The Five Components of Ice Cream

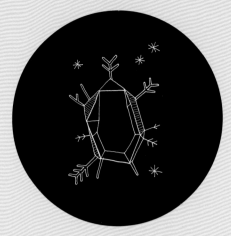

Ice

If I asked you what ice cream is, what would you tell me? It's creamy, cold, sweet, and delicious? Perhaps you'd tell me it's "the best thing on the planet" or simply "ice cream is life." Well, you're right! All these things are true, especially that last one. But what *is* ice cream?

Legally, ice cream is defined by the FDA as a food produced by freezing—while stirring—a pasteurized mix of dairy ingredients, caseinates, and suitable nondairy-derived ingredients. Mmmm, sounds delicious! It goes on to list specific requirements, like a butterfat content of no less than 10% and a total weight of no less than 4.5 pounds per gallon of ice cream.

It all sounds super-technical, but this simply means that for a manufacturer to be able to sell you a product labeled "ice cream," they can't neglect food safety, cheap out on the cream, or whip so much air into the ice cream that the size of the carton is misleading. These are good things! Because you'd be surprised what people will try to do to save a buck. Ever had a McDonald's "vanilla cone" and wonder why it's not listed as an "ice cream cone"? With only around 4% butterfat in the mix, it's not legally considered ice cream.

But this legal definition tells us only what ice cream needs to contain to be *sold* as "ice cream." To get a better idea of what ice cream actually *is*, we have to look at the five components that all come together to *make* ice cream: ice, fat, protein, sugar, and air.

It's called ice cream for a reason: ice makes up a substantial amount of each scoop. Because of this, we are going to talk a lot about it. Before you churn—that is, freeze—your ice cream, know that just under 50% of your ice cream base will be water. You probably won't find water in the list of ingredients, but water slips into your ice cream in the form of milk (87% water) and cream (51% water).

Not All Ice Is Equal

When you spin a fluid ice cream base in your ice cream machine, the temperature drops rapidly and the water begins to turn into ice. The churning motion of the machine's paddle helps break up the ice crystals as they form, making them smaller. Once the semi-frozen ice cream is moved from your ice cream maker to the freezer, where the temperature continues to drop, the ice crystals that have formed during churning become the seeds of larger ice crystals, as more water gathers around each seed and freezes to it. After your ice cream is completely frozen, most of the water will be locked away as ice.

Do you remember the last bite of ice cream you had that was icy? You might remember it being grainy, crunchy, coarse, and generally unpleasant. You could probably hear yourself eating it! Now, imagine a smooth, creamy, velvety ice cream soundlessly melting in your mouth. It would be easy to think the icy ice cream contains more water. Well, maybe, but it's more likely that the two share the *same* amount of water, but with different size ice crystals. The iciness in the icy scoop is called "perceived" iciness, since we can feel large ice crystals, and the process of making ice cream seeks to create small, undetectable ice crystals. To do this, you need to understand a few things about water.

Somewhere in my elementary schooling, I learned that the word *polar* was used to describe more than the ice caps where the big white bears live. *Polarity* refers to a molecule's ability to bond with other molecules like itself, by possessing both a positively charged end and a negatively charged end. We looked at magnets, easily observing the polar ends, and made magnet chains by connecting a positive end to a negative end. We were then taught that water is made up of a million tiny, clear magnets, all with the same desire to pull together. We saw polarity cause water to defy gravity, rising up over the rim of a glass as it was overfilled, and we watched small droplets of water pull together to form larger beads of water.

I'll spare you any more details of my fifth-grade studies (although watching Barbie fly off a toy car to demonstrate inertia was a thrill, and churning butter in a jam jar during Pioneer Days was riveting). But this basic lesson on the polar behavior of water leads directly into this discussion on ice cream and the size of the ice crystals.

Basically, the water in your ice cream wants to pull together, or "coalesce"—really, *really* badly. However, once frozen, the water is stuck in place and its polar ends can no longer join forces and coalesce. Bigger beads of water mean bigger ice crystals. To avoid large, perceivable ice crystals in your ice cream, you have to turn the water into ice before too much of it pulls together.

Making Tiny Crystals

So, how do you make tiny ice crystals in your ice cream? First, by freezing your ice cream base while agitating it. The motion of the paddle in an ice cream maker does two things to the ice: it physically breaks up ice crystals as they form on the edges of the canister, keeping them small; and it helps move the fluid base around as it cools, so it chills evenly and no one area of it freezes first.

Second, you freeze the base as fast as possible. Professional ice cream makers have large ice cream machines with giant compressors that can chill the ice cream base into a semi-frozen soft ice cream in 5 to 8 minutes, and giant, extremely cold freezers that finish locking the ice into place in just 2 more hours. This super-fast freezing doesn't give the free water time to travel through the mixture, find the seed ice crystals, and attach itself to freeze into a big crystal.

At home, we are not so lucky. Most home machines take between 20 and 30 minutes to turn liquid base into a semi-frozen ice cream, and home freezers can take anywhere from 4 to sometimes 12 hours to finish freezing the ice cream. This means the little seeds of ice created at home during churning will be more like medium seeds. And in the hours it takes to completely freeze the ice cream, the remaining water in the ice cream will have time to pull together, nucleating around those medium ice crystal seeds to become larger, more perceivable ice crystals by the time the ice cream is completely frozen.

If you've ever wondered why your homemade ice cream is icier than the stuff made by professionals, this is one of the biggest reasons. It may seem like a lost cause. But at least now you know what you are up against; and I promise, there are things you can do to help ensure smaller ice crystals in your homemade ice cream, with careful handling and specific ingredients that bind some of the water before it becomes ice. You can read about binding water with stabilizers (which are not a bad thing!) on page 26, or continue reading this section to learn how sugar and protein also help bind water.

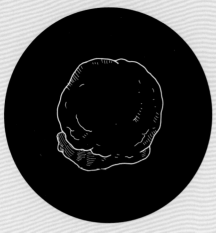

Fat

It's called ice *cream* for a reason; it contains cream, and cream is rich in butterfat. The butterfat in ice cream performs multiple functions. It adds flavor, creates a firmer texture, and stabilizes the air added during churning.

We know that ice cream needs over 10% butterfat to legally be called ice cream, but most ice creams have more than that. Ice cream makers have generally-agreed-upon marketing terms used to describe the butterfat content of their ice creams: *10 to 12% butterfat* is the commercial standard, considered "economy," and is what you'll find in half-gallon containers in your grocery store—ice creams like Blue Bell or Dryers; *12 to 14% butterfat* is considered "premium" ice cream (Turkey Hill, Whole Foods 365, your local old-fashioned scoop shop); *14 to 16% butterfat* is considered "super-premium," and is what you'll find in the top-of-the-line scoop shops like Jeni's, or brands like Häagen-Dazs and Ben and Jerry's; *17 to 20% butterfat* is beyond the scope of most commercial preparation—there is no common term for it, but think of it as "ultra-premium"; it is found mostly in home recipes or a very special kind of ice cream shop.

By the way, 20% is where we find the physical limit of butterfat in ice cream. More than that, and the ice cream feels flabby on the palate—more and more fat compounds on your cold tongue before your mouth has a chance to warm it and swallow it. Within a few bites, you'd notice your entire mouth has a slick of fat coating it. Texturally, overly fatty ice cream becomes too hard to scoop, and the ice cream appears crumbly.

Fat Is Flavor

Butterfat is key to ice cream's flavor, not only by contributing its own deliciousness but also by absorbing flavor from other ingredients like mint leaves or coffee beans. Because of this ability of butterfat, infusion is an efficient way to flavor ice cream. We can toss a handful of herbs, a spoonful of tea leaves, or any number of other ingredients into our ice cream base as it cooks, strain them out shortly after, and achieve a vibrant flavor.

Fat also plays a role in the way we *perceive* flavor. The more fat, the longer it takes for the flavor in the fat to present itself. An ice cream higher in butterfat has flavor that sneaks up on you and lingers on the palate, often long after you take a second bite. The flavor builds upon itself as you continue licking your scoops. Inversely, the less fat in an ice cream, the faster you can taste the flavor in it, and the more immediate impact it has.

Imagine eating a strawberry ice cream and a strawberry sorbet. The berry flavor of the ice cream is slow, gentle, and you can still taste it long after you have swallowed the ice cream. But in a sorbet, the flavor bursts and then disappears just in time for a second bite. You can use this fact to help you decide how much fat you want in your ice cream, depending on the flavor you are making. For example, you won't find a strawberry ice cream in this book, but you will find a strawberry sherbet. The sherbet is lower in butterfat, only 4%, which allows you to taste strawberry right away—an effect I prefer for the bright flavor of fruit.

On the other hand, you'll find this concept put into action in the other direction in the section on custard ice creams. The egg yolk–enriched custards are where I like to use flavors I want to cozy up to and spend some time with—like deep spices, rich coffees, dark sugars, brown liquors, and caramels. Likewise, you'll find cleaner, brighter flavors with more "pop" in the egg-free (Philadelphia-style) ice cream section—like fresh mint, lemon, bubblegum, and goat cheese.

Fat Is Texture, Too

The role of fat goes far beyond flavor in ice cream. Fat is the "hardest" thing in ice cream. But what does that mean? Imagine a stick of butter in the freezer. Pretty solid, right? Hardened butterfat helps the ice cream keep its shape outside the freezer even as the ice crystals melt. Imagine butter at room temperature. Soft, yes, but it won't melt into a liquid until you put it in a hot pan. As you know, the melting point of ice is 32°F, but the melting point of butter is 90°F, just below body temperature. This means the butterfat in ice cream won't melt until it's in your mouth. This is extremely helpful in keeping your scoops, well, scoops!

Most important is the way butterfat helps trap air in the ice cream, lightening it (for more on this, see page 20). It's the same way whipped cream is made, and indeed your ice cream is "whipping" when you churn it. To understand how butterfat does this, think of the butterfat as individual "globules." Each globule is like a tiny balloon filled with butter. The balloon-like surface surrounding the fat globule is slippery, acting like a little force field, repelling water and other fat globules as they float around the milk.

When cold, the butterfat inside the balloon globules is solid and firm. When you start to knock these little balloons around, you chip off parts of the fat globules' protective coating. Without the slippery coating, the hard butterfat is exposed, and it's sticky. This sticky fat then begins to adhere to things around it, which can mean other pieces of sticky butterfat or little bubbles of air. If enough banged-up butterfat globules stick to a bubble of air and completely surround it, the air bubble is trapped.

To visualize this concept, imagine putting cream in a jam jar and shaking it aggressively. (That fifth-grade Pioneer Day butter churning lesson *is* relevant!) The butterfat globules all start sticking together until you have a big blob of butter floating around in your jar. Now, imagine those same fat globules were instead knocked around by the wires of a whisk. Yes, the thin wires will chip the globules, and some will stick together. But the whisk is also dragging bubbles into the cream with it, which these recently chipped fat globules will latch on to. Drag your whisk through cold cream enough times, and you will have light, air-filled whipped cream.

Too much whisking, though, and the air will be knocked out of the whipped cream as the butterfat keeps finding more butterfat to stick to. If you've ever over-whipped cream, you have seen it start to look curdled, or chunky. Those are the fat globules starting to become butter. Likewise, in your ice cream, you can over-whip the fat and create butter. You'll know if you've tasted a "buttered" ice cream when you feel the little flecks of frozen butter on your tongue as you eat it.

Ice cream with lots of butterfat (over 18%) can easily become "buttered." But in the same way icier ice cream isn't necessarily made with more water, it's not the quantity of the butterfat that causes this to happen; rather, it's the size of the fat globules. The larger the globule, the less surface area it has relative to the fat it contains. Because of this, it can trap less air than many smaller globules. It will also quickly let go of an air bubble to connect to another oversized fat globule. Just like the ice crystals, we want small fat globules.

The naturally occurring size of the fat globules in fresh milk is so large and inconsistent that the fat easily coalesces and rises to the top of the milk, forming what is called the "cream-line." Old-timey milk drinkers once shook the milk to reincorporate the cream before drinking, but today we almost exclusively buy, sell, and drink homogenized milk, where the fat globules have been made small and uniform. To homogenize milk, the milk is forced between two plates with a very small gap between them. The fat globules have no choice but to break apart in order to squeeze through the microscopic passage. Once on the other side, proteins in the milk help re-create the membrane on these new, tinier fat globules. The fat globules are now too small to rise to the top of the milk, making homogenized milk and cream perfect for making ice cream.

That said, some farmstead milks are sold without being homogenized, and they are delicious. If you want to make ice cream out of one of these non-homogenized milks, more power to you. The flavor will be great! You can sort of hack a homogenizer at home by warming your milk above 100°F and spinning it in a blender for a couple minutes on high speed. You won't achieve the same results as a homogenizer, and you'll have to accept the possibility that there will be a little bit of buttered texture in your finished product. But that's a small price to pay for making ice cream with high-quality milk.

Whether you use homogenized dairy or not, your next step in keeping your fat globules small is to prevent them from coalescing. To do this, you emulsify the ice cream base. An emulsifier binds to both water and fat, disallowing the fat from joining with other fat globules. Custard ice cream bases are often considered the smoothest, and this is a direct result of the emulsifying properties of egg yolks. For eggless ice cream bases, the proteins in the dairy can assist in emulsifying the base if you cook them a little longer, and additional emulsifying agents can also be employed. You can read more about emulsifiers on page 24.

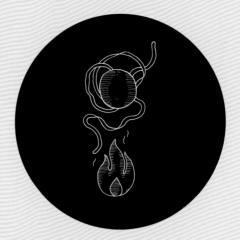

Protein

The protein in ice cream comes from the milk as well. It's not as substantial as the ice, or as glamorous as the flavorful, multitasking butterfat. But the small amount of protein in ice cream is crucial for texture and for binding the other structural components.

How Protein Works

Milk contains two different proteins: casein and whey. I know it's hard to envision casein and whey—all I can come up with is a gym rat's after-workout-drink powder. Instead, imagine another protein-filled fluid, an egg, and we can talk generally about how proteins behave. Imagine yourself adding heat to that egg, cooking it. As the transparent, fluid egg white becomes solid and opaque, and the bright yellow yolk hardens into the texture of fudge, you are seeing the proteins coagulate and become solid. This happens because heat causes the proteins to change their nature, or "denature." Technically, a protein is a long, coiled chain of amino acids. Imagine taking a long piece of yarn and wadding it up tightly. That's roughly what an individual protein looks like. When you apply heat, this scrunched-up amino acid chain unfurls into a long strand, and when these loosey-goosey strands touch each other, they connect, creating cross-links. If enough of the proteins connect to each other, they form a web that slows the flow of water. If cooked long enough, the cross-linked protein strands will stop the flow of water all together, turning the liquid egg solid.

Now, the proteins in milk behave just like the proteins in eggs. You might think, "Hey, I've cooked milk and it's never turned into a hard-boiled egg." That's partly because there's a lot more protein in an egg than there is in an equal amount of milk. Because of this, milk must be cooked much longer to evaporate water and denature enough proteins to cross-link and form a solid. But if you've ever had milk jam—dulce de leche—you've experienced the thick, semi-solid texture created by milk proteins that have denatured and bonded together.

Making Proteins Work for Your Ice Cream

While the cross-linked proteins disrupt the flow of water, solidifying eggs or "gelling" milk, something much more important is happening with dairy proteins. To understand what's going on, you need to know that these uncoiled protein strands aren't smooth threads. They have all sorts of little molecular branches on them, like a centipede's hands (or are they feet?). Many of the branches will *only* hold the hands of other proteins, forming those cross-links. However, other branches are hydrophilic and absolutely love to hold hands with water molecules, while others are hydrophobic and hate water, grabbing on to anything else they can find. The more the proteins unfurl, the more hands they have waving around looking for a loving embrace with water in the milk. The more water that binds *to* the proteins in your dairy, the less "free-roaming" water there is to pool together and create a large ice crystal.

To apply this concept, you'll notice that some of the recipes in this book require you to hold the ice cream base at a very low simmer for 2 minutes. By doing this, you are denaturing more and more of the proteins, thereby capturing some of the free-roaming water in the base, ultimately making the ice cream smoother and less icy. If you'd

like, you can amplify this effect and let your dairy slowly simmer for up to 10 minutes; but I give you the following two warnings.

First, too much water will evaporate from a 1-quart batch of ice cream base. If you are making 100 gallons of ice cream base at a time, simmering your ice cream base for as much as an hour will cause relatively little water loss, so large manufacturers can safely apply this technique. But in the batch size you make at home, a fair amount of water will evaporate in 10 minutes, throwing off the ratio of the recipe. If you want to simmer your small-batch base for longer than 2 minutes to denature more proteins, weigh your base before and after you cook it, then replace the water lost in evaporation.

Second, the ice cream will *taste* cooked. To be honest, this can be delicious, and I'd never turn down a scoop of ice cream with a cooked flavor. But it's not what I want for every scoop of ice cream I make. If you find you prefer a more cooked, rather than fresh, dairy flavor in your ice cream, prolong the low simmer and replace the water lost to evaporation, as above.

Professional ice cream makers go one step further and *add* a source of "concentrated milk protein" to ensure formation of tiny ice crystals. They either add nonfat milk powder or a liquid condensed milk (not the delicious sweet stuff in cans). At home, you can use powdered milk to increase the water-binding power of milk proteins, and you'll notice that many of the recipes in this book call for it. Another great source for concentrated milk proteins is cream cheese. Cream cheese is included in our list of stabilizers, and you can read more about it on page 31.

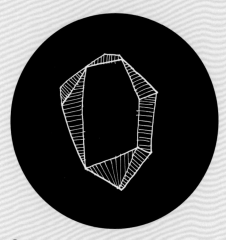

Sugar

Sugar isn't just what makes ice cream sweet—you actually can't make ice cream without it. (Commercial "sugar free" ice creams are both a misnomer and a true miracle of science.) Sugar is crucial to the physical structure of ice cream. Not only does it add body to the ice cream but it also bonds to some of the water in the ice cream base and actually *prevents* it from freezing, helping the ice cream stay scoopably soft.

The Sugar Family

The sweet white crystals in your pantry are what is commonly considered "sugar," but specifically it's sucrose. Sucrose is just one member of a big family called "sugar," and this distinction is important for understanding the role sugar plays in ice cream. While the recipes in this book use "sugar" to mean granulated white sugar, in this chapter I call it "sucrose" for sake of specificity, and I call the sugar family the "saccharides," as the scientists do.

There are the "monosaccharides," which are individual sugar molecules like glucose, dextrose, galactose, and fructose. When two of these monosaccharides join together, they create "disaccharides." For example, our good friend sucrose is a disaccharide made of a glucose molecule bonded to a fructose molecule. And lactose, the sugar naturally present in milk, is made of a glucose molecule bonded to a galactose molecule.

Each of these mono- or disaccharides has a unique amount of sweetness, called "relative sweetness." The scale of relative sweetness considers sucrose to be 100, which makes it easy to understand how much more or less sweet these other sugars are relative to sucrose:

RELATIVE SWEETNESS

Fructose (monosaccharide)	110
Sucrose (disaccharide)	100
Glucose/dextrose (monosaccharide)	74
Galactose (monosaccharide)	60
Lactose (disaccharide)	16

You can see that the sugar naturally present in milk—lactose—offers almost no sweetness to our ice cream, whereas sucrose adds a lot.

Sugar and Ice Cream Texture

Sugar isn't great for our bodies, and skimming a little off an ice cream recipe seems like a great way to make this indulgent dessert a bit more forgiving. Likewise, sugar is very sweet, and it's tempting to want to reduce the sweetness for the sake of flavor. But believe me when I say, "Don't do it!" (And believe me when I say there is a better way to reduce sweetness.)

Without sugar, ice cream would be like a fluffy, fatty ice cube. You see, sugar bonds with water and depresses its freezing point, keeping some of the water in the ice cream fluid below freezing temperatures. Or, to put it more simply, it keeps the ice cream soft and scoopable.

Much like the proteins have those little water-holding hands, sugar does, too—two of them. Imagine you are holding a water droplet in each hand. You'd be just like a monosaccharide, like glucose, neatly binding two molecules of water. Now, imagine you and your best friend are holding hands with each other. Even though you have four hands as a pair, you can still only hold two water molecules with your free hands. You and your BFF are a disaccharide, like sucrose.

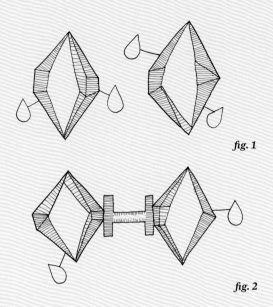

fig. 1: *Two monosaccharides holding four water molecules.*

fig. 2: *A disaccharide holding two water molecules.*

This means that an equal quantity of glucose will bind twice as much water as sucrose. So, by using a monosaccharide like glucose for a portion of the sugar in your ice cream, you ensure less of the water forms ice, and the ice cream is softer when frozen. As a bonus, glucose is also less sweet than sucrose and will tame the sweetness of your scoop without sacrificing texture. (Conversely, honey is almost entirely made of fructose, which is even sweeter than sucrose.)

Glucose and Its Counterparts

You'll notice that many of the recipes in this book call for glucose. You can order glucose online, and many craft stores with candy-making sections sell liquid glucose, as well as most local cake-decorating stores. But if you can't find it, you still have options. There is actually a way to split disaccharides like sucrose into two monosaccharides—kind of like forcing you and your best friend to stop holding hands. This is called "inverting" the sugar.

Professionals have access to inverted sugar syrup, sold to us in tubs of pearly white viscous goo.

However, you can easily make inverted sugar syrup at home by boiling sucrose with water and an acid. I've provided a recipe for inverted sugar syrup on page 214, and you can use it as a substitute for the glucose in any of the recipes in this book, but keep in mind it retains the same sweetness level as sucrose.

There is another sugar syrup full of monosaccharides that is much more widely available to the ice-cream-making public, and you might already have some! Corn syrup is made by processing a polysaccharide (so many saccharides!!!)—cornstarch—with an enzyme, cutting the giant sugar chain into very specific monosaccharides.

Pick up a bottle of corn syrup and turn it over, and you'll notice it has more than one ingredient. As corn syrup is mostly made of the monosaccharide glucose, it isn't naturally very sweet. The second ingredient is high fructose corn syrup, which is used to bring the sweetness of the syrup up to the same level as sucrose. High fructose corn syrup is where corn syrup gets in trouble with the public. It is corn syrup that is processed with enzymes that don't break apart the saccharide chains, but instead re-bond extra fructose molecules to the glucose until the syrup is really sweet. It's these franken-saccharides that are hard for our bodies to process and that give all corn syrups a bad rap.

Still, you can use corn syrup in place of the glucose in any of the ice cream recipes, and it will work textural wonders on your final results. If I found myself with a bottle of it, I'd likely use it, too. In fact, since it's so widely available, I recommend it as good textural solution. As to whether corn syrup is welcome in your home, I respectfully leave that decision up to you.

Finally, you can always replace the glucose called for in the recipe with the same weight of granulated sugar—good old sucrose. Your ice cream won't be as soft, and it will be more sweet. But it will still be fine, and cooking at home is often about making due with what is on hand. But please promise me, whatever you do, don't remove any of the sugar from the recipes!

Air

Air is an invisible ingredient in ice cream, added during the churning of the ice cream base by the mechanical motion of the ice cream maker's beater. We talked about how one of fat's key roles is to trap and stabilize air. But why do we need air in our ice cream?

For starters, if we didn't have air in our ice cream, we would have a solid treat—something like a Popsicle. The amount of air in an ice cream profoundly affects its mouthfeel and, in a sense, its flavor. If you've ever wondered what makes gelato technically different from ice cream, the short answer is that it has much less air whipped into it. This makes it feel denser and therefore creamier. Some people prefer an airier, fluffier ice cream, but air is the cheapest ingredient in the world, and the more air whipped in, the less your pint of ice cream costs the manufacturer to make. You'll find that premium ice creams, prizing a luxurious, dense mouthfeel, have less air whipped into them.

Try something next time you're in the grocery store. Take a pint of the most expensive ice cream in one hand and a pint of the cheapest in the other. The expensive one will feel heavier than the cheap one. The cheaper pint of ice cream, you'll come to realize, is cheaper because there's less of it in the carton.

The air in ice cream has a technical name; it's called "overrun." This term refers to the increase in volume that happens when air is whipped into the liquid ice cream base. To measure overrun, the volume of churned ice cream is compared to its weight. So, if a quart of ice cream is 32 ounces by volume but weighs 16 ounces, it has a 50% overrun. This is typical of the commercial ice creams sold in large half-gallons and in many scoop shops around the country. You might not notice how fluffy the ice cream is at your local scoop shop, however. The motion of an ice cream scoop compresses much of the air in the ice cream as it digs into the tubs. "Hand-packed" pints from those scoop shops have a good bit of the air pressed out; this can make a high-overrun ice cream feel like a low-overrun ice cream.

Incidentally, a benefit of the slow churn of a home machine is that it can't whip very much air into the ice cream. This is a great side effect that puts you well on your way to a delicious, dense ice cream!

The Texture Agents

Stabilizers and Emulsifiers

While not strictly a make-or-break addition to ice creams, particularly those made at home, all your ice cream recipes can be improved by stabilizers, which make them smoother and less icy. I always use them. Now, the word *stabilizer* has a really bad reputation. It has come to suggest anything artificial, used to alter wholesome food into unnatural, fake, processed food, for the purpose of extending its shelf life at the expense of your health so as to maximize profit. When you put it that way, yeah, stabilizers sound like jerks.

If that's how you feel, it's time we had The Talk. Keep an open mind while I shed some light on these texture agents.

Let's start by talking about what stabilizers are not. They are not poison. They are not necessarily "chemicals" (unless you consider that everything on this planet is a chemical, but that's a word fight for another day). And most important, they are not cheating.

A stabilizer is simply an ingredient that functions to keep the five components of ice cream stable. It does this by helping lock water into place, preventing it from shifting around and forming big ice crystals, which in turn makes ice cream smoother and more satisfying. And these helpful friends are often already in your ice cream—like milk proteins—or in your cupboards, like corn-starch and pectin. "Stabilizer" has also become a blanket term for anything in ice cream that helps with the texture, including their frequent bedfellows, emulsifiers and (ironically) *de*stabilizers. These two helpful agents do for butterfat what stabilizers do for water. They hold the fat in place, and help prepare it to capture air when you churn the ice cream. And again, many of these are already in your kitchen, like egg yolks. Feeling better about this yet?

But before we meet these texture agents, we need to talk about Mother Nature. She's a powerful force in this world, much stronger than you or I—or your ice cream machine, for that matter. Mother Nature prefers a condition of "low surface energy," and she achieves this by shrinking surface area whenever possible, condensing her energy, like juggling one big ball instead of ten small ones. Imagine a vinaigrette. The oil and vinegar appear combined when you shake them together; once your shaking efforts cease, Mother Nature steps back in and the little beads of oil in the vinaigrette start to coalesce into larger beads of oil, until you have a large pool of oil floating on top of the vinegar. You've just witnessed Mother Nature shrinking the "aggregated surface area" of the oil and water. Mother Nature will attempt to do the same with the water and butterfat in your ice cream. You, on the other hand, want your water and butterfat to stay in as many tiny droplets as you can get for a smooth, even ice cream full of tiny, imperceptible ice crystals.

For the small, quart-size batches of ice cream that the recipes in this book yield, you need tiny amounts of these texture agents. If you're working with grams, you must have a scale that measures below 1 gram, called a micro-scale. These tiny scales are often sold for illicit use doing things I would know nothing about, and are the only reason you'll ever find me in a head shop, where they are widely available. They can also be ordered online. If you don't have a micro-scale, use the standard measurements and just make sure you level off your teaspoons exactly.

XANTHAN GUM

LOCUST
BEAN GUM

GUAR GUM

CARRAGEENAN

MILK POWDER

LECITHIN

GELATIN

CREAM
CHEESE

TAPIOCA
STARCH

PECTIN

COMMERCIAL
STABILIZER

CORNSTARCH

MONO- AND
DIGLYCERIDE FLAKES

POLYSORBATE
80

EGG YOLK

Emulsifiers

Emulsifiers bond with both water and fat at the same time, which prevents them from drifting apart and coalescing with themselves. By binding the water and fat to each other instead of letting them puddle separately, emulsifiers help ensure your ice cream leaves no noticeable butter flakes or ice crystals on the tongue.

There are several agents especially skilled in the art of emulsifying the ice cream base, but generally speaking they are either proteins (amino acids) or fats (lipids).

Milk Powder

The proteins in milk are my favorite emulsifiers, because they are naturally a part of ice cream to begin with. As discussed on pages 16 and 17, proteins unravel with heat into long amino acid chains, with parts that bond with water and other parts that bond with anything *but* water, latching on to butterfat and therefore joining the two.

To enhance the emulsifying effect of milk proteins, I often add milk powder in addition to the liquid milk in the ice cream bases. Milk powder, a.k.a. powdered milk, is made by evaporating skim milk until all the water is removed. The powder is sold in most grocery stores. To use milk powder to help emulsify your ice cream base, use it in a concentration of 2% (i.e., use 20g in a 1000g batch of ice cream), simmering it with your ice cream base for at least 2 minutes. Flip to the chapter on Philadelphia-style ice creams for recipes that employ milk powder (page 75).

Egg Yolks

Egg yolks are jam-packed with proteins that thicken and emulsify the ice cream base in the same manner as the milk proteins. An ice cream base emulsified with egg yolks is called a custard ice cream, and we have an entire chapter dedicated to them (page 49)!

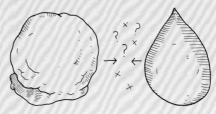

fig. 1

fig. 2

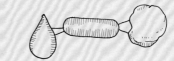

fig. 3

fig. 4

fig. 1: *Oil and water don't mix.*

fig. 2: *Left to their own devices, they will drift apart and coalesce.*

fig. 3: *An emulsifier bonds with both fat and water.*

fig. 4: *More efficient emulsifiers are used in commercial brands.*

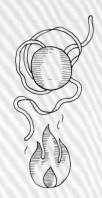

fig. 1

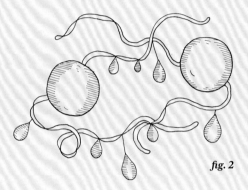

fig. 2

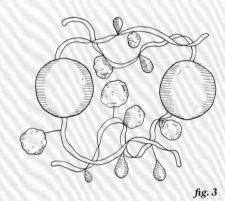

fig. 3

fig. 1: *When heated, the protein strand unravels, or denatures.*

fig. 2: *The denatured protein exposes hydrophilic parts that bond with water molecules, stabilizing them.*

fig. 3: *When further denatured, hydrophobic parts of the protein bond with fat, emulsifying the mixture.*

If you read through the instructions for a custard ice cream base, you'll see that the yolks get cooked. As this happens, the abundant proteins unravel and bond with both fat and water in the ice cream mix, but they *also* begin to cross-link with each other. When they do that, they form a web that slows the movement of the water in the ice cream base. Real talk: this ice cream base *thickens*. The thicker the ice cream base, the smoother it will be when churned. To use egg yolks to emulsify your ice cream, use them at a concentration of 5% to 10% of the total ice cream base weight, and follow the instructions for Blank Slate Custard Ice Cream (page 50).

You'll see other emulsifiers listed as ingredients in commercial ice creams, or mixed in with commercial blends. They are lecithin, mono- and diglycerides, and polysorbate 80. Each of these is a high-functioning ingredient, and unless you're employing a commercial stabilizer, you likely won't come across them individually.

Destabilizers

Okay, so if stabilizers help your ice cream's texture, why would you want to use a *destabilizer*? Well, it's a little bit of a linguistic paradox, but destabilizers in this case destabilize one very specific thing. A stable butterfat globule floating around your ice cream base has a full coating of nonstick proteins. Destabilizing agents erode this coating, exposing the fat globule's sticky insides, which can adhere to two things: an air bubble or another fat globule. The fat globules start to stick together two or three at a time, a process called "partial coalescence." Unlike the coalescing described earlier, where the oil droplets in the vinaigrette combined to form a big drop, partially coalesced butterfat globules have bumped up against each other and are stuck side by side, like conjoined twins. The conjoined butterfat globules now have *increased* surface area, and are therefore twice as ready to catch and hang on to an air bubble as it's churned into the ice cream. This makes for a lighter and smoother ice cream. If you read the section on Fat (page 14) in "The Five Components of Ice Cream," you'll remember that the fat is also destabilized mechanically when the fat globules collide with the blades of the dasher in the ice cream machine. By employing a destabilizer, you don't need to rely on the long process of bludgeoning fat globules in order to start whipping air into your ice cream; destabilizers let you whip air into the ice cream right away, lightening it more effectively.

I emphasize the importance of curing your ice cream base in the refrigerator several times throughout this book, and allowing time for the destabilizers to work is one of the biggest reasons. If you want to harness the destabilizing powers of one of these agents, you're in luck. Conveniently, the destabilizing agents are actually double agents that were introduced earlier as emulsifiers: egg yolks, lecithin, mono- and diglycerides, and polysorbate 80. For homemade ice cream recipes, I mostly use egg yolks, but often choose to use a commercial blend to bring the advantages of a destabilizer to my home ice cream bases. If you choose to do so as well, you absolutely *must* cure your ice cream base overnight before churning.

Stabilizers (and the Terror of the Freeze-Thaw Cycle)

Here we are, finally, at the actual stabilizers in this section on stabilizers. When the ice cream base is still fluid, these agents bind water, preventing it from coalescing and forming larger ice crystals when churned. While stabilizers are helpful in preventing large ice crystals from the get-go, they work their real magic after the ice cream is frozen.

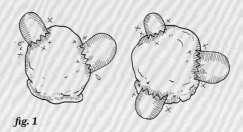

fig. 1

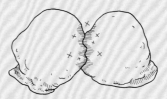

fig. 2

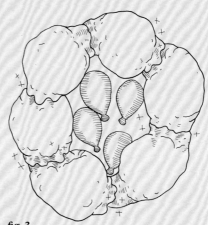

fig. 3

fig. 1: *Destabilizers erode the coating on fat globules, exposing the sticky interior.*

fig. 2: *The sticky interior allows fat globules to partially coalesce.*

fig. 3: *Destabilized fat globules also trap air, and partially coalesced fat globules are more efficient at the job.*

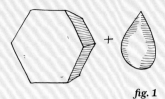

fig. 1

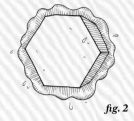

fig. 2

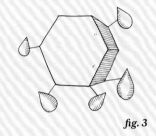

fig. 3

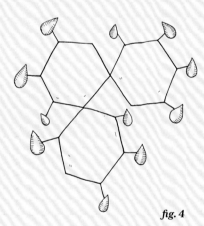

fig. 4

fig. 1: *A plant-based gum is added to the ice cream base in its dry state.*

fig. 2: *Once these gum-derived stabilizers absorb water, they are considered hydrated.*

fig. 3: *A hydrated stabilizer bonds with multiple water molecules, locking them in place.*

fig. 4: *When heated to the correct temperature, stabilizers also bond with each other, thickening the ice cream base for improved churning.*

Stabilizers are often plant-based gums like guar gum, or starches, like cornstarch. When a stabilizer is added to the ice cream base, it first hydrates, meaning it soaks up water. Then, it will start to form a gel, meaning it will cross-link and bond with itself. (Depending on the stabilizer, sometimes heat is required.) When the stabilizers bond with one another, they begin to disrupt the flow of water, much like the proteins do when egg yolks are cooked, thickening the ice cream base. Remember, a thicker ice cream base will be smoother and will trap more air when churned. And with our slow-churning home machines, we can use a little help getting air into our ice cream base.

But most important, stabilizers drastically slow the growth of ice crystals during the freeze-thaw cycle. Your freezer may feel cold all the time, but it actually goes through temperature fluctuations, whether from opening and closing the door or during the defrost cycle. Without a stabilizer, during a thaw cycle any ice that melts into water will coalesce, then freeze into a larger ice crystal when the freezer kicks back in and gets cold again. Even a fluctuation of five degrees is enough to cause the enlargement of ice crystals in this manner. With a stabilizer, the water is bound and can't coalesce during the thaw cycle. This means it refreezes into the same tiny ice crystal it melted from. In a home freezer, the temperature can fluctuate multiple times a day, wreaking havoc on ice cream.

If you employ only one of the texture agents, let it be a stabilizer. The scourge of homemade ice cream is the growth of large ice crystals, and using a stabilizer will make such a drastic improvement in your ice cream. Following is a list of many helpful stabilizers, and while they function differently, in the end they all do exactly the same thing. I'll leave it to you to decide which stabilizers to invite into your kitchen, based on your own comfort level.

Milk Powder

You may have already read about powdered milk as an emulsifier (page 24), but to use milk powder as a stabilizer, you add it to your recipes in a concentration of 3% (30g | ¼ cup per 1kg | 1-quart batch). But be warned: it's not necessarily easy to use milk as the sole stabilizer in a recipe.

As you'll recall, cooking milk unravels the proteins to expose the amino acid chains, which act as emulsifiers. To unravel enough protein to use milk powder as your only stabilizer, you will need to expose the milk to temperatures of 160°F or higher for 30 to 60 minutes. For small batches of homemade ice cream, simmering your ice cream base for 30 minutes often means drastic water loss and potentially burning your ice cream base. If you employ this technique at home, keep your ice cream base at a very low simmer, and monitor the loss of water periodically. You will need to measure the ice cream base after it is finished cooking and replace the water that has evaporated. If you have access to a sous-vide system, it is a great tool for holding the ice cream base at 160°F for 30 to 60 minutes without any water loss.

Cornstarch

Cornstarch is something most of us are quite familiar with, one of its greatest charms being that you probably already have some in your kitchen. Cornstarch granules begin soaking up water when added to cold liquid, and then they swell, absorbing more water when heat is applied. These swollen starch granules are big and bulky, and they slow the movement of water in the ice cream base. It's likely you've seen this happen if you've ever thickened a sauce or pudding with cornstarch.

However, cornstarch does begin to deteriorate when frozen, making it a wonderful thickener but less ideal for protecting ice creams from the freeze-thaw cycle over time. Use cornstarch at a concentration of 1% (10g | 1 tablespoon plus

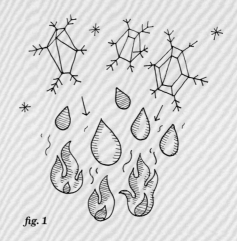

fig. 1

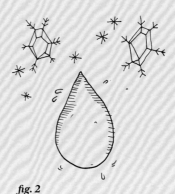

fig. 2

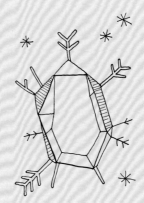

fig. 3

fig. 1: *When the temperature fluctuates above 32°F/0°C, ice reverts into water.*

fig. 2: *Unstabilized water coalesces into large droplets.*

fig. 3: *Each large water droplet creates a large, perceivable ice crystal.*

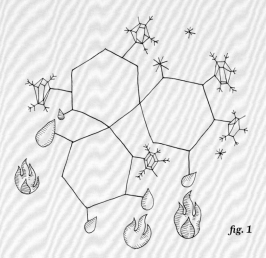

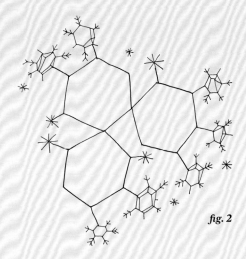

1 teaspoon per 1kg | 1-quart batch), dissolved in twice its weight in cold water to make a slurry.

Whisk the cornstarch slurry into an ice cream base as it finishes cooking, and hold the thickening ice cream base at a simmer for no more than 60 seconds. The cornstarch granules need to reach boiling temperatures to cook completely, but they are also at risk of over-cooking. Should you boil your cornstarch for too long, the starch granules will begin to rupture, and their thickening power then diminishes.

Tapioca Starch

Tapioca starch is similar to cornstarch but comes from the tuberous root of the cassava plant. The starch granules in tapioca starch swell at a lower temperature than cornstarch—140°F—and don't need to be boiled to cook through. This root starch can absorb more water than cornstarch, and it becomes translucent when cooked, a property that can be beneficial to you elsewhere in cooking, but goes unnoticed in opaque ice cream. Tapioca starch also performs better in the freezer than cornstarch, and doesn't lose strength when frozen.

Use tapioca starch at a concentration of .5% (5g | 2 teaspoons per 1kg | 1-quart batch), mixed with four times its weight in 2 tablespoons cold water to form a slurry. Just after an ice cream base has finished cooking, remove it from heat and whisk in the tapioca starch slurry, allowing the residual heat to cook the starch.

Locust Bean Gum

Locust bean sounds a little like the source of a biblical plague, and the pros who use this stabilizer like to shorten the name to LBG, while others call it by its other name, carob bean gum. This stabilizer is well known for its velvety texture when added to dairy. Use locust bean gum at a concentration of .2% (2g | ¾ teaspoon per 1kg | 1-quart batch) tossed with the sugar before it's added to the milk and cream.

When using locust bean gum, it's best to use a hand blender to incorporate the mixture into the milk and cream, ensuring it's evenly dispersed. Locust bean gum must reach near boiling temperatures to be activated, but since the instructions for most of these ice creams include boiling, you are safe to add locust bean gum to your recipe without taking any extra cooking steps.

Pectin

Pectin is a polysaccharide derived from the cell wall of plants—in particular, the pith of citrus fruits. If you've made jam, you've likely used pectin to thicken fruit to the point of delicious spreadability. Unfortunately, the pectin you use for many jams—high-esther pectin—is not suitable for ice cream.

Luckily, low-methoxy pectin is. This pectin requires calcium ions to form a gel, and we've got plenty of those in our ice cream recipes! Low-methoxy pectin is widely available to the public, sold in little blue boxes labeled Pamona's All-Natural Pectin. If you buy Pamona's pectin, you'll find two packets inside, one of pectin and a smaller one containing calcium powder. For these ice cream recipes, you can omit the extra calcium; there is enough in the dairy.

Use low-methoxy pectin at a concentration of .1% (1g | ¼ teaspoon per 1kg | 1-quart batch). To introduce the pectin into your ice cream base, toss the pectin with the sugar in the recipe before adding it to the milk and cream.

Guar Gum

Guar plants grow in arid regions and have long been a marketable crop in India, Pakistan, Africa, and more recently Texas. Guar gum is more soluble than locust bean gum, meaning it will soak up water faster. Guar gum works best below 80°F, so blend this stabilizer into your chilled ice cream base. It's also widely available now thanks to its popularity in gluten-free baking, and you can find it in grocery stores or online.

Use guar gum at a concentration of .1% (1g | ¼ teaspoon per 1kg | 1-quart batch). To introduce the guar gum, place your cooked, chilled ice cream base in a blender, turn it on to a medium speed, then sprinkle the guar gum into the spinning ice cream base. Once it's all added, continue blending on high for 1 minute, before proceeding with the next step in your recipe.

Xanthan Gum

Xanthan gum comes from a natural source, but it's a little different from the milled seeds that produce locust bean and guar gums. Xanthan gum is the secretion of a bacteria, produced by fermenting glucose or sucrose.

Use xanthan gum at a concentration of .1% (1g | ¼ teaspoon per 1kg | 1-quart batch). To introduce the xanthan gum, place your cooked, chilled ice cream base in a blender, turn it on to a medium speed, then sprinkle the xanthan gum into the spinning ice cream base. Once it's all added, continue blending on high for 1 minute, before proceeding with the next step in your recipe.

Carrageenan

A family of stabilizers extracted from seaweed, carrageenans have been used for culinary applications for over 2,000 years. People historically boiled this seaweed to harness its gelling capabilities in both ancient China and Ireland, and sometimes it is referred to as Irish moss.

Carrageenans are particularly useful with dairy because they can bond with protein as well as water. There are three types of carrageenan: kappa, iota, and lambda. Each type forms a different texture when cooked with milk; lambda and kappa are unsuitably brittle, however, so for ice cream, you only want the soft gel formed by iota carrageenan.

Use iota carrageenan at a concentration of .25% (2.5g | ¾ teaspoon per 1kg | 1-quart batch) and introduce it into the ice cream base by tossing it with the sugar, then cook it with the milk and cream. When adding iota carrageenan along with your sugar, it's best to use a hand blender to incorporate the mixture into the milk and cream, ensuring it's evenly dispersed. Iota carrageenan needs to be cooked to near boiling temperatures in order for its gelling capabilities to be activated; the boiling step in the ice cream recipes in this book is sufficient to do so.

Cream Cheese

Great and mighty cream cheese is a wonderful stabilizer for your ice cream. If you pick up a package of cream cheese and turn it over, you'll find a few of our new friends listed in the ingredients: whey proteins, locust bean gum, and xanthan gum. By adding cream cheese to your ice cream base, you gain the benefit of not one, but three stabilizers! Cream cheese makes for a very thick ice cream base as well, which is smoother and traps more air as it is churned.

To use cream cheese as a stabilizer, use it at a concentration of 5% (50g | ¼ cup per 1kg | 1-quart batch) replacing 5% of the cream in your recipe. Whisk softened cream cheese with the chilled ice cream base to prevent the acidic cheese from curdling the base as it cooks.

Gelatin

Gelatin is made of proteins extracted from collagen found in the bones and hides of animals raised for consumption. Gelatin was used as an ice cream stabilizer historically, but it lost popularity midway through the last century, pushed aside for less expensive, more efficient plant-based alternatives.

Because the strength of gelatin available on the market can vary, it will take trial and error on a dedicated ice cream maker's part to find the best concentration of the selected gelatin. We tested with Knox powdered gelatin and found that a concentration of .4% (4g | 1 teaspoon per 1kg | 1-quart batch) was quite sufficient to stabilize the ice cream.

To use powdered gelatin, place the cold milk and cream called for in the recipe into a pot and sprinkle the gelatin over the surface. Let the gelatin bloom, allowing it to absorb water for 5 minutes, then heat the cream and milk, whisking the gelatin until it's melted. Once the gelatin is melted, continue adding ingredients as the recipe suggests.

Commercial Ice Cream Stabilizers

A commercial ice cream stabilizer will contain a blend of stabilizers, emulsifiers, and destabilizers that all work together to create a smooth, stable ice cream. They are favored by professionals for their ease in use, and I myself use them. While I daydream about creating my own blend from these ingredients, pinpointing a texture that is decidedly mine and mine alone, I employ a commercial blend. I've used many over the years and find them all basically the same. You'll find the best texture in your ice creams at home if you employ a commercial blend, if it fits your comfort level.

To use a commercial blend, you can refer to the instructions given by the manufacturer, if they are given. Otherwise, use a commercial stabilizer blend at a concentration of .3% (3g | 1 teaspoon per 1kg | 1-quart batch), mixed with the sugar before it's cooked with the ice cream base.

The Process

The process of making ice cream looks similar no matter whose recipe you use, or whether you're making it professionally or at home. Here, we'll walk through the basic steps, and I'll explain what is happening in each, so you can peek behind the curtain to see how everything works.

Cooking the Ice Cream Base

The first step in making ice cream is to prepare a liquid ice cream base out of dairy products, sugar, and sometimes eggs. This step requires heating the dairy to temperatures above 200°F to achieve three things: to dissolve the sugars, to denature the proteins, and to infuse flavors.

First, you bring the milk, cream, and sugars to a boil. As the temperature of the dairy rises, its molecules begin to move and vibrate faster. This vibration makes it easier to completely dissolve the sugar into the ice cream base, breaking apart the sugar crystals into individual sucrose molecules. This, in turn, makes them free to bond with water molecules. As mentioned on page 18, once a water molecule is bonded with a sugar molecule, it will remain liquid at freezing temperatures, a very important factor in keeping the ice cream softer and less icy.

You also cook the ice cream base to denature the proteins in the milk—and eggs, if they are present. Again, the increased vibration of the hot water molecules begins to unravel the protein strands (see page 16). These strands have lots of little arms, and some of those arms are "hydrophilic," or water loving. Hiding in the very center of these knotted proteins are also little feet, and these feet *hate* water. They are called "hydrophobic," or water fearing.

By cooking the ice cream base, you are unraveling these proteins so their water-loving hands can grab on to more water, further reducing the free-roaming water in the ice cream base, and ultimately making for less icy ice cream. While that is happening, the water-hating feet are getting as far from the water as they can, and they sink themselves into any little globs of butterfat they can find. Because the protein is now holding both water and fat together, it is emulsifying the base.

The third reason to cook the ice cream base is to infuse flavors. We all know there are five generally observable tastes in our food: salty, sour, umami, bitter, and sweet. These tastes are all perceived by the tongue. Everything else—and I mean every other flavor you've ever tasted—is an aroma compound, and it is perceived by the olfactory gland. These aroma compounds are volatile, a word that refers to their ability to evaporate. As the temperature rises, these compounds become highly volatile, so, when submerged in hot liquid, the aroma compounds move from their original source into the liquid ice cream base, infusing it with their flavors.

Chilling the Ice Cream Base

After you cook the ice cream base, it needs to be chilled rapidly. This is primarily about microscopic little critters called bacteria that want to eat the delicious ice cream base. I love to share my ice cream, just not with things that will make me sick. So, an ice bath is used to rapidly bring the temperature of the ice cream base to 50°F, before any unwanted friends crash the party. Then, you quickly tuck away the cooled ice cream base in the refrigerator, where the temperature falls below 40°F, and the ice cream base is in the safety zone.

Milk has everything needed to sustain life—water, sugar, and protein—which is why bacteria flourish in dairy. In the best case, we can grow healthy bacteria, called dairy cultures, and get things like yogurt, sour cream, and kefir. In the worst case, we can grow *E. coli*, salmonella, and listeria. By boiling the ice cream base, you are killing any microbial hazard in the ice cream that tagged along in the dairy products from the store (very unlikely with modern pasteurization, but it happens), from our natural surroundings (wash your hands!), or riding on the back of the freshly cut mint leaves you infused into the ice cream base. It takes only four hours for enough bacteria to multiply to cause harm. These bacteria only grow at certain temperatures, so if you chill your ice cream base quickly to below 40°F, you can eliminate time spent in the temperatures of the danger zone, as we know it—or the party zone, as the bacteria like to call it. Once chilled, bacterial growth is slowed drastically, and when frozen, it's completely arrested. However, there are bacteria that make us sick when we eat them, and those that leave behind toxic waste after they have been eliminated.

Are you terrified of ice cream yet? Don't be. Just use an ice bath and chill your ice cream quickly. A quart of ice cream chilled in an ice bath will drop below 50°F in about 20 minutes—hours before anything bad can happen.

Curing the Ice Cream Base

After the ice cream base is cold, it benefits greatly from curing. This step is often overlooked, and if you don't want to wait to churn your ice cream, I'm not going to judge you; we all understand the need for instant ice cream gratification. However, you will be greatly rewarded if you do cure your ice cream base, which just means leaving it alone in the refrigerator for a minimum of four hours, or preferably overnight. During this time, many things happen to improve the texture and flavor of the ice cream.

Those proteins you worked so hard to denature in the cooking process will continue to take hold of the water and fat molecules during the curing period. This allows them maximum capability to strengthen your emulsion and help capture free-roaming water. Likewise, the sugar continues to grab on to the hands of water, binding it. And finally, the stabilizers you've added will continue to soak up water until they have reached full water-binding capacity. Remember, more bound water means smaller ice crystals.

The curing time also continues to cool the ice cream base after the ice bath. Adding cooler ice cream base to the ice cream machine makes better ice cream, since a faster churn and freeze means, again, less time for big ice crystals to form. (And you won't run the risk of overtaxing your machine's cooling capacity.)

But curing the base isn't *just* about ice. The aroma compounds that were infused use the curing time to fully integrate with all the ingredients in the ice cream base. When the aroma compounds are distributed evenly, they are perceived more clearly when we eat them. Which means the ice creams flat-out taste better!

And then there's the fat. The curing process gives the mono- and diglycerides time to strip the butterfat globules off of their slick surface. If you read the section on Fat (page 14), you understand that the fat globules are responsible for trapping the air bubbles whipped into the ice cream base. The air is trapped after the fat globules' slick surface has been nicked or chipped-off from a collision with the blades of the ice cream machine. Once the slick surface is damaged, the sticky fat underneath will adhere to these air bubbles, and when a bubble is completely surrounded by these banged-up fat globules, it is trapped in the ice cream. Well, to help with all that, mono- and diglycerides have the unique capability of stripping the surface of the fat globules without our having to physically agitate them, but they do need time. Mono- and diglycerides are found in

egg yolks, and are also added to commercial ice cream stabilizer blends. If you've added either of these things to your ice cream base, it's even more important to let it cure properly.

Churning the Ice Cream Base into Ice Cream

Churning is when you turn the base into ice cream by freezing and agitating it at the same time, and during this process many things are happening. While different ice cream machines chill the base using different cooling systems, they all share the same basic mechanics and physics and produce a similar ice cream.

(The exceptions are big commercial ice cream manufacturers that have a special kind of ice cream machine called a continuous freezer. It's a wild contraption not unlike something on Willy Wonka's factory floor, with pipes twisting around pipes, and an air pump to fluff the ice cream as it inches through the machine continuously. The ice cream starts as a fluid base in a tank on one side, and by the time it passes through the machine, it comes out a faucet on the other side as ice cream.)

For the rest of us, both professionals and home cooks, we have batch freezers. Every one of these employs a freezing canister that is filled with the liquid ice cream base. The base that comes in contact with the walls of the canister starts to freeze while a set of blades called the dasher turns in a circular motion, scraping the newly formed ice cream off the frozen canister walls, mixing it back into the ice cream base. As the dasher scrapes the frozen base, the churning motion breaks up the newly formed ice into individual ice crystals, which in turn become the seeds for the remainder of the ice to grow around.

As the blade scrapes and chops the newly formed ice on the walls of the canister, it also introduces air bubbles. The air bubbles added during the churning process help soften the ice cream when it hardens (see page 20). The speed of the dasher is what defines the amount of overrun, or air, in your ice cream. Professionals often have the option of choosing how fast the blades of their large ice cream makers spin, creating lighter or denser ice creams. At home, we are bound by the pre-set speed of our ice cream makers. (Only one home machine I know of, the Kitchen-Aid, gives you the option of changing speeds.)

After enough time churning, the ice cream will whip, like whipped cream, thickening from both the trapped air and the growing number of ice crystals. You see your ice cream base transform as it churns, growing in volume and thickening slowly, then starting to hold peaks, until it has the texture of soft-serve ice cream.

Professional batch freezers often have an automatic setting that turns the freezing mechanism off when the ice cream is finished churning, sounding a convenient alarm. The ice cream machine knows the ice cream is done churning when it reaches a temperature of 25°F. At home, you can take the temperature with a thermometer, or simply use the visual cue "looks like soft-serve" to determine if your ice cream is finished churning.

Hardening the Ice Cream

Once the ice cream has been churned into a soft-serve state, it needs to be hardened in the freezer to become American hard-pack–style ice cream. This hardening stage turns the soft-serve into the firm, chewy scoops we know and love. In Italy, hardening the ice cream is often skipped, and ice cream is sold freshly churned, smeared with a paddle in cones or cups, and called gelato. This soft, flexible texture is what differentiates gelato from ice cream the most. Gelato is more akin to soft serve than ice cream; it's meant to be eaten the day it's made. While you'll find pints of gelato in the freezer case of your grocery stores, they're hardened just like ice cream, and technically speaking are not true-to-form gelato. Because gelato isn't regulated the same way ice cream is in the United States, legally speaking, it's anything goes for "gelato." But ask any gelato maker worth their salt, and they will insist to you that gelato is made fresh daily, never hardened.

Your ice creams will be perfectly delicious if you eat them soft, immediately after you churn them. There are pastry chefs who believe you haven't truly lived until you've eaten ice cream this way. However, the recipes in this book were designed to be hardened into American hard-pack–style ice cream, and their texture truly shines after a night in the freezer.

Growing ice crystals seems counterintuitive, since we talked so much about preventing ice crystals, right? Not quite. We talked about managing the size of and quantity of ice crystals, but we still *need* ice. Without enough ice, ice cream loses the refreshing quality it should possess, and eats like a frozen pudding.

During the hardening phase, the butterfat also grows colder and harder. This makes the fat more stable, keeping the air whipped into the ice cream firmly in place. You can see this effect when you scoop cold ice cream and cut into these air bubbles. You're seeing the air that's been locked into place by hard butterfat.

Like curing your ice cream base, hardening your ice cream is a hands-off step that only requires patience. Professionals use hardening rooms, which are giant super-freezers with gale-force fans that force subzero air around the ice creams. Don't worry, I don't have one of those at home, either! Hardening your ice cream at home best happens in the coldest part of your freezer, away from the door. I've found that if I place my churned ice cream in a tall, slender container, I can tuck it inside the freezer bowl of my ice cream machine and create a small subzero chamber within my freezer. As the bowl refreezes, it keeps the container of ice cream extra cold inside.

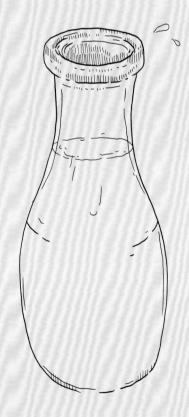

The Machines

If you want to make ice cream, you have to have an ice cream machine. There are no two ways about it. You do have choices, though, when you decide which ice cream maker to bring into your kitchen; they all have pros and cons for you to weigh. The various home models fall into three categories: machines with pre-frozen inserts, machines with built-in compressors, and machines with buckets filled with salt and ice. The physics behind all these machines is identical. In fact, the basic mechanics of ice cream machines haven't evolved much since the mid-nineteenth century, so let's start there.

Hand-Crank Salt and Ice Machines

The earliest ice cream makers depended on ice and salt to freeze the ice cream base. The styles vary, but basically these machines are made of an internal metal canister with a fixed double-blade dasher, a larger external bucket, and a top yoke that allows you to crank and turn the internal canister. You fill the canister with liquid ice cream base and submerge it in the bucket, which is then filled with a slush of ice and rock salt. The physical reaction between the salt and ice interferes with the freezing point of water, causing it to melt but stay liquid below 32°F (similar to how sugar prevents water from freezing in your ice cream!). This super-chilled water surrounds the canister, and the ice cream inside will freeze around the edges. As you crank, the canister rotates, and the blades of the dasher scrape the newly frozen ice cream from the walls, stirring it into the liquid ice cream mix. Historically, ice cream was consumed immediately after churning, as there was no refrigeration to further freeze and harden (or store) the frozen dessert.

You can still hand-churn your ice cream in this fashion by using an old-fashioned hand-crank machine. I have one at home, and it makes a wonderful group activity, especially when children are around. You'll need a large bag of ice, and rock salt (table, kosher, or other cooking salt is too small and just dissolves into the water).

The biggest advantage to this machine is the ability to churn more than one flavor a day, unlike the more-popular machines that use canisters you chill in the freezer a day ahead of time. You can just keep reloading the machine with more salt and ice, and churn ice cream all day long! These machines often can churn bigger batches, too—up to a gallon of ice cream at a time—allowing you to feed large groups of ice cream lovers.

Pre-Frozen Canisters

The most common home ice cream maker has a thick-walled bowl filled with a gel coolant, which requires a 24-hour pre-freeze. A mechanized base rotates the bowl while a plastic double-blade dasher churns inside. The frozen bowl usually retains temperatures below the freezing point of water for 30 to 40 minutes at room temperature.

In our recipe testing for this book, we purchased every home ice cream maker with a frozen insert we could find, ten in all. The prices ranged

*Left to right: Cuisinart 1½-quart ice cream maker with built-in compressor;
Kitchen-Aid stand mixer with ice cream maker attachment; Cuisinart 1½-quart
countertop model; hand-crank salt and ice machine.*

from $30 to $100, and all of them had the same basic mechanics. The differences in quality came in the bowl's ability to maintain cold temperatures when in use and the physical strength of the dasher. We had two clear favorites: the Cuisinart countertop model, in either 1½-quart or 2-quart capacity, and the ice cream maker attachment for Kitchen-Aid stand mixers.

The Cuisinart was our all-around favorite, with the best chilling and the strongest paddle. You might be surprised to learn that many professional pastry chefs without the funds for a large-batch freezer rely on these models. I used to make all the ice cream for Eva restaurant in Seattle with a trio of these machines.

The Kitchen-Aid's blade was strong, and the bowl also stayed cold for a long time, but it won our hearts as the only machine that allows you to churn at different speeds. If you refer to the section on Air in "The Five Components of Ice Cream" (page 20), you'll see that ice cream's texture is defined in large part by the amount of air whipped into it, referred to as overrun. Most home ice cream makers churn very slowly, making dense, chewy ice creams. This is great if you love a dense, chewy ice cream. However, there are those among us who like a lighter, softer ice cream, much like the scoops we get in old-fashioned ice cream shops. The Kitchen-Aid allows you to churn your ice cream at a little higher speed and whip a little more air into your scoops. If you do that, you'll get about 1½ quarts of churned ice cream with each of the recipes in this book, sometimes closer to 2 quarts, depending on the flavor.

The biggest advantages to this type of machine are the small footprint, taking up less of your precious cupboard or counter space, and their relatively low cost. The disadvantage is that it can only be used once in a 24-hour period. Unlike the ice-and-salt machines, or those with built-in compressors, the freezing capability decreases the longer you use it. This means a moderately warm ice cream base may never freeze if added to this machine, and you won't be able to fix it without freezing the bowl again for 24 hours. When I used these machines in a restaurant, I purchased extra bowls, allowing me more than one churn a day. They are much cheaper than the machine itself, and can live in the freezer until you need them. If you are serious about home-made ice cream, and have the room, an extra bowl will be a great advantage.

Also, if your ice cream needs to churn longer than 30 minutes, keep a watchful eye on it. After that time, the freezing capability of the frozen coolant diminishes greatly, and there will come a point when it no longer freezes. If you continue churning past this point, you will begin to melt your ice cream instead of freezing it. If you don't see any textural change for 2 minutes, you've reached the end of the bowl's freezing capability.

Built-in Compressors

Professional ice cream manufacturers all use machines with large compressor units that remove heat from the ice cream quickly as it churns with the dashers. There are a handful of ice cream machines with small compressors available to home cooks that work well, offering you the option of churning multiple batches of ice cream in one day, and they do not require planning ahead and pre-freezing an insert.

The capability of a compressor directly affects the quality of the ice cream. The better the compressor, the faster it freezes and the smoother and creamier the ice cream will be. And the bet-ter the compressor, generally the more expensive the machine.

The top-of-the-line home ice cream makers with built-in compressors will cost an arm and a leg. If you are a texture fanatic, and are willing to shell out the big bucks, these are your machines. There are also less expensive models, all with similar capabilities. But for every machine, we found the best results when we turned the compressor on 5 minutes before we added the ice cream base, ensuring the machine was cold when we started churning. This cut the churning time by about 10 minutes, and made noticeably less icy ice cream. Without taking this step, we found the ice cream churned in home compressor models was icier than the scoops we made with pre-frozen canisters.

The biggest advantage of an ice cream machine with a built-in compressor is its convenience. It allows you to churn ice cream without premeditation, becoming cold the moment you flip the switch. It also allows you to make multiple batches in one day. The quality of the ice cream increases with the pricier models, but the machines in the lower cost range made ice cream of equal quality to those made in our favorite pre-frozen canisters. They do take up quite a bit more space, though, and you'll need to dedicate a large portion of a shelf to house it between your ice cream–making adventures.

The Color of Flavor

It's a little shocking to realize how important color is to flavor. When I staged at The Fat Duck restaurant in England, I learned just how strongly color affects the way food tastes. The lesson came in the form of a little disk of gelée that each guest was treated to. The left half was orange and the right half was red, and the guests were told the flavors were orange and beet. Confusion set in when the guest realized the orange side was made of golden beets and the red side of blood oranges. Giggles ensued. This parlor trick taught me that we use color to help us determine what a flavor is, and the effect is so strong it can mislead us. Try this: Allow yourself to be blindfolded and have someone give you a cup of Coca-Cola and another of 7-Up. Taste them and guess which is which. Or, do the same with red and white wine. For a most people, it's nearly impossible to tell without cues from color.

While testing the recipes for this book, I found myself staring at a lot of the same color: white. With many of the recipes, I infused different ingredients into the milk and cream, but they imparted only their flavor, none of their telltale color. Mint ice cream was the same color as popcorn ice cream, and eggnog ice cream was indistinguishable from banana. Many of the ice creams you buy in the store are colored with food coloring to better help you recognize the flavors. And let's be honest, the colors make the scoops really pretty!

As a chef, I've learned to harness the power of a few brightly colored foods to help me tint my desserts. In doing so, I've found a stunning range of colors not available with food coloring. Here are some of the natural tints I use, with a rainbow of colors you can add to your scoops if you want them to look as good as they taste. Some of these ingredients will have an aroma and flavor when you are extracting and adding them, but the flavor will disappear when diluted in your ice cream. Remember, though, that these are tints, not dyes. If you want a more vividly colored ice cream, you'll need to use food coloring.

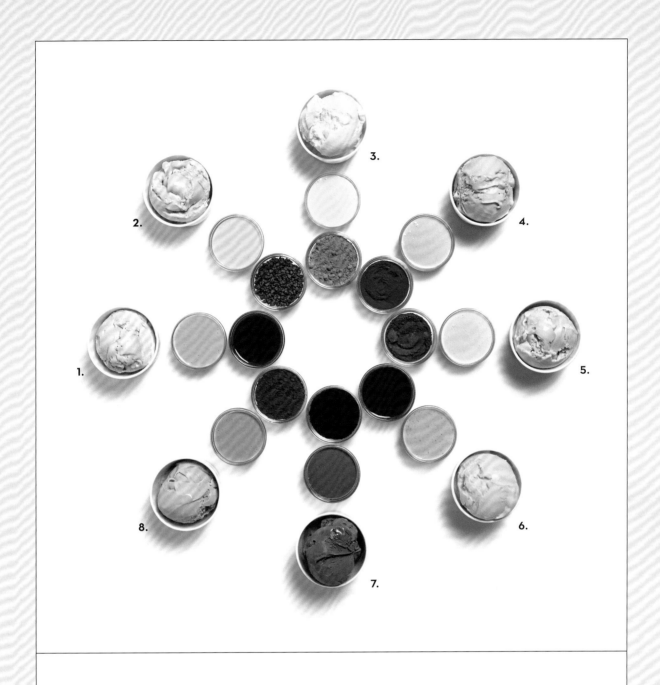

1. Beet juice   5. Blue Majik

2. Annatto   6. Blueberry juice

3. Turmeric   7. Activated charcoal

4. Spirulina   8. Cocoa powder

PINK | Beet juice

The juice of deep purple beets will stain your hands on contact, and tint your ice cream a pretty blushing pink. Add more, and you'll find yourself with a hot flamingo pink ice cream. To use beet juice to color your ice cream, peel a large beet and juice it in a juicer. For every 1000g | 1 quart of ice cream base, add 2g | ½ teaspoon of beet juice to the cooled base.

ORANGE | Annatto

This tiny, lumpy seed imparts a deeply orange color. You'll recognize it as the color of boxed macaroni and cheese. Buy 50g | ½ cup of whole seeds and slowly simmer with 1 cup water for 30 minutes, or until you have about 25g | 2 tablespoons of highly concentrated orange liquid. (Be careful not to evaporate all the water.) Strain out the seeds and let the liquid cool. To color 1000g | 1 quart of ice cream base, add 15g | 1 tablespoon of annatto coloring to the cooled base. Leftover tint keeps in the refrigerator for 1 week, or in the freezer for 3 months. If you can find powdered annatto seeds, often called achiote, use 1.5g | ½ teaspoon of annatto powder dissolved in 5g | 1 teaspoon water.

YELLOW | Turmeric

This yellow spice is responsible for the distinct color of yellow mustard. To color 1000g | 1 quart of ice cream base, mix 1.5g | ½ teaspoon of turmeric powder into 5g | 1 teaspoon of water until it is dissolved into a paste. Whisk the paste into your cooled base. The color will begin slightly orange, but after 30 minutes it will bloom into a lemony yellow.

GREEN | Spirulina

A blue-green algae sold as a health booster in many natural foods stores, this intensely green powder has a deeply vegetal, almost fish-food aroma that is enough to deter you from wanting it anywhere near your dessert. However, I promise you won't taste it once it is diluted into your ice cream! To color 1000g | 1 quart of ice cream base, mix 1g | ½ teaspoon of spirulina with 5g | 1 teaspoon of water and stir it into a paste. Whisk the paste into your cooled base. The color will deepen after 5 minutes, so wait before you add more if you desire a darker color.

BLUE | **Blue Majik**

This is a specific spirulina powder, proprietary to a company called E3live, and it imparts the most beautiful blue when added to ice cream. It's even stinkier than regular spirulina, but again I promise you won't taste a thing when it is mixed into your ice cream base. There aren't too many foods that are blue, but that's no reason not to have some fun. Add it to vanilla ice cream and call it cotton candy, or flavor your ice cream with almond and vanilla extract, and make the Italian favorite, Puffalo, which is what Italian children call Smurfs. To color 1000g | 1 quart of ice cream base, mix 1g | ½ teaspoon of Blue Majik with 5g | 1 teaspoon of water and stir it into a paste. Whisk the paste into your cooled base. The color will brighten after 5 minutes, so wait before you add more if you desire a brighter color.

PURPLE | **Blueberry juice**

The juice of blueberries can tint your ice cream a lovely periwinkle shade of purple without flavoring it, particularly if the berries are never cooked. In season, harvest blueberry juice by freezing the berries, then letting them thaw in a basket strainer set over a bowl. The freezer damages the tissue of the blueberries enough that you can squeeze the berries and wring them of their purple juice. Out of season, buy frozen berries instead. Blackberries will also work if blueberries aren't around; their color is slightly more lilac than periwinkle. To color 1000g | 1 quart of ice cream base with blueberry juice, whisk 15g | 1 tablespoon into your cooled base. I recommend adding the blueberry juice just before churning, as on occasion the blueberry color fades unless frozen immediately.

BLACK | **Activated charcoal**

This powder is as black as black can be. It is sold as an intestinal decontaminant, a fancy term for Pepto-Bismal, which is flooded with pink coloring to mask the black charcoal it contains. You can use it to tint your ice cream gray, if you so desire, and your black licorice ice cream might taste more like the candy if you choose to do so. To color 1000g | 1 quart of ice cream base with activated charcoal, stir .5g | ½ teaspoon into 5g | 1 teaspoon of water until it forms a paste. Stir this paste into your cooled base.

BROWN | **Cocoa powder**

I have often used a hint of cocoa powder to color coffee ice creams, Fernet Branca-flavored ice cream, or Danish licorice ice cream. You won't taste a teaspoon of cocoa powder in a quart of ice cream, but you'll see it! I recommend tinting ice creams brown if they are infused with whole spices or brown liquors, as well. If you use Dutch-processed cocoa powder, you will notice a red tint to the ice cream you are coloring. Unless this is desired, reach for a natural cocoa powder, as dark as you can find. To color 1000g | 1 quart of ice cream base with cocoa powder, stir 2g | 1 teaspoon of cocoa powder into 10g | 2 teaspoons of hot water until it forms a paste. Whisk this paste into your cooled base.

THE RECIPES

A Few Things to Know When Making These Recipes

Milk

The recipes in this book are intended for use with homogenized whole milk (the standard 4% butterfat). If you use a non-homogenized creamline milk from your local dairy, make sure you warm it and blend it in a blender at high speed for 3 minutes just before you use it. This will disperse the fat.

Cream cheese

When cream cheese is called for in a recipe, use blocks of full-fat cream cheese, leaving the low-fat, fat-free, whipped, and spreadable variations for your bagels.

Eggs

Unless specified, these recipes call for large eggs, which are 2 ounces or about 60 grams each.

Cream

All cream in this book is heavy cream, with 40% butterfat content. If you can't find the percentage of fat listed on the label, you can calculate it yourself by dividing the grams of fat in a serving by the gram weight of a serving.

Buttermilk

While true buttermilk, strained off of churned butter, is a culinary delight, the recipes in this book use standard, cultured low-fat buttermilk.

Glucose

Glucose is a key ingredient in these recipes, offering the textural benefits of sugar while tasting much less sweet (see page 19). Glucose syrup is sold in craft stores, in the candy-making section, or online. You can also substitute corn syrup (the easiest choice) or homemade inverted sugar syrup (see page 214), though both are noticeably sweeter.

Coconut oil

Many of the add-in recipes use coconut oil, which makes the add-ins melt in your mouth instantly, even when frozen. There are many coconut oils available, and several of them taste like coconut. Surprise, surprise. I recommend searching out expeller-pressed coconut oil, which doesn't add any coconut flavor when used in a recipe.

Kitchen thermometer

While I offer visual cues to look for in most recipes, it is a great idea to have a kitchen thermometer—either a probe-style digital-read thermometer or mercury-style candy thermometer—around for some of the recipes, especially the caramels and ribbons.

Grated citrus zest

Whenever the recipe calls for grated citrus zest, my preferred method is to grate the peel with a small Microplane grater, which produces very fine zest, and then pack it into the teaspoon to measure it.

Malic acid

Malic acid, derived from apples, is my preferred powdered acid, as it imparts a clean flavor. It can be special-ordered online; I get mine from Terra Spice.

Citric acid

Available widely for use in canning jams and jellies, citric acid is a powdered acid derived from citrus fruits. It can be used anywhere malic acid is called for in this book.

Custard Ice Creams

Ice cream made with egg yolks is called custard ice cream (or French-style ice cream), and is the richest-tasting ice cream you can make. It is also some of the smoothest. Upon first bite, you'll notice that custard-style ice cream is dense and a little chewy, the kind of ice cream you can really sink your teeth into. When the egg yolks are added, they occupy space in your ice cream that would otherwise be taken up by watery milk, which in turn replaces the ice crystals with fat. Fat becomes hard in your freezer, adding firmness to the ice cream and creating that bitable quality many of us love in a scoop.

Another characteristic of fat is its ability to delay flavor release. The flavors in this rich custard-style ice cream take a moment to present themselves, but once they do, they linger. Because of this, I use a custard-style ice cream to embody flavors I like to cozy up to and spend some time with—deep flavors, like roasted coffee, black teas, vanilla beans, complex whole spices, or robust herbs like rosemary and sage.

A custard ice cream is also a great canvas for different sugars, like caramel, molasses, brown sugar, maple, or honey. These sugars are rich and deep, and at times a little angular, a quality that complements the extra richness of the egg yolks. To add the flavor of an alternative sugar, you can exchange it for some of the granulated sugar in the recipe—generally speaking, one to one by weight.

(If you're using maple syrup, I recommend boiling the maple syrup until it is reduced by half before adding it, as real maple syrup is high in water.) Another thing to note, when adding an alternative sugar, is that it can often be slightly acidic. If you add it while the dairy is hot, it may curdle your milk. Most of the alternative sugars are in liquid form, which is convenient; you simply stir them into the ice cream base when it cools down. For brown sugar, you can create a syrup of your own, as I do for the Bourbon Butterscotch Ice Cream (page 54), and add the cooled syrup to the cooled ice cream base.

Finally, if you want to use a nip of liquor—rum, bourbon, brandy, Scotch, and sweeter liqueurs or eau de vie like Grand Marnier or Poire Williams—in your ice cream, add it to a custard-style ice cream. You must be careful when adding liquor to ice cream, though, as the alcohol quickly lowers the freezing point of ice cream, meaning that it will melt more easily. Should you add too much liquor, you'll find yourself with creamy mush. I recommend replacing no more than 2 tablespoons (30g) of milk with booze for every quart of ice cream base. Another technique is to first cook off some of the alcohol in the liquor; if you look at the Bourbon Butterscotch Ice Cream, you'll notice this technique. If you want a stronger flavor, just drown your finished scoops with a jigger or two, like an affogato.

Blank Slate Custard Ice Cream

Makes between 1 and 1½ quarts ice cream

Cream (30%)
300g | 1½ cups

Milk (40%)
400g | 2 cups

Glucose syrup (5%)
50g | ¼ cup

Sugar (15%)
150g | ¾ cup

Egg yolks (10%)
100g | about 5 large yolks

Texture agent of your choice
(see below)

This recipe is a blank slate, created so you can adapt it to any flavor you like. All the recipes in this chapter stem from this basic recipe; armed with this formula, you can invent any flavor of custard-style ice cream you like. I recommend using it when you want to flavor your ice cream with deep, rich flavors like vanilla beans, whole spices, black teas, dark sugars, caramels, licorice, and brown liquors.

Prepare an ice bath. Fill a large bowl two-thirds of the way with very icy ice water and place it in the refrigerator.

Boil the dairy and sugars. Put the cream, milk, glucose, and sugar ① in a medium heavy-bottomed saucepan, and place it over medium-high heat. Cook, whisking occasionally to discourage the milk from scorching, until the mixture comes to a full rolling boil ④, then remove the pot from heat.

Temper the yolks and cook the custard. In medium bowl, whisk the yolks. Add ½ cup of the hot dairy mixture to the yolks while whisking so the hot milk doesn't scramble the yolks. Pour the tempered yolks back into the pot of hot milk while whisking. Place the pot over medium-low heat and cook, stirring and scraping the bottom of the pot constantly with a rubber spatula to avoid curdling.

Chill. When you notice the custard thickening, or the temperature reaches 180°F on a thermometer, immediately pour the custard into a shallow metal or glass bowl ③. Nest the hot bowl into the ice bath, stirring occasionally until it cools down.

Strain. When the custard is cool to the touch (50°F or below) ②, strain it through a fine-mesh sieve to remove any bits of egg yolk. (This step is optional, but will help ensure the smoothest ice cream possible.)

Cure. Transfer the cooled base to the refrigerator to cure for 4 hours, or preferably overnight. (This step is also optional, but the texture will be much improved with it.)

Churn. Place the base into the bowl of an ice cream maker and churn according to the manufacturer's instructions. The ice cream is ready when it thickens into the texture of soft-serve ice cream and holds its shape, typically 20 to 30 minutes.

Harden. To freeze your custard ice cream in the American hard-pack style, immediately transfer it to a container with an airtight lid. Press plastic wrap directly on the surface of the ice cream to prevent ice crystals from forming, cover, and store it in your freezer until it hardens completely, between 4 and 12 hours. Or, feel free to enjoy your ice cream immediately; the texture will be similar to soft-serve.

TEXTURE AGENTS

① Best texture
Commercial stabilizer
3g | 1 teaspoon mixed with the sugar before it is added to the dairy.

② Least icy
Guar or xanthan gum
1g | ¼ teaspoon whirled in a blender with the custard base after it is chilled in the ice bath.

③ Easiest to use
Tapioca starch
5g | 2 teaspoons mixed with 20g | 2 tablespoons of cold milk, whisked into the custard base after it is finished cooking.

④ Most accessible
Cornstarch
10g | 1 tablespoon plus 1 teaspoon, mixed with 20g | 2 tablespoons of cold milk, whisked into the simmering dairy, then cooked for 1 minute.

fig. 1

fig. 2

fig. 3

fig. 4

fig. 1: *Boil the dairy and sugar.*

fig. 2: *Temper the yolks.*

fig. 3: *Cook the custard.*

fig. 4: *Strain the custard, then cure.*

Vanilla Ice Cream

Makes between 1 and 1½ quarts ice cream

Cream (30%)
300g | 1½ cups

Milk (40%)
400g | 2 cups

Glucose syrup (5%)
50g | ¼ cup

Sugar (15%)
150g | ¾ cup

Vanilla
1 whole bean (or 2 tablespoons vanilla extract)

Egg yolks (10%)
100g | about 5 large yolks

Texture agent of your choice
(see below)

Vanilla has come to imply plain or boring. I have a feeling that has to do with artificial vanilla flavor, a cheap liquid that contains a single flavor molecule called vanillin. Vanilla beans do contain vanillin, but they also contain myriad other flavor molecules, all developed during the nine months that the vanilla beans spend fermenting and drying in the equatorial sun, where they are hand-massaged and blanketed every night. When you consider that vanilla is the seedpod of an orchid that only grows near the equator, you'll begin to understand how exotic this flavor truly is.

Bourbon vanilla beans grow in Madagascar and Mexico, and have brown sugary, bourbon notes, with a masculine, leather-like fragrance. This is most likely the vanilla you've tasted. When these South American orchids were carried to Tahiti, they mutated. Tahitian vanilla beans taste bright and perfumed compared to the smoky flavors of the bourbon vanilla bean. To me, the Tahitian vanilla bean tastes of wildflower honey and saffron, with a feminine floral fragrance reminiscent of the flowers the seeds in this pod were to become.

To use a vanilla bean, carefully split it lengthwise to reveal the cache of tiny, flavorful seeds inside. Use the tip of a knife to scrape them out and collect them. The vanilla seeds are added to the ice cream (or directly to any recipe in which vanilla extract is called for); for ice cream, I also infuse the dried fruit-flavored pod in the dairy.

Vanilla extracts are made by blending the entire bean, pod and seeds, then soaking the mash in alcohol to extract the flavor. If you can't get your hands on vanilla beans to make this ice cream, real vanilla extract is an appropriate substitution. But I strongly urge you to find a vanilla bean—it will make your ice cream sing!

TEXTURE AGENTS

① Best texture
Commercial stabilizer
3g | 1 teaspoon mixed with the sugar before it is added to the dairy.

② Least icy
Guar or xanthan gum
1g | ¼ teaspoon whirled in a blender with the custard base after it is chilled in the ice bath.

③ Easiest to use
Tapioca starch
5g | 2 teaspoons mixed with 20g | 2 tablespoons of cold milk, whisked into the custard base after it is finished cooking.

④ Most accessible
Cornstarch
10g | 1 tablespoon plus 1 teaspoon, mixed with 20g | 2 tablespoons of cold milk, whisked into the vanilla flavored dairy after it's reheated, then cooked for 1 minute.

Prepare an ice bath. Fill a large bowl two-thirds of the way with very icy ice water and place it in the refrigerator.

Boil the dairy and sugars. Put the cream, milk, glucose, and sugar ① in a medium heavy-bottomed saucepan, and place it over medium-high heat. Cook, whisking occasionally to discourage the milk from scorching, until the mixture comes to a full rolling boil, then remove the pot from heat.

Infuse the vanilla. Cut the vanilla bean in half lengthwise and use the tip of a paring knife to scrape the seeds from the pod. Stir both the vanilla seeds and the pod into the hot dairy, and allow the vanilla bean to infuse for 30 minutes. (If using vanilla extract, wait to add it to the cooled ice cream base or the flavor will disappear during cooking.)

Remove the vanilla and reheat. Remove and discard the empty vanilla pod. Reheat the dairy over medium-high heat. Cook until the liquid comes to a full rolling boil ④, then remove from the heat.

Temper the yolks and cook the custard. In a medium bowl, whisk the yolks. Add ½ cup of the hot dairy mixture to the yolks while whisking so the hot milk doesn't scramble the yolks. Pour the tempered yolks back into the pot of hot milk while whisking. Place the pot over medium-low heat and cook, stirring and scraping the bottom of the pot constantly with a rubber spatula to avoid curdling.

Chill. When you notice the custard thickening, or the temperature reaches 180°F on a kitchen thermometer, immediately pour the custard into a shallow metal or glass bowl ③. Nest the hot bowl into the ice bath, stirring occasionally until it cools down.

Strain. When the custard is cool to the touch (50°F or below) ②, strain it through a fine-mesh sieve to remove any bits of egg yolk. (This step is optional, but will help ensure the smoothest ice cream possible.)

Cure. Transfer the cooled base to the refrigerator to cure for 4 hours, or preferably overnight. (This step is also optional, but the texture will be much improved with it.)

Churn. Place the base into the bowl of an ice cream maker and churn according to the manufacturer's instructions. The ice cream is ready when it thickens into the texture of soft-serve ice cream and holds its shape, typically 20 to 30 minutes.

Harden. To freeze your custard ice cream in the American hard-pack style, immediately transfer it to a container with an airtight lid. Press plastic wrap directly on the surface of the ice cream to prevent ice crystals from forming, cover, and store it in your freezer until it hardens completely, between 4 and 12 hours. Or, feel free to enjoy your ice cream immediately; the texture will be similar to soft-serve.

Bourbon Butterscotch Ice Cream

Makes between 1 and 1½ quarts ice cream

Butter (1%)
10g | 2 teaspoons

Cream (29%)
290g | 1½ cups

Dark brown sugar (15%)
150g | ¾ cup tightly packed

Bourbon (2%)
20g | 2 tablespoons

Kosher or sea salt
3g | ½ teaspoon

Milk (38%)
380g | 2 cups

Glucose syrup (5%)
50g | ¼ cup

Egg yolks (10%)
100g | about 5 large yolks

Texture agent of your choice
(see below)

The name butterscotch doesn't actually refer to the smoky Scotch whiskey, as I thought for years. Shuna Fish Lydon is a pastry chef and butterscotch historian, and from her I learned the word *scotch*, when used as a suffix, meant *to cut* or *to score* in Old English. Originally, butterscotch was a hard candy made from butter and unrefined molasses-rich sugar, which was cut, or "scotched," into pieces. This buttery, brown sugary flavor lives on in this ice cream, with a boost of flavor from bourbon, a nod toward to my delicious misunderstanding.

Brown sugar is rich in molasses, like the unrefined sugars of yore, but it is acidic and will curdle the milk if the two are cooked together. To combat this, cook the brown sugar, bourbon, and cream into a sauce that is added to the custard when both are cool. Cooking the bourbon with the sauce helps cook out the alcohol in the bourbon, too, which prevents the alcohol from depressing the freezing point of the ice cream and ultimately making it too soft to scoop. And if you'd like to leave out the bourbon entirely, I think you'll find this flavor is quite delicious even without it.

TEXTURE AGENTS

① **Best texture**
Commercial stabilizer
3g | 1 teaspoon mixed with 15g | 1 tablespoon of sugar and added to the milk, and remove 15g | 1 tablespoon brown sugar from the recipe.

② **Least icy**
Guar or xanthan gum
1g | ¼ teaspoon whirled in a blender with the custard base after it is chilled in the ice bath.

③ **Easiest to use**
Tapioca starch
5g | 2 teaspoons mixed with 20g | 2 tablespoons of cold milk, whisked into the custard base after it is finished cooking.

④ **Most accessible**
Cornstarch
10g | 1 tablespoon plus 1 teaspoon, mixed with 20g | 2 tablespoons of cold milk, whisked into the milk and glucose after they come to a boil, then cooked for 1 minute.

Prepare the bourbon butterscotch.
Place the butter in a medium heavy-bottomed saucepan over medium heat. Cook until the butter melts, sizzles, and begins to take on a brown, nutty color. When it's richly browned but not burnt, add the cream, brown sugar, bourbon, and salt. Cook the sauce, stirring occasionally to help dissolve the sugar, over medium-high heat until it comes to a boil. Transfer the sauce to a bowl and put it in the refrigerator to cool below 100°F, or body temperature.

Prepare an ice bath. Fill a large bowl two-thirds of the way with very icy ice water and place it in the refrigerator.

Boil the milk and glucose. Put the milk ① and glucose in a medium heavy-bottomed saucepan, and place it over medium-high heat. Cook, whisking occasionally to discourage the milk from scorching, until the mixture comes to a full rolling boil ④, then remove the pot from heat.

Temper the yolks and cook the custard. In a medium bowl, whisk the yolks. Add ½ cup of the hot dairy mixture to the yolks while whisking so the hot milk doesn't scramble the yolks. Pour the tempered yolks back into the pot of hot milk while whisking. Place the pot over medium-low heat and cook, stirring and scraping the bottom of the pot constantly with a rubber spatula to avoid curdling.

Chill. When you notice the custard thickening, or the temperature reaches 180°F on a kitchen thermometer, immediately pour the custard into a shallow metal or glass bowl ③. Nest the hot bowl into the ice bath, stirring occasionally until it cools down.

Mix the butterscotch into the custard and strain. When the custard is cool to the touch (50°F or below) ②, remove the bowl from the ice bath and add the chilled butterscotch sauce, whisking until evenly combined. Strain it through a fine-mesh sieve to remove any bits of egg yolk. (Straining is optional, but will help ensure the smoothest ice cream possible.)

Cure. Transfer the cooled base to the refrigerator to cure for 4 hours, or preferably overnight. (This step is also optional, but the texture will be much improved with it.)

Churn. Place the custard base into the bowl of an ice cream maker and churn according to the manufacturer's instructions. The ice cream is ready when it thickens into the texture of soft-serve ice cream and holds its shape, typically 20 to 30 minutes.

Harden. To freeze your custard ice cream in the American hard-pack style, immediately transfer it to a container with an airtight lid. Press plastic wrap directly on the surface of the ice cream to prevent ice crystals from forming, cover, and store it in your freezer until it hardens completely, between 4 and 12 hours. Or, feel free to enjoy your ice cream immediately; the texture will be similar to soft-serve.

Cold-Press Coffee Ice Cream

Makes between 1 and 1½ quarts ice cream

Cream (20%)
200g | 1 cup

Milk (40%)
400g | 2 cups

Glucose syrup (5%)
50g | ¼ cup

Sugar (15%)
150g | ¾ cup

Egg yolks (10%)
100g | about 5 large yolks

Coffee beans
30g | ½ cup

Crème fraîche (10%)
100g | ½ cup

Texture agent of your choice
(see below)

TEXTURE AGENTS

① Best texture
Commercial stabilizer
3g | 1 teaspoon mixed with the sugar before it is added to the dairy.

② Least icy
Guar or xanthan gum
1g | ¼ teaspoon whirled in a blender with the custard base after it is chilled in the ice bath.

③ Easiest to use
Tapioca starch
5g | 2 teaspoons mixed with 20g | 2 tablespoons of cold milk, whisked into the custard base after it is finished cooking.

④ Most accessible
Cornstarch
10g | 1 tablespoon plus 1 teaspoon, mixed with 20g | 2 tablespoons of cold milk, whisked into the simmering dairy, then cooked for 1 minute.

Coffee was my mother's favorite ice cream flavor, and one I pretended to like as a child out of sheer admiration for her. As I grew into a coffee-swilling adult, though, I too found a deep appreciation for this flavor. Most ice cream shops add concentrated coffee to their ice cream, making a recognizable tan-colored scoop. As a pastry chef, I learned to flavor coffee ice cream by infusing whole coffee beans into the dairy, giving me a pale-colored scoop with a deep coffee flavor.

As cold-press came onto the coffee shop scene, promising a smoother, less acidic brew, it too changed the way I thought about flavoring my coffee ice cream. Heat changes coffee's flavor, and as it brews, bitter, briny, acidic notes come with it. When I started making a cold-press coffee ice cream, I cooled my ice cream base completely before I introduced the beans. I let them infuse slowly, over the course of a full day and night. The resulting ice cream tastes the way coffee smells, and has the unique quality of being white. I stir in a small amount of tart crème fraîche at the end, and its acidic quality makes this coffee ice cream a very special version of a commonplace flavor—one you won't forget.

For a more classic-tasting coffee ice cream, or if you are short on time, go ahead and add the coffee beans to the milk and cream as they are heating up, and let them steep for 10 minutes before straining them out. You can also replace the crème fraîche with an equal amount of cream, added with the milk in the beginning of the recipe.

Prepare an ice bath. Fill a large bowl two-thirds of the way with very icy ice water and place it in the refrigerator.

Boil the dairy and sugars. Put the cream, milk, glucose, and sugar ① in a medium heavy-bottomed saucepan, and place it over medium-high heat. Cook, whisking occasionally to discourage the milk from scorching, until the mixture comes to a full rolling boil ④, then remove the pot from heat.

Temper the yolks and cook the custard. In a medium bowl, whisk the yolks. Add ½ cup of the hot dairy mixture to the yolks while whisking so the hot milk doesn't scramble the yolks. Pour the tempered yolks back into the pot of hot milk while whisking. Place the pot over medium-low heat and cook, stirring and scraping the bottom of the pot constantly with a rubber spatula to avoid curdling.

Chill. When you notice the custard thickening, or the temperature reaches 180°F on a kitchen thermometer, immediately pour the custard into a shallow metal or glass bowl ③. Nest the hot bowl into the ice bath, stirring occasionally until it cools down.

Strain. When the custard is cool to the touch (50°F or below) ②, strain it through a fine-mesh sieve to remove any bits of egg yolk. (This step is optional, but will help ensure the smoothest ice cream possible.)

Infuse the coffee. Stir the coffee beans into the cooled custard, and transfer it to the refrigerator to infuse for 12 hours.

Strain the custard and add the crème fraîche. When you are ready to churn your custard, strain out the coffee beans through a fine-mesh sieve. Take ¼ cup of the cold custard and stir it into the crème fraîche until smooth, and then stir this back into the custard.

Churn. Place the base into the bowl of an ice cream maker and churn according to the manufacturer's instructions. The ice cream is ready when it thickens into the texture of soft-serve ice cream and holds its shape, typically 20 to 30 minutes.

Harden. To freeze your custard ice cream in the American hard-pack style, immediately transfer it to a container with an airtight lid. Press plastic wrap directly on the surface of the ice cream to prevent ice crystals from forming, cover, and store it in your freezer until it hardens completely, between 4 and 12 hours. Or, feel free to enjoy your ice cream immediately; the texture will be similar to soft-serve.

Salted Crème Fraîche Caramel Ice Cream

Makes between 1 and 1½ quarts ice cream

Cream (20%)
200g | 1 cup

Sugar (15%)
150g | ¾ cup

Milk (40%)
400g | 2 cups

Glucose syrup (5%)
50g | ¼ cup

Egg yolks (10%)
100g | 6 large yolks

Crème fraîche (10%)
100g | ½ cup

Sea salt
10g | 2 teaspoons

Texture agent of your choice
(see below)

Salted caramel is a new standard, and there is hardly an ice cream shop without their spin on this flavor. This version is finished with crème fraîche, which adds a bright dimension to the wonderfully deep flavor of the caramelized sugars. This recipe also features a dry caramel, whereby the sugar is added to a hot pan bit by bit. The flavor grows deeper and deeper as each successive spoonful of sugar is added, until you have a complex layered caramel.

Take extra caution when adding liquid to caramelized sugar—caramel can cause really bad burns! (I can show you the divots in my right forearm, where hot caramel landed over ten years ago.) The cream will sputter less if it's warmed before it's added to the molten sugar, but just in case, keep a little bowl of ice water at the ready. You can also take precautionary measures and cover your hand with an oven mitt or dish towel as you add the cream.

Crème fraîche can be purchased from a grocery store, or you can make your own (see page 215). The crème fraîche is acidic, and if you cook it with the ice cream base, it will curdle. Instead, wait to add the crème fraîche until the ice cream base has cooled completely.

TEXTURE AGENTS

① **Best texture**
Commercial stabilizer
3g | 1 teaspoon mixed with 5g | 1 teaspoon granulated sugar and added to the milk.

② **Least icy**
Guar or xanthan gum
1g | ¼ teaspoon whirled in a blender with the ice cream base after it is chilled in the ice bath.

③ **Easiest to use**
Tapioca starch
5g | 2 teaspoons mixed with 20g | 2 tablespoons of cold milk, whisked into the custard base after it is finished cooking.

④ **Most accessible**
Cornstarch
10g | 1 tablespoon plus 1 teaspoon, mixed with 20g | 2 tablespoons of cold milk, whisked into the simmering caramel flavored dairy, then cooked for 1 minute.

Make the caramel. Place the cream in a small saucepan and bring it to a boil over medium-high heat, then remove it from the heat. Place a medium heavy-bottomed saucepan over medium heat and sprinkle 2 tablespoons of sugar over the bottom of the pot. When the sugar has started to take on color, sprinkle 2 more spoons of sugar over the bottom of the pot and stir gently with a heatproof spatula. Continue this process, 2 spoonfuls at a time, until all the sugar has been added to the pot and the sugar is a deep amber. To test the color of the caramel, carefully dip the corner of a piece of white paper into it. When the color of the caramel is no lighter than a newborn fawn and no darker than a cup of black tea, remove it from heat and immediately add the warm cream, bit by bit, carefully avoiding any hot splatters that might come from the pot. Place the pot back over medium-high heat, and whisk until the caramel is smooth and even. Remove the pot from heat.

Prepare an ice bath. Fill a large bowl two-thirds of the way with very icy ice water and place it in the refrigerator.

Boil the dairy and caramel. Whisk the milk ① and glucose into the caramel. Cook over medium-high heat, whisking occasionally to discourage the milk from scorching. When the mixture comes to a full rolling boil, ④ remove the pot from heat.

Temper the yolks and cook the custard. In a medium bowl, whisk the yolks. Add ½ cup of the hot dairy mixture to the yolks while whisking so the hot milk doesn't scramble the yolks. Pour the tempered yolks back into the pot of hot milk while whisking. Place the pot over medium-low heat and cook, stirring and scraping the bottom of the pot constantly with a rubber spatula to avoid curdling.

Chill. When you notice the custard thickening, or the temperature reaches 180°F on a kitchen thermometer, immediately pour the custard into a shallow metal or glass bowl ③. Nest the hot bowl into the ice bath, stirring occasionally until it cools down.

Add the crème fraîche and salt, then strain. When the custard is cool to the touch (50°F or below), add the crème fraîche and salt, and stir until evenly combined ②. Strain it through a fine-mesh sieve to remove any bits of egg yolk. (Straining is optional, but will help ensure the smoothest ice cream possible.)

Cure. Transfer the cooled base to the refrigerator to cure for 4 hours, or preferably overnight. (This step is also optional, but the texture will be much improved with it.)

Churn. Place the base into the bowl of an ice cream maker and churn according to the manufacturer's instructions. The ice cream is ready when it thickens into the texture of soft-serve ice cream and holds its shape, typically 20 to 30 minutes.

Harden. To freeze your custard ice cream in the American hard-pack style, immediately transfer it to a container with an airtight lid. Press plastic wrap directly on the surface of the ice cream to prevent ice crystals from forming, cover, and store it in your freezer until it hardens completely, between 4 and 12 hours. Or, feel free to enjoy your ice cream immediately; the texture will be similar to soft-serve.

Toasted Hay Ice Cream

Makes between 1 and 1½ quarts ice cream

Hay
50g | 2 ounces (1 large handful)

Cream (30%)
300g | 1½ cups

Milk (40%)
400g | 2 cups

Glucose syrup (5%)
50g | ¼ cup

Kosher or sea salt
2g | ¼ teaspoon

Sugar (15%)
150g | ¾ cup

Egg yolks (10%)
100g | about 5 large yolks

Texture agent of your choice
(see below)

Yes, this ice cream is flavored with the same hay we feed horses and cows, an outlandish flavor I first experienced while staging at Noma restaurant in Copenhagen.

It might not *sound* like a good idea, but don't let this flavor pass you by. The smell of toasted hay is intoxicating, and chefs have been capitalizing on this for centuries, roasting cuts of meat in nests of the dried grass, and wrapping cheeses to age in the fragrant straw.

I know there is no section for hay in your local produce department. Getting your hands on good-quality fresh hay takes some doing. I usually get mine by asking every farmer at the farmers' market until someone agrees to bring me some the following week. At times I've had to dry the hay myself, laying freshly cut grasses out on a sheet pan and tucking them in the oven on its lowest setting until it's dry and crackly. Once you find yourself with hay in hand, toasting it in the oven unlocks golden, nutty, grassy, green tea notes that are unlike anything else.

Prepare an ice bath. Fill a large bowl two-thirds of the way with very icy ice water and place it in the refrigerator.

Toast the hay. Preheat the oven to 350°F. Lay the hay on a sheet pan in a single layer, and toast it for 15 minutes, until very fragrant. While the hay is toasting, begin the next step; you'll want to infuse the dairy and hay while both are hot.

Boil the dairy and sugars. Put the cream, milk, glucose, salt, and sugar ① in a medium heavy-bottomed saucepan, and place it over medium-high heat. Cook, whisking occasionally to discourage the milk from scorching, until the mixture comes to a full rolling boil, then remove the pot from heat.

Infuse. When the hay comes out of the oven, immediately stir it into the hot dairy, and allow it to infuse for 30 minutes.

Strain and reheat the milk. Pour the mixture through a fine-mesh strainer, discarding the hay. Place the dairy in a clean pot over medium-high heat. Cook until the liquid comes to a full rolling boil ④, then remove from the heat.

Temper the yolks and cook the custard. In a medium bowl, whisk the yolks. Add ½ cup of the hot dairy mixture to the yolks while whisking so the hot milk doesn't scramble the yolks. Pour the tempered yolks back into the pot of hot milk while whisking. Place the pot over medium-low heat and cook, stirring and scraping the bottom of the pot constantly with a rubber spatula to avoid curdling.

TEXTURE AGENTS

① **Best texture**
Commercial stabilizer
3g | 1 teaspoon mixed with the granulated sugar before it is added to the dairy.

② **Least icy**
Guar or xanthan gum
1g | ¼ teaspoon whirled in a blender with the custard base after it is chilled in the ice bath.

③ **Easiest to use**
Tapioca starch
5g | 2 teaspoons mixed with 20g | 2 tablespoons of cold milk, whisked into the custard base after it is finished cooking.

④ **Most accessible**
Cornstarch
10g | 1 tablespoon plus 1 teaspoon, mixed with 20g | 2 tablespoons of cold milk, whisked into the simmering hay-flavored dairy, then cooked for 1 minute.

Chill. When you notice the custard thickening, or the temperature reaches 180°F on a kitchen thermometer, immediately pour the custard into a shallow metal or glass bowl ③. Nest the hot bowl into the ice bath, stirring occasionally until it cools down.

Strain. When the custard is cool to the touch (50°F or below) ②, strain it through a fine-mesh sieve to remove any bits of egg yolk. (This step is optional, but will help ensure the smoothest ice cream possible.)

Cure. Transfer the cooled base to the refrigerator to cure for 4 hours, or preferably overnight. (This step is also optional, but the texture will be much improved with it.)

Churn. Place the base into the bowl of an ice cream maker and churn according to the manufacturer's instructions. The ice cream is ready when it thickens into the texture of soft-serve ice cream and holds its shape, typically 20 to 30 minutes.

Harden. To freeze your custard ice cream in the American hard-pack style, immediately transfer it to a container with an airtight lid. Press plastic wrap directly on the surface of the ice cream to prevent ice crystals from forming, cover, and store it in your freezer until it hardens completely, between 4 and 12 hours. Or, feel free to enjoy your ice cream immediately; the texture will be similar to soft-serve.

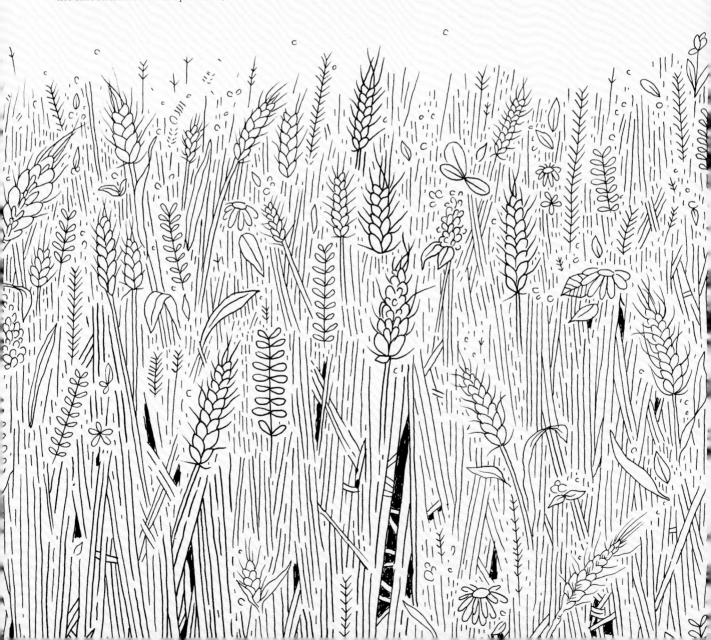

Burnt Honey Ice Cream

Makes between 1 and 1½ quarts ice cream

Cream (30%)
300g | 1½ cups

Honey (10%)
100g | ½ cup

Kosher or sea salt
2g | ¼ teaspoon

Milk (30%)
300g | 1½ cups

Glucose syrup (5%)
50g | ¼ cup

Sugar (5%)
50g | ¼ cup

Egg yolks (10%)
100 g | about 5 large yolks

Buttermilk (10%)
100g | ½ cup

Texture agent of your choice
(see below)

Burnt flavors are all the rage right now in haute cuisine, defying generations of cooks who attempted to do everything *but* burn their food. While "burning" the honey for this ice cream will cause it to smoke and turn a suspicious shade of dark, what's happening inside the pot is pure caramel magic.

Honey is rich to begin with, but caramelizing it pushes it over the edge. So much so, that I've found a dose of lean, sour buttermilk is the only thing that can bring this flavor back to solid ground. I don't recommend making this flavor without it.

We kept this sophisticated flavor on the rotating gelato menu at Avec restaurant in Chicago when I was the pastry chef there, and often flecked it with Classic Chocolate Chunks (page 156), made with a touch of toasted sesame oil. The flavor was outrageous, and we sold out every time we stocked our freezers with it. Now that I think about it, a few drops of sesame oil added to this ice cream would also be delicious!

TEXTURE AGENTS

① **Best texture**
Commercial stabilizer
3g | 1 teaspoon mixed with the sugar before it is added to the dairy.

② **Least icy**
Guar or xanthan gum
1g | ¼ teaspoon whirled in a blender with the custard base after it is chilled in the ice bath.

③ **Easiest to use**
Tapioca starch
5g | 2 teaspoons mixed with 20g | 2 tablespoons of cold milk, whisked into the custard base after it is finished cooking.

④ **Most accessible**
Cornstarch
10g | 1 tablespoon plus 1 teaspoon, mixed with 20g | 2 tablespoons of cold milk, whisked into the simmering dairy, then cooked for 1 minute.

Prepare the burnt honey. Place the cream in a small pot, and cook until very hot but not boiling (150°F or above), then set aside. Place the honey and salt in a medium heavy-bottomed saucepan over medium-high heat and cook, stirring occasionally as the honey bubbles and boils. When the burnt honey becomes quite dark and visibly starts smoking, reaching 275°F, remove the pot from the heat. Working carefully to avoid splatters, add the warm cream to the burnt honey, bit by bit, whisking between additions until smooth and even. Transfer the burnt honey sauce to the refrigerator to cool.

Prepare an ice bath. Fill a large bowl two-thirds of the way with very icy ice water and place it in the refrigerator.

Boil the milk and sugars. Put the milk, glucose, and sugar ① in a medium heavy-bottomed saucepan, and place it over medium-high heat. Cook, whisking occasionally to discourage the milk from scorching, until the mixture comes to a full rolling boil ④, then remove the pot from heat.

Temper the yolks and cook the custard. In a medium bowl, whisk the yolks. Add ½ cup of the hot dairy mixture to the yolks while whisking so the hot milk doesn't scramble the yolks. Pour the tempered yolks back into the pot of hot milk while whisking. Place the pot over medium-low heat and cook, stirring and scraping the bottom of the pot constantly with a rubber spatula to avoid curdling.

Chill. When you notice the custard thickening, or the temperature reaches 180°F on a kitchen thermometer, immediately pour the custard into a shallow metal or glass bowl ③. Nest the hot bowl into the ice bath, stirring occasionally until it cools down.

Mix in the burnt honey base and the buttermilk, then strain. When the custard is cool to the touch (50°F or below), remove the bowl from the ice bath and add the reserved burnt honey sauce, as well as the buttermilk, whisking until evenly combined ②. Strain it through a fine-mesh sieve to remove any bits of egg yolk. (Straining is optional, but will help ensure the smoothest ice cream possible.)

Cure. Transfer the cooled base to the refrigerator to cure for 4 hours, or preferably overnight. (This step is also optional, but the texture will be much improved with it.)

Churn. Place the base into the bowl of an ice cream maker and churn according to the manufacturer's instructions. The ice cream is ready when it thickens into the texture of soft-serve ice cream and holds its shape, typically 20 to 30 minutes.

Harden. To freeze your custard ice cream in the American hard-pack style, immediately transfer it to a container with an airtight lid. Press plastic wrap directly on the surface of the ice cream to prevent ice crystals from forming, cover, and store it in your freezer until it hardens completely, between 4 and 12 hours. Or, feel free to enjoy your ice cream immediately; the texture will be similar to soft-serve.

Green Cardamom Ice Cream

Makes between 1 and 1½ quarts ice cream

Cream (30%)
300g | 1½ cups

Milk (40%)
400g | 2 cups

Glucose syrup (5%)
50g | ¼ cup

Sugar (10%)
100g | ½ cup

Honey (5%)
50g | ¼ cup

Green cardamom
40 pods, cracked open

Egg yolks (10%)
100g | about 5 large yolks

Texture agent of your choice
(see below)

I used to *hate* cardamom. But somewhere outside my personal distaste for its flavor, I *knew* it was quite good. It's warm and spicy, like flavors we find in pies and gingerbreads, with a bracing quality like black pepper and mint. I could taste all these things, and knew it paired very well with honey, nuts, fruits, and rich custards.

After years of working with it, something magical happened. I began to reluctantly admit that I enjoyed cardamom, particularly when whole pods are steeped in milk and cream. Today I consider myself a member of the Society for the Appreciation of Cardamom, and if you too are in the club, then you'll delight in the flavor of this ice cream. Skip ground cardamom, which is made from just the seeds. Instead, make this ice cream with whole, crackly green cardamom pods. Place them in a plastic baggie and pound them to crack them open.

I've replaced part of the sugar in this recipe with honey, a sweetener used heavily in the parts of the world where cardamom grows. You'll find the richness of the honey enhances the flavor of cardamom quite nicely. However, feel free to replace it with an equal amount of sugar.

TEXTURE AGENTS

① **Best texture**
Commercial stabilizer
3g | 1 teaspoon mixed with the sugar before it is added to the dairy.

② **Least icy**
Guar or xanthan gum
1g | ¼ teaspoon whirled in a blender with the custard base after it is chilled in the ice bath.

③ **Easiest to use**
Tapioca starch
5g | 2 teaspoons mixed with 20g | 2 tablespoons of cold milk, whisked into the custard base after it is finished cooking.

④ **Most accessible**
Cornstarch
10g | 1 tablespoon plus 1 teaspoon, mixed with 20g | 2 tablespoons of cold milk, whisked into the cardamom-flavored dairy after it's reheated, then cooked for 1 minute.

Prepare an ice bath. Fill a large bowl two-thirds of the way with very icy ice water and place it in the refrigerator.

Boil the dairy and sugars. Put the cream, milk, glucose, sugar ①, and honey in a medium heavy-bottomed saucepan, and place it over medium-high heat. Cook, whisking occasionally to discourage the milk from scorching, until the mixture comes to a full rolling boil, then remove the pot from heat.

Infuse the cardamom. Stir the cracked cardamom pods into the hot dairy, and allow them to infuse for 30 minutes.

Strain and reheat the milk. Pour the mixture through a fine-mesh strainer, discarding the cardamom seeds and pods. Place the infused dairy in a clean pot, and place it over medium-high heat. Cook until the liquid comes to a full rolling boil ④, then remove from heat.

Temper the yolks and cook the custard. In a medium bowl, whisk the yolks. Add ½ cup of the hot dairy mixture to the yolks while whisking so the hot milk doesn't scramble the yolks. Pour the tempered yolks back into the pot of hot milk while whisking. Place the pot over medium-low heat and cook, stirring and scraping the bottom of the pot constantly with a rubber spatula to avoid curdling.

Chill. When you notice the custard thickening, or the temperature reaches 180°F on a kitchen thermometer, immediately pour the custard into a shallow metal or glass bowl ③. Nest the hot bowl into the ice bath, stirring occasionally until it cools down.

Strain. When the custard is cool to the touch (50°F or below) ②, strain it through a fine-mesh sieve to remove any bits of egg yolk. (This step is optional, but will help ensure the smoothest ice cream possible.)

Cure. Transfer the cooled base to the refrigerator to cure for 4 hours, or preferably overnight. (This step is also optional, but the texture will be much improved with it.)

Churn. Place the base into the bowl of an ice cream maker and churn according to the manufacturer's instructions. The ice cream is ready when it thickens into the texture of soft-serve ice cream and holds its shape, typically 20 to 30 minutes.

Harden. To freeze your custard ice cream in the American hard-pack style, immediately transfer it to a container with an airtight lid. Press plastic wrap directly on the surface of the ice cream to prevent ice crystals from forming, cover, and store it in your freezer until it hardens completely, between 4 and 12 hours. Or, feel free to enjoy your ice cream immediately; the texture will be similar to soft-serve.

Eggnog Ice Cream

Makes between 1 and 1½ quarts ice cream

Dark rum (1%)
10g | 1 tablespoon

Cream (30%)
300g | 1½ cups

Milk (39%)
390g | 2 cups

Glucose syrup (5%)
50g | ¼ cup

Sugar (15%)
150g | ¾ cup

Fresh bay leaf
1 leaf

Nutmeg
½ whole nutmeg, freshly grated

Egg yolks (10%)
100g | about 5 large yolks

Texture agent of your choice
(see below)

TEXTURE AGENTS

(1) Best texture
Commercial stabilizer
3g | 1 teaspoon mixed with the
granulated sugar before it is
added to the dairy.

(2) Least icy
Guar or xanthan gum
1g | ¼ teaspoon whirled in a
blender with the ice cream base
after it is chilled in the ice bath.

(3) Easiest to use
Tapioca starch
5g | 2 teaspoons mixed with
20g | 2 tablespoons of cold milk,
whisked into the custard base
after it is finished cooking.

(4) Most accessible
Cornstarch
10g | 1 tablespoon plus 1 teaspoon,
mixed with 20g | 2 tablespoons
of cold milk, whisked into the
simmering bay leaf–flavored dairy,
then cooked for 1 minute.

Sometime around Thanksgiving, the annual cartons of artificially flavored eggnog appear in grocery stores. Thickened to the texture of latex paint, the stuff pales in comparison to classic homemade eggnog: flavored with fresh nutmeg, spiked with brandy, bourbon, or rum, and yolk-thickened into a velvety custard. It is a relic of days before refrigeration, when milk and eggs would be mixed with alcohol and sugar before the winter limited their availability. This concoction would be left to cure through the winter, and often was heavily spiced to mask any off flavors. While we no longer need eggnog to preserve these nourishing products, it's still the perfect winter beverage.

When I first tried flavoring a dessert with true bay laurel leaves, not the dried California bay leaves commonly sold in grocery stores, I found they had a flavor strikingly similar to eggnog, so I use it to boost the eggnogginess of this ice cream. (If you can't find fresh bay leaf, omit it rather than using a dried bay leaf—that's likely a member of the eucalyptus family and not eggnoggy at all.) Do make the effort, though, to use freshly grated nutmeg—the flavor is remarkably better than the preground spice. If you prefer not to add alcohol to your ice cream, the rum can be omitted and replaced with rum extract.

Prepare an ice bath. Fill a large bowl two-thirds of the way with very icy ice water and place it in the refrigerator.

Boil the rum, dairy, and sugars. Put the rum, cream, milk, glucose, and sugar (1) in a medium heavy-bottomed saucepan, and place it over medium-high heat. Cook, whisking occasionally to discourage the milk from scorching, until the mixture comes to a full rolling boil, then remove the pot from heat.

Infuse. Stir the bay leaf and grated nutmeg into the hot dairy, and allow them to infuse for 30 minutes.

Remove the bay leaf and reheat the milk. Pluck out and discard the bay leaf. Reheat the dairy over medium-high heat until it comes to a full rolling boil (4), then remove from the heat.

Temper the yolks and cook the custard. In a medium bowl, whisk the yolks. Add ½ cup of the hot dairy mixture to the yolks while whisking so the hot milk doesn't scramble the yolks. Pour the tempered yolks back into the pot of hot milk while whisking. Place the pot over medium-low heat and cook, stirring and scraping the bottom of the pot constantly with a rubber spatula to avoid curdling.

Chill. When you notice the custard thickening, or the temperature reaches 180°F on a kitchen thermometer, immediately pour the custard into a shallow metal or glass bowl (3). Nest the hot bowl into the ice bath, stirring occasionally until it cools down.

Strain. When the custard is cool to the touch (50°F or below) (2), strain it through a fine-mesh sieve to remove any bits of yolk. (This is optional, but will help ensure the smoothest ice cream possible.)

Cure. Transfer the cooled base to the refrigerator to cure for 4 hours, or preferably overnight. (This step is also optional, but the texture will be much improved with it.)

Churn. Place the base into the bowl of an ice cream maker and churn according to the manufacturer's instructions. The ice cream is ready when it thickens into the texture of soft-serve ice cream and holds its shape, typically 20 to 30 minutes.

Harden. To freeze your custard ice cream in the American hard-pack style, immediately transfer it to a container with an airtight lid. Press plastic wrap directly on the surface of the ice cream to prevent ice crystals from forming, cover, and store it in your freezer until it hardens completely, between 4 and 12 hours. Or, feel free to enjoy your ice cream immediately; the texture will be similar to soft-serve.

Banana Ice Cream

Makes between 1 and 1½ quarts ice cream

Bananas, extremely ripe
4 medium or 3 large

Cream (30%)
300g | 1½ cups

Milk (40%)
400g | 2 cups

Glucose syrup (5%)
50g | ¼ cup

Sugar (15%)
150g | ¾ cup

Egg yolks (10%)
100g | about 5 large yolks

Kosher or sea salt
2g | ¼ teaspoon

Vanilla extract
5g | 1 teaspoon

Texture agent of your choice
(see below)

A banana is like a candy bar made for you by trees. But honestly, this fruit is downright weird. A banana is actually quite acidic, although you'd hardly notice that when eating one. A banana changes texture as it ripens, as its abundant starches convert into sugars as the fruit matures. Depending on the day, a banana might be mostly bland and starchy, or syrupy-sweet and loaded with the flavor molecules that scream "BANANA." (That's isoamyl acetate, in case you wanted to know.)

You can start to see that it's not easy to combine this inconsistent, starchy, acidic pudding of a fruit into ice cream. But Jason Jones, a sous chef at Poppy restaurant in Seattle (from the savory side even!) taught me to infuse the bananas into the ice cream, then strain them out.

This technique sidestepped the starchy quality that had plagued my banana ice creams, and gave me the smoothest, most banana-y ice cream ever. Since then, I've been overripening bananas until they are mostly black, then letting them soak in milk and cream. (The calcium in the milk firms up the squishy bananas, making them a snap to remove.) This recipe has you infusing the bananas for 2 to 24 hours, which is a pretty big window: 2 hours impart a lovely light flavor; 24 hours gives you maximum banana.

I plan ahead for this ice cream, wrapping a bunch of bananas in plastic wrap and leaving them in a warm spot in my kitchen for a week. If you don't have this kind of time on your hands, you can roast your bananas in the oven at 250°F for 30 minutes. The bananas won't be as flavorful as those left to ripen for a week, but it will give you a similar effect in a fraction of the time.

TEXTURE AGENTS

① **Best texture**
Commercial stabilizer
3g | 1 teaspoon mixed with the granulated sugar before it is added to the dairy.

② **Least icy**
Guar or xanthan gum
1g | ¼ teaspoon whirled in a blender with the custard base after it is chilled in the ice bath.

③ **Easiest to use**
Tapioca starch
5g | 2 teaspoons mixed with 20g | 2 tablespoons of cold milk, whisked into the custard base after it is finished cooking.

④ **Most accessible**
Cornstarch
10g | 1 tablespoon plus 1 teaspoon, mixed with 20g | 2 tablespoons of cold milk, whisked into the simmering banana-flavored dairy, then cooked for 1 minute.

Prepare the bananas. Peel and place the bananas in a 2-quart heatproof container.

Boil the dairy and sugars. Put the cream, milk, glucose, and sugar ① in a medium heavy-bottomed saucepan, and place the pan over medium-high heat. Cook, whisking occasionally to discourage the milk from scorching, until the mixture comes to a full rolling boil, then remove the pot from heat.

Infuse. Pour the hot dairy over the bananas, and transfer the container to the refrigerator, allowing them to infuse for 2 to 24 hours. The longer you let this infusion sit, the better the flavor will be.

Prepare an ice bath. Fill a large bowl two-thirds of the way with very icy ice water and place it in the refrigerator.

Strain and reheat the milk. Stir the dairy mixture to wash any fat that's clinging to the bananas back into the dairy. Pour the mixture through a fine-mesh strainer, discarding the bananas. Place the dairy in a clean pot, and place it over medium-high heat. Cook until the liquid comes to a full rolling boil ④, then remove from the heat.

Temper the yolks and cook the custard. In a medium bowl, whisk the yolks. Add ½ cup of the hot dairy mixture to the yolks while whisking so the hot milk doesn't scramble the yolks. Pour the tempered yolks back into the pot of hot milk while whisking. Place the pot over medium-low heat and cook, stirring and scraping the bottom of the pot constantly with a rubber spatula to avoid curdling.

Chill. When you notice the custard thickening, or the temperature reaches 180°F on a kitchen thermometer, immediately pour the custard into a shallow metal or glass bowl ③. Nest the hot bowl into the ice bath, stirring occasionally until it cools down.

Mix in the salt and vanilla, then strain. When the custard is cool to the touch (50°F or below) ②, remove the bowl from the ice bath and whisk in the salt and vanilla. Strain it through a fine-mesh sieve to remove any bits of egg yolk. (Straining is optional, but will help ensure the smoothest ice cream possible.)

Cure. Transfer the cooled base to the refrigerator to cure for 4 hours, or preferably overnight. (This step is also optional, but the texture will be much improved with it.)

Churn. Place the base into the bowl of an ice cream maker and churn according to the manufacturer's instructions. The ice cream is ready when it thickens into the texture of soft-serve ice cream and holds its shape, typically 20 to 30 minutes.

Harden. To freeze your custard ice cream in the American hard-pack style, immediately transfer it to a container with an airtight lid. Press plastic wrap directly on the surface of the ice cream to prevent ice crystals from forming, cover, and store it in your freezer until it hardens completely, between 4 and 12 hours. Or, feel free to enjoy your ice cream immediately; the texture will be similar to soft-serve.

Danish Licorice Ice Cream

Makes between 1 and 1½ quarts ice cream

Dark brown sugar (5%)
50g | ¼ cup tightly packed

Water (5%)
50g | ¼ cup

Licorice extract
1g | ¼ teaspoon

Kosher or sea salt
5g | 1 teaspoon

Cream (30%)
300g | 1½ cups

Milk (35%)
350g | 1¾ cups

Glucose syrup (5%)
50g | ¼ cup

Granulated sugar (10%)
100g | ½ cup

Star anise
3 pods

Anise seeds
10g | 1 tablespoon

Fennel seeds
10g | 1 tablespoon

Egg yolks (10%)
100g | about 5 large yolks

Texture agent of your choice
(see below)

Black licorice is a polarizing confection. Those who dislike it wrinkle their noses at the thought of it, but for a true licorice lover, it's ride-or-die. There is a range of flavor within the world of black licorice, starting with the sweet black vines sold in the states. The closer you get to Scandinavia, the more profound the licorice flavor becomes, and the candies are often heavily salted. I spent two summers cooking in Denmark, where I fell hard for lakrids, as these candies are called there. My favorite are the chewy chocolate-covered lakrids from Johan Bullow, whose original shop is on the island of Bornholm, where I lived. The local scoop shop, Svaneke Is, made a lakrids ice cream with Johan's candies, and my double-scoop cone always included room for this flavor. My favorite combo was a scoop of licorice alongside a scoop of raspberry ice cream. (Licorice and coffee is pretty great, too.)

It often goes unnoticed that licorice candy contains brown sugar—so much so, you'd hardly recognize licorice without it. The deep flavor of the molasses warms the abrasive licorice. For this ice cream I've used dark brown sugar, made into a syrup, and added it to the finished ice cream base, to avoid curdling the milk.

I use licorice extract to give this ice cream its distinct flavor, which you can buy online from Terra Spice. However, you'll notice that I also use three different anise-flavored spices to round out the flavor. Feel free to use any combination of them, or if you like the direct punch of zesty black licorice, leave them out to let the licorice extract shine. The salt, however, is crucial.

TEXTURE AGENTS

(1) **Best texture**
Commercial stabilizer
3g | 1 teaspoon mixed with the sugar before it is added to the dairy.

(2) **Least icy**
Guar or xanthan gum
1g | ¼ teaspoon whirled in a blender with the custard base after it is chilled in the ice bath.

(3) **Easiest to use**
Tapioca starch
5g | 2 teaspoons mixed with 20g | 2 tablespoons of cold milk, whisked into the custard base after it is finished cooking.

(4) **Most accessible**
Cornstarch
10g | 1 tablespoon plus 1 teaspoon, mixed with 20g | 2 tablespoons of cold milk, whisked into the anise-flavored dairy after it's reheated, then cooked for 1 minute.

Cook the brown sugar–licorice syrup. Place the brown sugar and water in a small saucepan over high heat and cook, stirring occasionally, to dissolve the brown sugar into a clear syrup. When the syrup comes to a boil, remove it from the heat and stir in the licorice extract and salt. Transfer the syrup to a heatproof container and place it in the refrigerator to cool.

Prepare an ice bath. Fill a large bowl two-thirds of the way with very icy ice water and place it in the refrigerator.

Boil the dairy and sugars. Put the cream, milk, glucose, and granulated sugar ① in a medium heavy-bottomed saucepan, and place it over medium-high heat. Cook, whisking occasionally to discourage the milk from scorching, until the mixture comes to a full rolling boil, then remove the pot from heat.

Infuse the spices. Stir the star anise, anise seeds, and fennel seeds into the hot dairy, and infuse for 30 minutes.

Strain and reheat the milk. Pour the mixture through a fine-mesh strainer, discarding the seeds, and bring it back to a boil over medium-high heat ④. Remove it from the heat.

Temper the yolks and cook the custard. In a medium bowl, whisk the yolks. Add ½ cup of the hot dairy mixture to the yolks while whisking so the hot milk doesn't scramble the yolks. Pour the tempered yolks back into the pot of hot milk while whisking. Place the pot over medium-low heat and cook, stirring and scraping the bottom of the pot constantly with a rubber spatula to avoid curdling.

Chill. When you notice the custard thickening, or the temperature reaches 180°F on a kitchen thermometer, immediately pour the custard into a shallow metal or glass bowl ③. Nest the hot bowl into the ice bath, stirring occasionally until it cools down.

Mix in the syrup and strain. When the custard is cool to the touch (50°F or below) ②, remove the bowl from the ice bath and add the reserved brown sugar syrup, whisking until evenly combined. Strain it through a fine-mesh sieve to remove the bits of egg yolk membrane that remain intact. (Straining is optional, but will help ensure the smoothest ice cream possible.)

Cure. Transfer the cooled base to the refrigerator to cure for 4 hours, or preferably overnight. (This step is also optional, but the texture will be much improved with it.)

Churn. Place the base into the bowl of an ice cream maker and churn according to the manufacturer's instructions. The ice cream is ready when it thickens into the texture of soft-serve ice cream and holds its shape, typically 20 to 30 minutes.

Harden. To freeze your custard ice cream in the American hard-pack style, immediately transfer it to a container with an airtight lid. Press plastic wrap directly on the surface of the ice cream to prevent ice crystals from forming, cover, and store it in your freezer until it hardens completely, between 4 and 12 hours. Or, feel free to enjoy your ice cream immediately; the texture will be similar to soft-serve.

Pumpkin-Sage Ice Cream

Makes between 1 and 1½ quarts ice cream

Roasted Pumpkin Puree (15%)
150g | ¾ cup (page 218)

Dark brown sugar (5%)
50g | ¼ cup, tightly packed

Salt
1g | ¼ teaspoon

Cream (30%)
300 g | 1½ cups

Milk (25%)
250g | 1¼ cups

Glucose syrup (5%)
50g | ¼ cup

Granulated sugar (10%)
100g | ½ cup

Fresh sage
15 leaves

Egg yolks (10%)
100g | about 5 large yolks

Texture agent of your choice
(see below)

TEXTURE AGENTS

① Best texture
Commercial stabilizer
3g | 1 teaspoon mixed with the granulated sugar before it is added to the dairy.

② Least icy
Guar or xanthan gum
1g | ¼ teaspoon whirled in a blender with the custard base after it is chilled in the ice bath.

③ Easiest to use
Tapioca starch
5g | 2 teaspoons mixed with 20g | 2 tablespoons of cold milk, whisked into the custard base after it is finished cooking.

④ Most accessible
Cornstarch
10g | 1 tablespoon plus 1 teaspoon, mixed with 20g | 2 tablespoons of cold milk, whisked into the simmering sage-flavored dairy, then cooked for 1 minute.

The flavor of pumpkin is deep and earthy, which can also be said of sage, and the marriage makes a wonderful flavor for ice cream. Canned pumpkin or almost any hard orange-fleshed squash can stand in for the pumpkin in this recipe; the texture will be the same.

If the flavor of sage doesn't tickle your fancy, swap the sage leaves for 10g | 2 teaspoons of pumpkin pie spice, cooked over the stovetop with the brown sugar and pumpkin.

Prepare the pumpkin. Place the pumpkin puree, brown sugar, and salt in a small saucepan over medium heat. Cook, stirring frequently, until the pumpkin begins to simmer and the brown sugar is dissolved. Transfer the mixture to a heatproof container and place it in the refrigerator.

Prepare an ice bath. Fill a large bowl two-thirds of the way with very icy ice water and place it in the refrigerator.

Boil the dairy and sugars, and infuse the sage. Put the cream, milk, glucose, and granulated sugar ① in a heavy-bottomed saucepan over medium-high heat. Cook, whisking, until the mixture comes to a full boil, then remove from heat. Stir in the sage and leave to infuse for 30 minutes.

Strain and reheat the milk. Pour the dairy through a fine-mesh strainer, discarding the sage. Place the dairy in a clean pot over medium-high heat until the liquid comes to a full boil ④; remove from the heat.

Temper the yolks and cook the custard. In a medium bowl, whisk the yolks. Add ½ cup of the hot dairy mixture to the yolks while whisking. Pour the tempered yolks back into the pot while whisking. Place the pot over medium-low heat and cook, scraping the bottom of the pot constantly with a rubber spatula to avoid curdling.

Chill. When you notice the custard thickening, or the temperature reaches 180°F, immediately pour it into a shallow metal or glass bowl ③. Nest the hot bowl into the ice bath, stirring occasionally until it cools down.

Strain and mix in the pumpkin. When the custard is cool to the touch (50°F or below) ②, strain it through a fine-mesh sieve to remove any bits of egg yolk. (This step is optional, but will help ensure the smoothest ice cream possible.) Whisk in the pumpkin.

Cure. Transfer the cooled custard to the refrigerator to cure for 4 hours, or preferably overnight. (This step is also optional, but the texture will be much improved.)

Churn. Place the base into the bowl of an ice cream maker and churn according to the manufacturer's instructions. The ice cream is ready when it thickens into the texture of soft-serve ice cream and holds its shape, typically 20 to 30 minutes.

Harden. To freeze your custard ice cream in the American hard-pack style, immediately transfer it to a container with an airtight lid. Press plastic wrap directly on the surface of the ice cream to prevent ice crystals from forming, cover, and store it in your freezer until it hardens completely, between 4 and 12 hours. Or, feel free to enjoy your ice cream immediately; the texture will be similar to soft-serve.

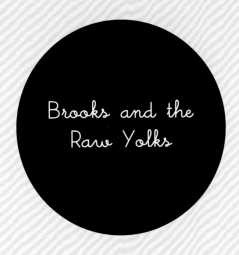

Brooks and the Raw Yolks

Brooks Headley owns a burger joint, but don't let that fool you: he's an amazing pastry chef. He's got a reputation for being punk rock, possibly from his longstanding career as a drummer in punk rock bands. I have to be honest: I don't really know what being punk means. I came of age in Seattle in the '90s, and we had a different kind of angst. If I listen to stereotypes, being punk means, "F*** the man, we do whatever we want, anarchy for everyone!" Which sounds pretty aggressive, and anti-everything. But if I base punk on what I know of Brooks, I would think it means, "Super-nice, talented vegetarians with fierce independent streaks who always wear black hoodies." But then again, what do I know about being punk?

If you go to Brooks's burger joint, you'll notice that he makes burgers without any meat, which is a slap in the face to the entire beefy genre. Brooks does something equally punk rock with his ice cream. When making custard ice creams, the ice cream establishment firmly requires you to cook the egg yolks until they thicken into a custard. Brooks doesn't do that. Instead, he lets his ice cream base cool, then blends in raw egg yolks, breaking every rule about making custard ice creams. It shouldn't work, and Brooks admitted he's not sure why it does, but folks, these anti-establishment ice creams are outright delicious.

When his book *Fancy Desserts* came out, my cooks immediately started cooking from it. Their first question was "Why does he add raw egg yolks to his gelatos?" I had no idea. I'd never seen anyone do that before. So I asked him. He told us that he likes how the egg yolk adds richness but no cooked flavor. He compared it to that luscious yolkiness on eggs Benedict, where the yolk is warm but basically raw, and freaking delicious.

Unlike a cooked custard, these yolks don't thicken the ice cream base, but they do work as an emulsifier. The egg yolk contains lecithin, which is amphiphilic, meaning it loves to hold on to both water and fat at the same time, thus helping everything stick together in the ice cream base, the same way raw egg yolk binds mayonnaise. The lecithin contains triglycerides, which destabilize the surface of the fat globules, and help prepare the butterfat to trap air in the ice cream when it's churned.

I asked Brooks if I could share his technique with the readers of this book, because I wanted to give those of us who don't want to risk curdling the eggs while cooking our custard bases another option. More so, I want the world to know about his unique approach. You can apply this technique to any of the custard recipes in this book. Simply hold on to the egg yolks and chill the ice cream base after the sugar and dairy are cooked together. Once they are cold, whisk in the raw egg yolks.

The only drawback to Brooks's raw custard is that the eggs never get to the temperature at which germs like salmonella die. This means all of Brooks's raw egg ice creams need to come with a warning label. It's the same warning label that's on sushi, eggs sunny side up, and beef tartare, which is that eating undercooked foods could be—on some small and unlikely level—hazardous to your health. But, I mean, an ice cream with a warning label? That's pretty punk rock.

Philadelphia-Style Ice Creams

It's likely you've never heard of Philadelphia-style ice cream, but I know you've had it. Philly-style is made without eggs and is the prevailing style in the United States. It is so common that it's rarely referred to as anything other than "ice cream." I'd never heard of it until my very first restaurant pastry job, at Eva in Seattle. I started exploring recipes beyond the classic French custard bases I learned in culinary school, and discovered the beauty of an ice cream made with just milk and cream. Without the richness of the eggy custard to mute them, the flavors in Philly-style ice creams really pop, making this the perfect backdrop for more delicate, subtle flavors.

Because of the clean flavor of Philadelphia-style ice cream, it's my favorite base to use when infusing fresh herbs like mint, basil, or lemon verbena, or flowers like chamomile, rose, or lavender. If you're using green teas to flavor your ice cream, this base lets the grassy notes shine! If you have a loose-leaf tea like jasmine pearls, you can steep them in the dairy, or use bright green matcha powder blended into the base when it's cooled.

Philly-style ice cream base is also my go-to for making ice cream that features dairy products like fresh goat cheese, crème fraîche, or mascarpone. I've included recipes that use many different dairy products in this chapter, but if you want to explore beyond the recipes here, use these rules of thumb: If the ingredient is high in fat, like sour cream, substitute it for a portion of the cream. If it's lower in fat, like ricotta, substitute it for a portion of the milk. Alternative dairy products often have more milk solids, and you'll do well to omit the milk powder in these recipes and replace it with an equal weight of milk. Finally, most alternative dairy products are cultured, and therefore acidic. If you add them with the dairy when you cook it, they will curdle the ice cream base. Instead, add them to the base after it's chilled.

Every ice cream book has to have chocolate ice cream, of course, and you'll find that recipe in this chapter, as I've come to prefer Philly-style bases for my chocolate flavors. This is particularly true if you are using one of those fancy-schmancy chocolates with deep, nuanced flavors.

One of my favorite quirky uses for Philly-style ice cream base is to blend in baked goods. Seemingly small additions of cookies, cake, blueberry muffins, or whatever you like make instantly recognizable, if surprising, flavors. Magical things happen when you simmer these bakery treats into milk; their starches act as stabilizers, making for velvety smooth ice creams.

Which brings me to my last point about Philly-style ice creams. Texturally speaking, these ice cream bases are at a small disadvantage. Unlike the egg yolks in custard-style ice creams, there are only a few naturally occurring emulsifiers in the milk protein, so my recipes include a protein boost from nonfat milk powder. Using milk powder allows you to use a little less liquid milk, and the protein in the milk powder helps to bind some of the water in the base, again reducing iciness. This makes for a denser, firmer scoop of ice cream. Still, if you don't have powdered milk on hand, or simply don't want to add it, replace the milk powder with an equal weight of milk. Your ice cream will be a touch icier without it, but it will still taste delicious.

Blank Slate Philadelphia-Style Ice Cream

Makes between 1 and 1½ quarts ice cream

Milk powder (2%)
20g | 3 tablespoons

Sugar (15%)
150g | ¾ cup

Cream (38%)
380g | 2 cups

Milk (40%)
400g | 2 cups

Glucose (5%)
50g | ¼ cup

Texture agent of your choice
(see below)

This recipe is a blank slate, created so you can adapt it to any flavor you like. All the recipes in this chapter are based on this formula, with adjustments made to both the ingredients and the technique. Armed with this basic recipe, you can invent any flavor of Philadelphia-style ice cream you like. I recommend it for making ice creams with bright, fresh flavors, such as herbs and flowers; teas; citrus; chocolate; alternative dairy products; and blended-in baked goods.

Combine the milk powder and sugar. Mix the milk powder and sugar ① in a small bowl.

Boil the dairy. Place the cream, milk, and glucose in a medium heavy-bottomed saucepan over medium-high heat and cook, whisking occasionally to discourage the milk from scorching, until it comes to a full rolling boil.

Add and cook the milk powder. Whisk the milk powder mixture into the pot. Reduce the heat to a low simmer and continue cooking for 2 minutes ④, whisking to prevent scorching ③.

Chill. Immediately pour the ice cream base into a shallow metal or glass bowl. Working quickly, fill a large bowl two-thirds of the way with very icy ice water. Nest the hot bowl into this ice bath, stirring occasionally until it cools down ②.

Strain. When the base is cool to the touch (50°F or below), strain it through a fine-mesh sieve. (This step is optional, but will help ensure the smoothest ice cream possible.)

Cure. Transfer the base to the refrigerator to cure for 4 hours, or preferably overnight. (This step is also optional, but the texture will be much improved with it.)

Churn. Place the base into the bowl of an ice cream maker and churn according to the manufacturer's instructions. The ice cream is ready when it thickens into the texture of soft-serve ice cream and holds its shape, typically 20 to 30 minutes.

Harden. To freeze your ice cream in the American hard-pack style, immediately transfer it to a container with an airtight lid. Press plastic wrap directly on the surface of the ice cream to prevent ice crystals from forming, cover, and store it in your freezer until it hardens completely, between 4 and 12 hours. Or, feel free to enjoy your ice cream immediately; the texture will be similar to soft-serve.

TEXTURE AGENTS

① Best texture
Commercial stabilizer
3g | 1 teaspoon mixed with the sugar before it is added to the dairy.

② Least icy
Guar or xanthan gum
1g | ¼ teaspoon whirled in a blender with the ice cream base after it is chilled in the ice bath.

③ Easiest to use
Tapioca starch
5g | 2 teaspoons mixed with 20g | 2 tablespoons of cold milk, whisked into the ice cream base after it is finished cooking.

④ Most accessible
Cornstarch
10g | 1 tablespoon plus 1 teaspoon, mixed with 20g | 2 tablespoons of cold milk, whisked into the simmering ice cream base, and cooked for 1 more minute.

fig. 1: Boil the dairy.

fig. 2: Strain the ice cream base.

fig. 3: Cure the ice cream base.

fig. 4: Churn the ice cream.

Blue Ribbon Chocolate Ice Cream

Makes between 1 and 1½ quarts ice cream

Dark chocolate (10%)
100g | 4 ounces, chopped

Milk chocolate (5%)
50g | 2 ounces, chopped

Cocoa powder (2%)
20g | 3 tablespoons

Kosher or sea salt
3g | ½ teaspoon

Milk powder (2%)
20g | 3 tablespoons

Sugar (15%)
150g | ¾ cup

Cream (16%)
160g | ¾ cup

Milk (45%)
450g | 2¼ cups

Glucose (5%)
50g | ¼ cup

Texture agent of your choice
(see below)

As a child, the closest scoop shop to our house was Baskin-Robbins. It's where most of my early childhood ice cream memories were created; my wide eyes stared at the ice cream cakes shaped like castles, with cones for turrets, while my sisters decided on a flavor. I never needed time to decide; I was a die-hard chocolate-fudge fan; it was twice as chocolaty as the regular chocolate ice cream next to it, and so dark it seemed black.

As a lifetime member of the chocolate ice cream fan club, I've added chocolate to ice cream in just about every way imaginable, and this is the crown jewel in my collection. After tasting many a chocolate ice cream and gelato in Europe, I realized the fudgy flavor of the ice creams I grew up with was unique. This is because American ice cream makers use cocoa powder, whereas ice cream makers in Europe favor melted chocolate. I combine both styles, making for a super-chocolate flavor, and I'd like to think this ice cream would be worthy of the highest American praise, a blue ribbon at a state fair.

You can substitute all milk or dark chocolate for the three chocolates, perhaps using a fancy single-origin, bean-to-bar chocolate. The unique flavor of the chocolate you choose will ring true here.

Milk chocolate has a lot more sugar in it than dark chocolate, so while you can use all milk chocolate in this recipe, you will end up with a very sweet, soft scoop. If it were me, I'd reduce the sugar to 10% (100g | ½ cup) and increase the cream to 23% (230g | 1 cup plus 2 tablespoons).

TEXTURE AGENTS

① **Best texture**
Commercial stabilizer
3g | 1 teaspoon mixed with the sugar before it is added to the dairy.

② **Least icy**
Guar or xanthan gum
1g | ¼ teaspoon whirled in a blender with the ice cream base after it is chilled in the ice bath.

③ **Easiest to use**
Tapioca starch
5g | 2 teaspoons mixed with 20g | 2 tablespoons of cold milk, whisked into the ice cream base after it is finished cooking.

④ **Most accessible**
Cornstarch
10g | 1 tablespoon plus 1 teaspoon, mixed with 20g | 2 tablespoons of cold milk, whisked into the simmering dairy, then cooked for 1 minute.

Melt the chocolates. Fill a medium pot with 2 inches of water, and place the pot over high heat until it comes to a boil, then reduce the heat to a simmer. Place the dark chocolate, milk chocolate, cocoa powder, and salt in a metal or glass bowl with a rim about 2 inches higher than the pot and nest it over the pot of simmering water, making sure the bottom of the bowl does not touch the water. Melt the chocolates, stirring occasionally, until smooth. Remove the bowl from the pot, wipe the bottom dry of any condensation, and set aside in a warm place.

Combine the milk powder and sugar. Mix the milk powder and sugar ① in a small bowl.

Boil the dairy. Place the cream, milk, and glucose in a medium heavy-bottomed saucepan over medium-high heat and cook, whisking occasionally to discourage the milk from scorching, until it comes to a full rolling boil.

Add and cook the milk powder. Whisk the milk powder mixture into the pot. Reduce the heat to a low simmer and continue cooking for 2 minutes ④, whisking to prevent scorching ③.

Combine the ice cream base and chocolate. Whisk one-third of the hot base into the bowl of melted chocolate. Add the remaining dairy in two more additions, whisking between each. (By adding the hot ice cream base to the chocolate gradually, you ensure there are no minuscule flecks of unmixed chocolate in the final ice cream, which feel grainy when frozen.)

Chill. Fill a large bowl two-thirds of the way with a lot of ice and a little water. Nest the bowl of warm chocolate base into this ice bath, stirring occasionally until it cools down ②.

Strain. When the ice cream base is cool to the touch (50°F or below), strain it through a fine-mesh sieve. (This step is optional, but will help ensure the smoothest ice cream possible.)

Cure. Transfer the base to the refrigerator to cure for 4 hours, or preferably overnight. (This step is also optional, but the texture will be much improved with it.)

Churn. Place the base into the bowl of an ice cream maker and churn according to the manufacturer's instructions. The ice cream is ready when it thickens into the texture of soft-serve ice cream and holds its shape, typically 20 to 30 minutes.

Harden. To freeze your ice cream in the American hard-pack style, immediately transfer it to a container with an airtight lid. Press plastic wrap directly on the surface of the ice cream to prevent ice crystals from forming, cover, and store it in your freezer until it hardens completely, between 4 and 12 hours. Or, feel free to enjoy your ice cream immediately; the texture will be similar to soft-serve.

Cinnamon Basil Ice Cream

Makes between 1 and 1½ quarts ice cream

Milk powder (2%)
20g | 3 tablespoons

Sugar (15%)
150g | ¾ cup

Cream (38%)
380g | 2 cups

Milk (40%)
400g | 2 cups

Glucose (5%)
50g | ¼ cup

Fresh basil, leaves and stems
25g | 1 ounce (about a handful)

Cinnamon stick
2 pieces, each about
3 inches long

Texture agent of your choice
(see below)

TEXTURE AGENTS

① **Best texture**
Commercial stabilizer
3g | 1 teaspoon mixed with the sugar before it is added to the dairy.

② **Least icy**
Guar or xanthan gum
1g | ¼ teaspoon whirled in a blender with the ice cream base after it is chilled in the ice bath.

③ **Easiest to use**
Tapioca starch
5g | 2 teaspoons mixed with 20g | 2 tablespoons of cold milk, whisked into the ice cream base after it is finished cooking.

④ **Most accessible**
Cornstarch
10g | 1 tablespoon plus 1 teaspoon, mixed with 20g | 2 tablespoons of cold milk, whisked into the simmering ice cream base, then cooked for 1 minute.

The flavor of cinnamon and basil together is brilliant and unexpected, which is exactly the kind of thing I'd love to be credited for inventing! However, Mother Nature beat me to this one. Cinnamon basil is a type of basil that tastes exactly like it sounds. Jerry Traunfeld, the chef and owner of Poppy restaurant, in Seattle, planted it specifically for me to use in ice cream. I gladly obliged, and became such a fan of this flavor that I started using basil leaves and cinnamon sticks when our gardens stopped producing the specialty herb.

While not essential, it's worth seeking out true cinnamon sticks, often labeled Ceylon or Vietnamese cinnamon, rather than the cassia bark that is often labeled and sold as cinnamon in grocery stores. If you have cinnamon basil growing in your garden, call me—I need some! Also, use just the fresh leaves, omitting the cinnamon stick from this ice cream. I have also made cinnamon-less basil ice creams with this recipe, using globe basil, purple basil, or Thai basil, all with great success.

Summer fruits like peaches and nectarines are a perfect foil for basil ice cream, and nothing is finer than topping it all off with a drizzle of aged balsamic vinegar.

Combine the milk powder and sugar. Mix the milk powder and sugar ① in a small bowl.

Boil the dairy. Place the cream, milk, and glucose in a medium heavy-bottomed saucepan over medium-high heat, and cook, whisking occasionally to discourage the milk from scorching, until it comes to a full rolling boil.

Add and cook the milk powder. Whisk the milk powder mixture into the pot. Reduce the heat to a low simmer and continue cooking for 2 minutes ④, whisking to prevent scorching ③.

Infuse. Remove the pot from the heat. Stir the basil and cinnamon into the hot dairy, and allow it to infuse for 30 minutes.

Strain and chill. Strain the base through a fine-mesh sieve, into a shallow metal or glass bowl, discarding the basil and cinnamon. Fill a large bowl two-thirds of the way with a lot of ice and a little water. Nest the hot bowl into this ice bath, stirring occasionally until it cools down ②.

Cure. When the ice cream base is cool to the touch (50°F or below), transfer it to the refrigerator to cure for 4 hours, or preferably overnight. (This step is optional, but the texture will be much improved with it.)

Churn. Place the base into the bowl of an ice cream maker and churn according to the manufacturer's instructions. The ice cream is ready when it thickens into the texture of soft-serve ice cream and holds its shape, typically 20 to 30 minutes.

Harden. To freeze your ice cream in the American hard-pack style, immediately transfer it to a container with an airtight lid. Press plastic wrap directly on the surface of the ice cream to prevent ice crystals from forming, cover, and store it in your freezer until it hardens completely, between 4 and 12 hours. Or, feel free to enjoy your ice cream immediately; the texture will be similar to soft-serve.

Donut Ice Cream

Makes between 1 and 1½ quarts ice cream

Cream (38%)
380g | 2 cups

Milk (37%)
370g | 1¾ cups

Sugar (15%)
150g | ¾ cup

Glucose (5%)
50g | ¼ cup

Glazed donut (5%)
50g | 2 ounces (about ½ large donut or 1 small)

Vanilla extract
3g | ½ teaspoon

Kosher or sea salt
2g | ⅓ teaspoon

Texture agent of your choice
(see below)

TEXTURE AGENTS

① Best texture
Commercial stabilizer
3g | 1 teaspoon mixed with the sugar before it is added to the ice cream base.

② Least icy
Guar or xanthan gum
1g | ¼ teaspoon whirled in a blender with the ice cream base after it is chilled in the ice bath.

③ Easiest to use
Tapioca starch
5g | 2 teaspoons mixed with 20g | 2 tablespoons of cold milk, whisked into the ice cream base after it is finished cooking.

④ Most accessible
Cornstarch
10g | 1 tablespoon plus 1 teaspoon, mixed with 20g | 2 tablespoons of cold milk, whisked into the simmering ice cream base, then cooked for 1 minute.

Baked goods do something peculiar when boiled with milk: they dissolve and become stretchy and elastic. Throw the mixture into a blender, and this strange concoction becomes velvety and thick, like pudding. I first encountered this magic trick at a restaurant full of them, called Alinea. There, a pudding made by boiling brioche and cream was served with raspberries for an elegant "toast-and-jam" bite. Since then, I've applied the same principle to just about every other kind of bakery treat I can get my hands on—like gingerbread or devil's food cake. Most recently, I've been reducing glazed donuts to a velvety pudding to flavor ice cream.

Buy the most delicious glazed donut you can find. This might be from a local shop where donuts are hand-forged, or from Krispy Kreme, or even from your grocery store's bakery case. And don't stop at donuts; you can use this recipe with any cake, cookie, or pastry you desire.

Boil the dairy. Place the cream, milk, sugar ①, and glucose in a medium heavy-bottomed saucepan over medium-high heat and cook, whisking occasionally to discourage the milk from scorching, until it comes to a full rolling boil.

Cook the donut. Add the donut to the dairy, breaking it up with a whisk while you stir it in. Reduce the heat and cook at a low simmer for 2 minutes ④, whisking occasionally to help break up the donut.

Blend the base. Remove the pot from heat and carefully transfer the hot base to a blender. Add the vanilla and salt, and start blending on low speed at first, increasing gradually to full speed, to avoid the hot liquid jumping out the top. When the blender is on high, continue blending for 1 to 2 minutes, until very smooth ③.

Chill. Immediately pour the base into a shallow metal or glass bowl. Working quickly, fill a large bowl two-thirds of the way with very icy ice water. Nest the hot bowl into this ice bath, stirring occasionally until it cools down ②.

Strain. When the ice cream base is cool to the touch (50°F or below), strain it through a fine-mesh sieve.

(This step is optional, but will help ensure the smoothest ice cream possible.)

Cure. Transfer the ice cream base to the refrigerator to cure for 4 hours, or preferably overnight. (This step is also optional, but the texture will be much improved with it.)

Churn. Place the base into the bowl of an ice cream maker and churn according to the manufacturer's instructions. The ice cream is ready when it thickens into the texture of soft-serve ice cream and holds its shape, typically 20 to 30 minutes.

Harden. To freeze your ice cream in the American hard-pack style, immediately transfer it to a container with an airtight lid. Press plastic wrap directly on the surface of the ice cream to prevent ice crystals from forming, cover, and store it in your freezer until it hardens completely, between 4 and 12 hours. Or, feel free to enjoy your ice cream immediately; the texture will be similar to soft-serve.

Goat Cheese Ice Cream

Makes between 1 and 1½ quarts ice cream

Goat cheese (10%)
100g | ½ cup

Lactic acid
3g | ½ teaspoon (optional; or lemon juice, to taste)

Cream (38%)
380g | 2 cups

Milk (32%)
320g | 1½ cups

Sugar (15%)
150g | ¾ cup

Glucose (5%)
50g | ¼ cup

Texture agent of your choice
(see below)

TEXTURE AGENTS

① **Best texture**
Commercial stabilizer
3g | 1 teaspoon mixed with the sugar before it is added to the ice cream base.

② **Least icy**
Guar or xanthan gum
1g | ¼ teaspoon whirled in a blender with the ice cream base after it is chilled in the ice bath.

③ **Easiest to use**
Tapioca starch
5g | 2 teaspoons mixed with 20g | 2 tablespoons of cold milk, whisked into the ice cream base after it is finished cooking.

④ **Most accessible**
Cornstarch
10g | 1 tablespoon plus 1 teaspoon, mixed with 20g | 2 tablespoons of cold milk, whisked into the simmering ice cream base, then cooked for 1 minute.

Goat cheese is one of those flavors still considered "savory," although I never could figure out why. Perhaps it's just my own love of the tangy soft cheese, but I've been lacing cheesecakes, puddings, and ice creams with it since I started making desserts. Any fresh goat cheese, sometimes called chèvre, will make a delicious scoop of ice cream.

Goat cheese ice cream was a staple at Avec, a restaurant dedicated to the cuisine surrounding the Mediterranean—hot, arid regions low in cows but high in goats. We would swirl ribbons of seasonal fruit jam through the ice cream, or serve scoops over slices of warm honey-soaked cakes and squares of sticky baklava. I'm sure you, too, will find plenty of sweet reasons to make this "savory" flavor.

Because goat cheese is made with lean goat's milk, it replaces a portion of the cow's milk in this recipe. The milk powder is also unnecessary, thanks to the extra protein in the goat cheese. Just remember, don't stir the acidic cheese into the ice cream base until it has chilled. If you special-order lactic acid, it offers a wonderful dairy-specific brightness to this ice cream. Feel free to brighten the ice cream to taste with lemon juice as well, if you don't mind adding the citrus flavor.

Prepare the goat cheese. Crumble the goat cheese into 1-inch pieces, place in a small bowl, and add the lactic acid if you're using it. Loosely cover with plastic wrap, and set it aside on the counter, allowing it to come to room temperature.

Boil the dairy. Place the cream, milk, sugar ①, and glucose in a medium heavy-bottomed saucepan over medium-high heat, and cook, whisking occasionally to discourage the milk from scorching, until it comes to a full rolling boil ④.

Chill. Immediately pour the base into a shallow metal or glass bowl ③. Working quickly, fill a large bowl two-thirds of the way with very icy ice water. Nest the hot bowl into this ice bath, stirring occasionally until it cools down ②.

Blend in the goat cheese and strain. When the base is cool to the touch (50°F or below), whisk in the softened goat cheese. Transfer to a blender and blend on medium-high speed for 1 minute, until very smooth.

Strain through a fine-mesh sieve to remove any unmixed pieces of goat cheese.

Cure. Transfer the ice cream base to the refrigerator to cure for 4 hours, or preferably overnight. (This step is optional, but the texture will be much improved with it.)

Churn. Place the base into the bowl of an ice cream maker and churn according to the manufacturer's instructions. The ice cream is ready when it thickens into the texture of soft-serve ice cream and holds its shape, typically 20 to 30 minutes.

Harden. To freeze your ice cream in the American hard-pack style, immediately transfer it to a container with an airtight lid. Press plastic wrap directly on the surface of the ice cream to prevent ice crystals from forming, cover, and store it in your freezer until it hardens completely, between 4 and 12 hours. Or, feel free to enjoy your ice cream immediately; the texture will be similar to soft-serve.

Garden Mint Ice Cream

Makes just over 1 quart of ice cream

Milk powder (2%)
20g | 3 tablespoons

Sugar (15%)
150g | ¾ cup

Cream (38%)
380g | 2 cups

Milk (40%)
400g | 2 cups

Glucose (5%)
50g | ¼ cup

Fresh mint, stems and leaves
25g | 1 ounce (about 1 handful)

Peppermint oil or extract
1g | ¼ teaspoon

Texture agent of your choice
(see below)

Mint ice cream is rarely eaten without chips of chocolate and a squeeze of green food dye. It's really too bad, because the flavor of fresh mint leaves steeped in ice cream is light, fresh, and a far cry from the bracing green scoops. The flavor in conventional mint ice creams has little to do with the mint leaf and more to do with the menthol compounds that make peppermint flavoring.

If you have fresh peppermint leaves, lucky you! Use them in this recipe and omit the peppermint extract. However, for most of us there is no peppermint patch out the back door, and we must employ both the fresh spearmint leaves (a.k.a. standard grocery-store mint), and a touch of peppermint extract. (If you can find peppermint oil, use that instead! It's cleaner flavored than the extract, which often combines peppermint oil and alcohol.)

I think a white mint ice cream is quite lovely, but if mint ice cream doesn't taste like mint to you unless it's green, you have options. Green food coloring is obvious, or you can follow the instructions for tinting ice cream green with spirulina on page 42. Sam Mason at Oddfellows Ice Cream in Brooklyn blends a portion of his mint ice cream base with fresh mint leaves moments before the ice cream is churned, capturing the chlorophyll from the green leaves before it oxidizes. (If you do this, be sure not to run the blender for more than a few seconds, or you may turn the cream to butter.)

TEXTURE AGENTS

① Best texture
Commercial stabilizer
3g | 1 teaspoon mixed with the sugar before it is added to the dairy.

② Least icy
Guar or xanthan gum
1g | ¼ teaspoon whirled in a blender with the ice cream base after it is chilled in the ice bath.

③ Easiest to use
Tapioca starch
5g | 2 teaspoons mixed with 20g | 2 tablespoons of cold milk, whisked into the ice cream base after it is finished cooking.

④ Most accessible
Cornstarch
10g | 1 tablespoon plus 1 teaspoon, mixed with 20g | 2 tablespoons of cold milk, whisked into the simmering ice cream base, then cooked for 1 minute.

Combine the milk powder and sugar. Mix the milk powder and sugar ① in a small bowl.

Boil the dairy. Place the cream, milk, and glucose in a medium heavy-bottomed saucepan over medium-high heat and cook, whisking occasionally to discourage the milk from scorching, until it comes to a full rolling boil.

Add and cook the milk powder. Whisk the milk powder mixture into the pot. Reduce the heat to a low simmer and continue cooking for 2 minutes ④, whisking to prevent scorching ③.

Infuse the mint. Remove the pot from the heat. Stir in the fresh mint, and allow it to infuse for 30 minutes.

Strain and chill. Strain the base through a fine-mesh sieve into a shallow metal or glass bowl, discarding the mint. Working quickly, fill a large bowl two-thirds of the way with very icy ice water. Nest the hot bowl into this ice bath, stirring occasionally until it cools down ②.

Add the peppermint oil. When the base is cool to the touch (50°F or below), stir in the peppermint oil.

Cure. Transfer the ice cream base to the refrigerator to cure for 4 hours, or preferably overnight. (This step is optional, but the texture will be much improved with it.)

Churn. Place the base into the bowl of an ice cream maker and churn according to the manufacturer's instructions. The ice cream is ready when it thickens into the texture of soft-serve ice cream and holds its shape, typically 20 to 30 minutes.

Harden. To freeze your ice cream in the American hard-pack style, immediately transfer it to a container with an airtight lid. Press plastic wrap directly on the surface of the ice cream to prevent ice crystals from forming, cover, and store it in your freezer until it hardens completely, between 4 and 12 hours. Or, feel free to enjoy your ice cream immediately; the texture will be similar to soft-serve.

Earl Grey Ice Cream

Makes between 1 and 1½ quarts ice cream

Milk powder (2%)
20g | 3 tablespoons

Sugar (15%)
150g | ¾ cup

Cream (38%)
380g | 2 cups

Milk (40%)
400g | 2 cups

Glucose (5%)
50g | ¼ cup

Earl Grey tea
10g | 2 tablespoons
(or about 8 tea bags)

Dried lavender buds
1g | ½ teaspoon, packed

Grated lemon zest
1g | ¼ teaspoon, tightly packed

Texture agent of your choice
(see below)

TEXTURE AGENTS

① Best texture
Commercial stabilizer
3g | 1 teaspoon mixed with the sugar before it is added to the dairy.

② Least icy
Guar or xanthan gum
1g | ¼ teaspoon whirled in a blender with the ice cream base after it is chilled in the ice bath.

③ Easiest to use
Tapioca starch
5g | 2 teaspoons mixed with 20g | 2 tablespoons of cold milk, whisked into the ice cream base after it is finished cooking.

④ Most accessible
Cornstarch
10g | 1 tablespoon plus 1 teaspoon, mixed with 20g | 2 tablespoons of cold milk, whisked into the simmering ice cream base, then cooked for 1 minute.

My mother did housework like no one I've ever seen. She would have a sink full of hot soapy water in the kitchen, laundry half-folded on the couch, an art project on the dining room table, and the vacuum halfway down the hallway where she had stopped cleaning the carpet, all the while listening to a book on tape on her Walkman, with only one ear covered by the headphones, and the TV on in two rooms. As she flitted about the house from one task to the next, there was never a mug of Earl Grey tea far from her. She would add so much sugar and milk that it was practically dessert. No doubt her three daughters loved stealing sips when she was around the corner tending to one of the five things she was doing. To this day, the flavor of Earl Grey takes me right back to her, and I wish she could have tasted this ice cream.

Earl Grey tea is a simple black tea distinguished by the addition of oil of bergamot orange. The fragrance of this citrus oil is remarkably like lavender. I've embellished my Earl Grey ice cream with a few lavender buds, enhancing the lovely floral quality.

Combine the milk powder and sugar. Mix the milk powder and sugar ① in a small bowl.

Boil the dairy. Place the cream, milk, and glucose in a medium heavy-bottomed saucepan over medium-high heat and cook, whisking occasionally to discourage the milk from scorching, until it comes to a full rolling boil.

Add and cook the milk powder. Whisk the milk powder mixture into the pot. Reduce the heat to a low simmer and continue cooking for 2 minutes ④, whisking to prevent scorching ③.

Infuse. Remove the pot from the heat. Stir the tea, lavender buds, and lemon zest into the hot dairy, and allow it to infuse for 30 minutes.

Strain and chill. Strain the base through a fine-mesh sieve into a shallow metal or glass bowl, discarding the tea, lavender, and zest. Fill a large bowl two-thirds of the way with very icy ice water. Nest the hot bowl into this ice bath, stirring occasionally until it cools down ②.

Cure. When the base is cool to the touch (50°F or below), transfer it to the refrigerator to cure for 4 hours, or preferably overnight. (This step is optional, but the texture will be much improved with it.)

Churn. Place the base into the bowl of an ice cream maker and churn according to the manufacturer's instructions. The ice cream is ready when it thickens into the texture of soft-serve ice cream and holds its shape, typically 20 to 30 minutes.

Harden. To freeze your ice cream in the American hard-pack style, immediately transfer it to a container with an airtight lid. Press plastic wrap directly on the surface of the ice cream to prevent ice crystals from forming, cover, and store it in your freezer until it hardens completely, between 4 and 12 hours. Or, feel free to enjoy your ice cream immediately; the texture will be similar to soft-serve.

Parmesan Ice Cream

Makes between 1 and 1½ quarts ice cream

Cream (38%)
380g | 2 cups

Milk (37%)
370g | 1½ cups

Sugar (15%)
150g | ¾ cup

Glucose (5%)
50g | ¼ cup

Parmesan cheese (5%)
50g | ½ cup, freshly grated, lightly packed

Texture agent of your choice
(see below)

TEXTURE AGENTS

① Best texture
Commercial stabilizer
3g | 1 teaspoon mixed with the sugar before it is added to the dairy.

② Least icy
Guar or xanthan gum
1g | ¼ teaspoon whirled in a blender with the ice cream base after it is chilled in the ice bath.

③ Easiest to use
Tapioca starch
5g | 2 teaspoons mixed with 20g | 2 tablespoons of cold milk, whisked into the ice cream base after it is finished cooking.

④ Most accessible
Cornstarch
10g | 1 tablespoon plus 1 teaspoon, mixed with 20g | 2 tablespoons of cold milk, whisked into the simmering dairy, then cooked for 1 minute.

Parmesan ice cream is kind of "out there," but I made a career in fine dining restaurants based on "out there" flavors. I found that for every "Oh, this flavor is unexpected, interesting, and pleasant to eat—just this once," there was another flavor that made me think "Holy crap, why didn't I think of this sooner?" Parmesan Ice Cream falls into this second category, and makes for a cheesy, nutty ice cream that is downright delicious. I bring it out for special moments, like when an apple crumble is coming out of the oven.

It doesn't take much Parmesan cheese to flavor this ice cream, but it's *gotta* be the good stuff. Splurge and buy the aged Parmigiano Reggiano they hold behind the cheese counter; for the love of all that is holy, don't buy the pre-grated stuff! The surface of cheese starts to dry out when it is exposed to air, making it next to impossible to melt the cheese into your ice cream.

To blend the Parmesan into the ice cream base until smooth, you need the powerful blades of a blender, rather than a hand-blending wand. Still, even if all you have is a whisk, this ice cream can be made; you'll just feel tiny flecks of the cheese when it's frozen.

Boil the dairy. Place the cream, milk, sugar ①, and glucose in a medium heavy-bottomed saucepan over medium-high heat, and cook, whisking occasionally to discourage the milk from scorching, until it comes to a full rolling boil.

Add the cheese. Whisk in the cheese. Reduce the heat to a low simmer and continue cooking for 2 minutes ④, whisking frequently to prevent the cheese from settling to the bottom of the pot and scorching. Remove the pot from the heat ③.

Blend the cheese. Transfer the ice cream base to a blender and blend, starting on low speed and increasing gradually to high. Blend on high for 1 to 2 minutes, until the base is very smooth.

Chill. Immediately pour the ice cream base into a shallow metal or glass bowl. Working quickly, fill a large bowl two-thirds of the way with very icy ice water. Nest the hot bowl into this ice bath, stirring occasionally until it cools down ②.

Strain. When the base is cool to the touch (50°F or below), strain it through a fine-mesh sieve to remove any unblended cheese.

Cure. Transfer the base to the refrigerator to cure for 4 hours, or preferably overnight. (This step is optional, but the texture will be much improved with it.)

Churn. Place the base into the bowl of an ice cream maker and churn according to the manufacturer's instructions. The ice cream is ready when it thickens into the texture of soft-serve ice cream and holds its shape, typically 20 to 30 minutes.

Harden. To freeze your ice cream in the American hard-pack style, immediately transfer it to a container with an airtight lid. Press plastic wrap directly on the surface of the ice cream to prevent ice crystals from forming, cover, and store it in your freezer until it hardens completely, between 4 and 12 hours. Or, feel free to enjoy your ice cream immediately; the texture will be similar to soft-serve.

Lemon Crème Fraîche Ice Cream

Makes between 1 and 1½ quarts ice cream

Milk powder (2%)
20g | 3 tablespoons

Sugar (15%)
150g | ¾ cup

Cream (10%)
100g | ½ cup

Milk (38%)
380g | 2 cups

Glucose (5%)
50g | ¼ cup

Grated lemon zest
10g | 2 teaspoons, tightly packed
(from 1 large lemon)

Crème fraîche (28%)
280g | 1½ cups

Fresh lemon juice (strained of flesh or pits) (2%)
20g | 1 tablespoon

Texture agent of your choice
(see below)

TEXTURE AGENTS

① **Best texture**
Commercial stabilizer
3g | 1 teaspoon mixed with the sugar before it is added to the dairy.

② **Least icy**
Guar or xanthan gum
1g | ¼ teaspoon whirled in a blender with the ice cream base after it is chilled in the ice bath.

③ **Easiest to use**
Tapioca starch
5g | 2 teaspoons mixed with 20g | 2 tablespoons of cold milk, whisked into the ice cream base after it is finished cooking.

④ **Most accessible**
Cornstarch
10g | 1 tablespoon plus 1 teaspoon, mixed with 20g | 2 tablespoons of cold milk, whisked into the simmering dairy, then cooked for 1 minute.

Pastry chefs prize crème fraîche for its dual richness and acidity, adding it to desserts with great abandon. Ice cream is no exception, though crème fraîche ice cream is something rarely seen. This is really too bad, because it's one of the most versatile and delicious flavors you can make.

Crème fraîche is made by inoculating cream with a selective set of live cultures, which convert lactose into lactic acid, thickening the cream and giving it a wonderful, sour cream–like tartness. Many stores sell crème fraîche, but it can be rather expensive. If you have a little time on your hands, crème fraîche can also be made at home (see page 215). For a more accessible but no less delicious ice cream, you can substitute sour cream for the crème fraîche.

I love a hint of lemon in this crème fraîche ice cream. Meyer lemons, a cross between a lemon and a tangerine, would make a wonderful choice for this ice cream. For a plain crème fraîche ice cream, just omit the lemon zest and juice.

Combine the milk powder and sugar. Mix the milk powder and sugar ① in a small bowl.

Boil the dairy. Place the cream, milk, and glucose in a medium heavy-bottomed saucepan over medium-high heat, and cook, whisking occasionally to discourage the milk from scorching, until it comes to a full rolling boil.

Add and cook the milk powder. Whisk the milk powder mixture into the pot. Reduce the heat to a low simmer and continue cooking for 2 minutes ④, whisking to prevent scorching ③.

Infuse. Remove the pot from the heat. Stir the lemon zest into the hot dairy, and allow it to infuse for 30 minutes.

Strain and chill. Strain the base through a fine-mesh sieve, into a shallow metal or glass bowl, discarding the zest. Fill a large bowl two-thirds of the way with a lot of ice and a little water. Nest the hot bowl into this ice bath, stirring occasionally until it cools down ②.

Add the crème fraîche and lemon juice. When the base is cool to the touch (50°F or below), whisk in the crème fraîche and lemon juice.

Cure. Transfer the ice cream base to the refrigerator to cure for 4 hours, or preferably overnight. (This step is optional, but the texture will be much improved with it.)

Churn. Place the base into the bowl of an ice cream maker and churn according to the manufacturer's instructions. The ice cream is ready when it thickens into the texture of soft-serve ice cream and holds its shape, typically 20 to 30 minutes.

Harden. To freeze your ice cream in the American hard-pack style, immediately transfer it to a container with an airtight lid. Press plastic wrap directly on the surface of the ice cream to prevent ice crystals from forming, cover, and store it in your freezer until it hardens completely, between 4 and 12 hours. Or, feel free to enjoy your ice cream immediately; the texture will be similar to soft-serve.

Cream Cheese Ice Cream

Makes between 1 and 1½ quarts ice cream

Cream cheese (15%)
150g | ¾ cup

Cream (25%)
250g | 1¼ cups

Milk (40%)
400g | 2 cups

Sugar (15%)
150g | ¾ cup

Glucose (5%)
50g | ¼ cup

Texture agent of your choice
(see below)

TEXTURE AGENTS

① Best texture
Commercial stabilizer
3g | 1 teaspoon mixed with the
sugar before it is added to the
dairy.

② Least icy
Guar or xanthan gum
1g | ¼ teaspoon whirled in a
blender with the ice cream base
after it is chilled in the ice bath.

③ Easiest to use
Tapioca starch
5g | 2 teaspoons mixed with
20g | 2 tablespoons of cold milk,
whisked into the ice cream base
after it is finished cooking.

④ Most accessible
Cornstarch
10g | 1 tablespoon plus 1 teaspoon,
mixed with 20g | 2 tablespoons
of cold milk, whisked into the
simmering dairy, then cooked for
1 minute.

While cream cheese ice cream has a lovely tang that goes with, um, everything, you'll want to make this ice cream for its texture. Dense, rich cream cheese replaces some of the cream in this recipe. In doing so, you replace the water in the cream with so much milk protein that the scoop gets delightfully chewy. You might not realize how important the chew factor of ice cream is, but remember, the hallmark of American hard-pack ice cream is a scoop you can bite into. My sister, who lives among shops selling soft *eis* and gelato in Germany, can attest to this, as it's the thing she misses most as she licks her scoops.

You can flavor this ice cream by infusing the milk before combining it with the cream cheese. You'll end up with the most bite-worthy ice cream on the block. The tang and texture of cream cheese also makes this ice cream the perfect foil for add-ins of all kinds. We feature this ice cream in our Gooey Butter Cake composed scoop (page 188), but don't stop there! Fruit ribbons and ripples, carrot cake, or brownies—all will feel at home in this tangy Cream Cheese Ice Cream.

Cut and temper the cream cheese. Cut the cream cheese into 1-inch pieces and place in a large bowl. Cover the surface with plastic wrap, and allow it to come to room temperature.

Boil the dairy. Place the cream, milk, sugar ①, and glucose in a medium heavy-bottomed saucepan over medium-high heat, and cook, whisking occasionally to discourage the milk from scorching, until it comes to a full rolling boil ④.

Chill. Immediately pour the ice cream base into a shallow metal or glass bowl ③. Working quickly, fill a large bowl two-thirds of the way with very icy ice water. Nest the hot bowl into this ice bath, stirring occasionally until it cools down ②.

Mix in the cream cheese. When the base is cool to the touch (50°F or below), whisk in the softened cream cheese. Transfer to a blender and blend on medium-high speed for 1 minute, until very smooth.

Strain. Strain the base through a fine-mesh strainer into a shallow metal or glass bowl. Use a rubber spatula to push any unincorporated lumps of cream cheese through the strainer, then scrape the bottom side of the strainer to collect any cream cheese that has accumulated there, whisking it back into the base.

Cure. When the base is cool to the touch (50°F or below), transfer the base to the refrigerator to cure for 4 hours, or preferably overnight. (This step is optional, but the texture will be much improved with it.)

Churn. Place the base into the bowl of an ice cream maker and churn according to the manufacturer's instructions. The ice cream is ready when it thickens into the texture of soft-serve ice cream and holds its shape, typically 20 to 30 minutes.

Harden. To freeze your ice cream in the American hard-pack style, immediately transfer it to a container with an airtight lid. Press plastic wrap directly on the surface of the ice cream to prevent ice crystals from forming, cover, and store it in your freezer until it hardens completely, between 4 and 12 hours. Or, feel free to enjoy your ice cream immediately; the texture will be similar to soft-serve.

Cheesecake Ice Cream

Makes between 1 and 1½ quarts ice cream

Milk (40%)
400g | 2 cups

Sugar (10%)
100g | ½ cup

Glucose (5%)
50g | ¼ cup

Cheesecake, no crust (45%)
450g | 2¼ cups, packed (page 170)

Lactic acid
5g | 1 teaspoon (optional)

Vanilla extract
5g | 1 teaspoon

Kosher or sea salt
2g | ⅓ teaspoon

Texture agent of your choice
(see below)

TEXTURE AGENTS

① Best texture
Commercial stabilizer
3g | 1 teaspoon mixed with the
sugar before it is added to the
milk.

② Least icy
Guar or xanthan gum
1g | ¼ teaspoon whirled in a
blender with the ice cream base
after it is chilled in the ice bath.

③ Easiest to use
Tapioca starch
5g | 2 teaspoons mixed with
20g | 2 tablespoons of cold milk,
whisked into the ice cream base
after it is finished cooking.

④ Most accessible
Cornstarch
10g | 1 tablespoon plus 1 teaspoon,
mixed with 20g | 2 tablespoons
of cold milk, whisked into the
simmering milk, then cooked for
1 minute.

This ice cream requires a little extra effort on your part, because you're going to have to bake a cheesecake, sans crust. Then, after you proudly admire the fruits of your labor, you're going to place it in a blender and puree it into oblivion. It's a little like stomping on your own sandcastle. I wouldn't ask you to do this unless it was worth it—and it's *really* worth it. This cheesecake ice cream is dense and rich, unlike store-bought cheesecake ice creams, which rely on an artificial cheesecake flavoring. With this ice cream you can make one of my personal favorite scoops ever, the Cheesecake Neapolitan (page 196).

If making a cheesecake just isn't happening today, no problem! Go ahead and buy one, I won't tell. Keep in mind you'll need to separate the cake from the crust. Buy a cheesecake that weighs at least 1½ pounds, or a few slices from a bakery that total about the same. After you remove the crust, you'll have just about the right amount. And perhaps that crust can be saved and folded into the cheesecake ice cream when you've churned it! I like to add a little lactic acid to make the cheesecake ice cream taste more like cheesecake. If you don't have it around, the ice cream will still be wonderful.

Boil the dairy. Place the milk, sugar ①, and glucose in a medium heavy-bottomed saucepan over medium-high heat, and cook, whisking occasionally to discourage the milk from scorching, until it comes to a full rolling boil ④.

Chill. Immediately pour the base into a shallow metal or glass bowl ③. Working quickly, fill a large bowl two-thirds of the way with very icy ice water. Nest the hot bowl into this ice bath, stirring occasionally until it cools down ②. When cool to the touch (50°F or below), remove the bowl from the ice bath.

Blend in the cheesecake. Place the cheesecake, lactic acid if using, vanilla, and salt in a blender and add half the base. Blend on high for 1 minute, until it looks like a cheesecake smoothie. Pour the cheesecake mixture into the rest of the dairy and whisk together.

Strain. Strain the base through a fine-mesh sieve to remove any particles of cheesecake that may be present. (This step is optional, but will help ensure that you have the smoothest ice cream possible.)

Cure. Transfer the base to the refrigerator to cure for 4 hours, or preferably overnight. (This step is also optional, but the texture will be much improved with it.)

Churn. Place the base into the bowl of an ice cream maker and churn according to the manufacturer's instructions. The ice cream is ready when it thickens into the texture of soft-serve ice cream and holds its shape, typically 20 to 30 minutes.

Harden. To freeze your ice cream in the American hard-pack style, immediately transfer it to a container with an airtight lid. Press plastic wrap directly on the surface of the ice cream to prevent ice crystals from forming, cover, and store it in your freezer until it hardens completely, between 4 and 12 hours. Or, feel free to enjoy your ice cream immediately; the texture will be similar to soft-serve.

Popcorn Ice Cream

Makes between 1 and 1½ quarts ice cream

Cream (37%)
370g | 2 cups

Milk (40%)
400g | 2 cups

Sugar (15%)
150g | ¾ cup

Glucose (5%)
50g | ¼ cup

Clarified butter or oil (1%)
10g | 2 teaspoons

Raw popcorn kernels (2%)
20g | 2 tablespoons

Salt
4g | ¾ teaspoon

Texture agent of your choice
(see below)

When it came time for Dan, my main squeeze, to celebrate his mother's birthday, he made it clear that she wasn't a cake person. Lucky for me, Holli *is* an ice cream person, and a popcorn lover as well, so I set myself to the task of making a buttered popcorn ice cream for her birthday. This was my first chance to make an impression on her, and I was determined it be a delicious one.

I had made a popcorn sorbet at Poppy restaurant as the base of a caramel corn sundae, and had enough experience to know better than to blend popped corn with hot liquid. The starches in the popcorn form long gummy chains and make it kind of snotty—yuck! I blended popped corn into a chilled ice cream base, but it wasn't quite right—and this ice cream had to be just right. After a team powwow, Harry Flagger, pastry cook supreme, said it was missing the flavor of the toasted oil. And boy, was he right. I popped the popcorn in clarified butter on the stovetop, then I added the ice cream base to the pot—and it perfectly captured the aroma of popcorn.

Clarified butter is butter that is cooked until the water simmers away; the milk solids sink to the bottom and are strained and discarded. You can often find ghee, the Indian style of clarified butter, for sale in little jars at grocery stores, which are perfect for this recipe!

TEXTURE AGENTS

① Best texture
Commercial stabilizer
3g | 1 teaspoon mixed with the sugar before it is added to the ice cream base.

② Least icy
Guar or xanthan gum
1g | ¼ teaspoon whirled in a blender with the ice cream base after it is chilled in the ice bath.

③ Easiest to use
Tapioca starch
5g | 2 teaspoons mixed with 20g | 2 tablespoons of cold milk, whisked into the ice cream base after it is finished cooking.

④ Most accessible
Cornstarch
10g | 1 tablespoon plus 1 teaspoon, mixed with 20g | 2 tablespoons of cold milk, whisked into the simmering ice cream base, then cooked for 1 minute.

Boil the dairy. Place the cream, milk, sugar ①, and glucose in a medium heavy-bottomed saucepan over medium-high heat, and cook, whisking occasionally to discourage the milk from scorching, until it comes to a full rolling boil. Reduce the heat to a low simmer and continue cooking for 2 minutes ④, then set the pot aside in a warm place ③.

Pop the popcorn. Place the clarified butter and popcorn in a large heavy-bottomed pot over medium-high heat. Cover with a lid and cook until you hear the sound of the corn popping. Use pot holders to take hold of the handle in one hand and the lid in the other. Gently shake and swirl the pot around, keeping the bottom flush with the burner, to encourage even popping and avoid burnt spots. Continue until the sound of popping corn has slowed to less than one pop per second. Immediately remove the popcorn from the heat.

Infuse. Working quickly, remove the lid from the popcorn pot and pour the dairy into it. Stir the popcorn, watching it dissolve. Let the popcorn-dairy mixture cool to room temperature, about 1 hour.

Blend. Transfer the popcorn mixture to a blender. Add the salt and start blending on low speed at first, increasing gradually to full speed, to avoid the liquid's jumping out of the blender cup. Continue blending for 1 to 2 minutes, until the ice cream base is very smooth.

Chill. Transfer the base to a shallow metal or glass bowl. Working quickly, fill a large bowl two-thirds of the way with very icy ice water. Nest the hot bowl into this ice bath, stirring occasionally until it cools down ②.

Strain. When the ice cream base is cool to the touch or a thermometer reads 50°F or below, strain it through a fine-mesh sieve to remove the bits of hull.

Cure. Transfer the ice cream base to the refrigerator to cure for 4 hours, or preferably overnight. (This step is optional, but the texture will be much improved with it.)

Churn. Place the base into the bowl of an ice cream maker and churn according to the manufacturer's instructions. The ice cream is ready when it thickens into the texture of soft-serve ice cream and holds its shape, typically 20 to 30 minutes.

Harden. To freeze your ice cream in the American hard-pack style, immediately transfer it to a container with an airtight lid. Press plastic wrap directly on the surface of the ice cream to prevent ice crystals from forming, cover, and store it in your freezer until it hardens completely, between 4 and 12 hours. Or, feel free to enjoy your ice cream immediately; the texture will be similar to soft-serve.

Bubblegum Ice Cream

Makes between 1 and 1½ quarts ice cream

Strawberry Puree (10%)
100g | ½ cup (page 216)

Banana extract
5g | 1 teaspoon

Vanilla extract
5g | 1 teaspoon

Milk powder (2%)
20g | 3 tablespoons

Sugar (15%)
150g | ¾ cup

Cream (38%)
380g | 2 cups

Milk (30%)
300g | 1½ cups

Glucose (5%)
50g | ¼ cup

Grated orange zest
1g | ¼ teaspoon, tightly packed

Grated lemon zest
1g | ¼ teaspoon, tightly packed

Texture agent of your choice
(see below)

TEXTURE AGENTS

① Best texture
Commercial stabilizer
3g | 1 teaspoon mixed with the sugar
before it is added to the dairy.

② Least icy
Guar or xanthan gum
1g | ¼ teaspoon whirled in a
blender with the ice cream base
after it is chilled in the ice bath.

③ Easiest to use
Tapioca starch
5g | 2 teaspoons mixed with 20g |
2 tablespoons of cold milk, whisked
into the dairy after cooking.

④ Most accessible
Cornstarch
10g | 1 tablespoon plus 1 teaspoon,
mixed with 20g | 2 tablespoons of
cold milk, whisked into the simmering dairy, then cooked for 1 minute.

Bubblegum is a fantasy flavor, which is an industry term to describe flavors that don't resemble anything in the natural world. Turns out, bubblegum doesn't grow on trees! But fantasy flavors, as imaginary as they are, must still be made from flavors that *do* exist in nature. After all, you can't create something out of nothing.

While working in Seattle, I staged with the team at Modernist Cuisine, and I asked Chris Young, the chef then heading the project, how bubblegum was made. The answer I got didn't lead me to making my own bubblegum as I had hoped, but I got something even better. He gave me the real flavors that are used to create the backbone of bubble-gum flavor: banana, vanilla, orange, and lemon. I quickly set to playing with these familiar ingredients and was amazed when I landed on a for-mula that did, sure enough, taste exactly like bubblegum! The addition of strawberry gives this ice cream the signature pink color.

Mix the flavorings. Stir together the strawberry puree, banana extract, and vanilla extract in a small bowl. Set in the refrigerator.

Combine the milk powder and sugar. Mix the milk powder and sugar ① in a small bowl.

Boil the dairy. Place the cream, milk, and glucose in a medium heavy-bottomed saucepan over medium-high heat and cook, whisking to discourage the milk from scorching, until it comes to a full boil.

Add and cook the milk powder. Whisk the milk powder mixture into the saucepan. Reduce the heat to a low simmer and continue cooking for 2 minutes ④, whisking to prevent scorching ③.

Infuse the zests. Remove the pot from the heat and stir in the orange and lemon zests. Let these infuse for 30 minutes.

Strain and chill. Strain the infused ice cream base through a fine-mesh sieve into a shallow metal or glass bowl, discarding the zest. Working quickly, fill a large bowl two-thirds of the way with very icy ice water. Nest the bowl of hot base into this ice bath, stirring occasionally until it cools ②.

Mix in the flavorings and strain the base. When the base is cool to the touch (50°F or below), remove the bowl from the ice bath and whisk in the strawberry puree. Strain through a fine-mesh sieve. (This step is optional, but will help ensure the smoothest ice cream.)

Cure. Transfer the ice cream base to the refrigerator to cure for 4 hours, or preferably overnight. (This step is also optional, but the texture will be much improved.)

Churn. Place the base into the bowl of an ice cream maker and churn according to the manufacturer's instructions. The ice cream is ready when it thickens into the texture of soft-serve ice cream, 20 to 30 minutes.

Harden. To freeze your ice cream in the American hard-pack style, immediately transfer it to a container with an airtight lid. Press plastic wrap directly on the surface of the ice cream, cover, and store it in your freezer until it hardens completely, between 4 and 12 hours. Or, feel free to enjoy your ice cream immediately; the texture will be similar to soft-serve.

Jeni and the Cream Cheese

The first time I heard of Jeni Britton Bauer was during a period of my career when traditionally crafted ice cream and I diverged. I found myself in a kitchen with a Paco Jet, a high-speed ice-shaving machine that required me to completely change all my recipes, leaving behind the kinds of ice creams I'd always made, the kinds Jeni was writing about in her book *Jeni's Splendid Ice Creams at Home*.

I set aside Jeni's book and picked up industrial manuals on the science of ice cream, but Jeni just wouldn't stay out of my head. A few years later, Jeni opened a scoop shop in Chicago. I was in line on opening week, and I was immediately smitten. Who wouldn't be? The texture was out-of-this-world dense and chewy, and the flavors were bold and unique. And Jeni captured color in her ice creams with the grace of an artist.

When I got home, I dug out her book and took an afternoon to rediscover it. Her story is amazing, and it made me want to jump out the window and open my own ice cream shop immediately. I also took a closer look at her cream cheese–laced ice creams, this time with the eye of a seasoned ice cream maker. What she does is pure genius.

The commercial ice cream manufacturers that create our favorite dense, chewy ice creams rely on a few things we don't have access to at home. Every manufacturer uses what is called a "concentrated source of milk solids" and a "concentrated source of butter fat." We can easily buy a concentrated source of butter fat by purchasing heavy cream. But a concentrated source of milk solids is harder to come by. The recipes in this book use milk powder as a concentrated source of milk solids. But Jeni uses cream cheese, solving the problem for the home cook in a very friendly and flavorful way.

Jeni also addresses the issue of what we call free-roaming water, which tends to freeze into big crystals—the icy plague of homemade ice cream. Manufacturers bind free-roaming water with the help of specially designed food gums, which you can read about in the section "The Texture Agents" (page 21). These gums are extremely efficient at binding water, and once the water is bound, it has no choice but to form tiny ice crystals. Jeni replicates this by adding a common household ingredient, cornstarch.

Jeni also cooks her ice cream base for longer than usual to help unlock the milk proteins so they can bind more water. All in all, Jeni has created an ice cream base with common household ingredients that is just as dense and chewy as the professional scoops.

If you want one of her recipes, you'll have to buy her book! No, seriously, you should. Her flavors are inspiring. But you can also Jeni-fy any of the recipes in this chapter, in three easy steps:

1. Replace 5% (50g | ¼ cup) of the milk in any of these recipes with an equal amount of soft cream cheese, mixed in when the base is chilled.
2. Increase the simmering time of the dairy from 2 minutes to 5 minutes.
3. Follow the instructions in each recipe to use cornstarch as the stabilizer.

With these cues from Jeni, you can turn any ice cream base into the dense, chewy, smooth ice creams she's famous for. And when you try your homemade ice cream made with her technique, tip a scoop to her and say thanks.

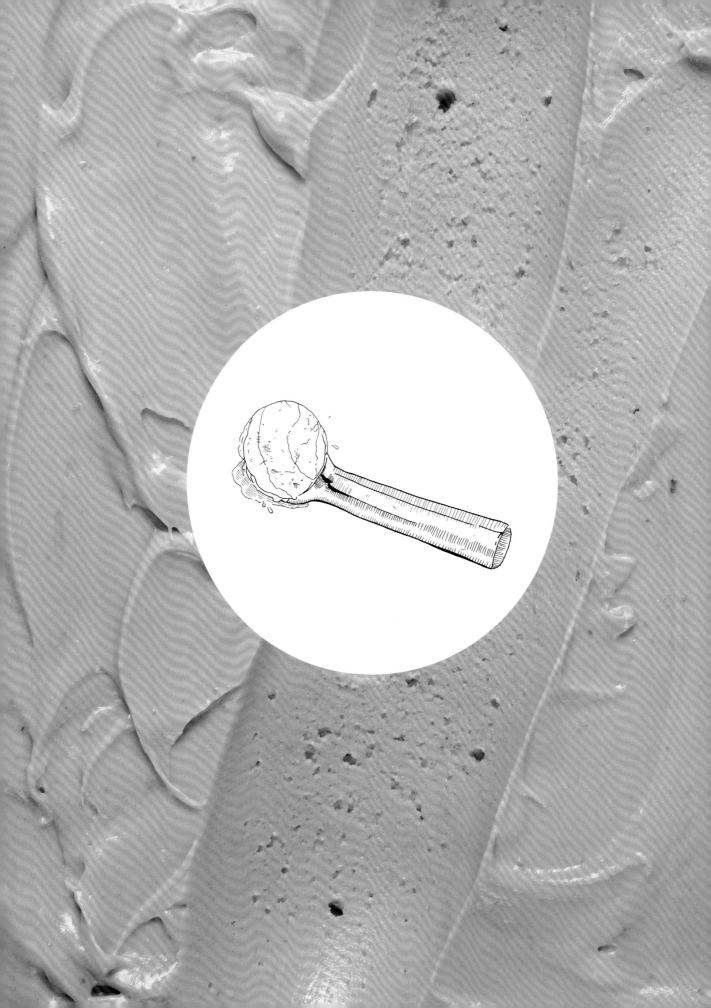

Sherbets

Sherbet is a sadly overlooked family of frozen desserts that lives somewhere between a sorbet and an ice cream. Legally speaking, a sherbet can have no less than 2 percent butterfat and no more than 4 percent, which is to say that you can think of them as creamy fruit sorbets—or as I like to see them, as the fruitiest ice creams you've ever had. They have just enough richness to add body but not too much to dull the fresh flavors of fruit; I believe that you, too, will agree these sherbets are the best way to make fruit-flavored ice cream.

This sherbet base is made in two easy pieces. First, the milk, cream, and sugars are cooked together and cooled, much like a Philadelphia-style ice cream base. To this, you add pureed fruit and a dose of tangy buttermilk—the latter a personal touch I add to all my sherbets to lift the fruit flavors into the spotlight.

There is one quirk, though, that I insist on with regard to these recipes. They each call for an exact amount of *fruit puree*, instead of a quantity of *fruit*; this ensures the ratio of fruit to dairy is correct, which is vital for the intended flavor and texture. If you have access to good-quality fruit purees, you can of course use those, but I usually prefer making the purees myself. See "Fruit Purees" in Fruit Purees and Other Basics (page 216) for techniques and recipes.

Some fruits require you to cook them before they are blended, while others can go directly into the blender raw. And there are fruits that can go either way, like peaches, which I prefer cooked, but you may prefer untouched by heat. Do what your heart and mind tell you! After all, your ice creams belong to you.

Of course, flavoring a sherbet doesn't stop at the fruit, and the best way to add a complementary flavor to a sherbet is to infuse it in the milk and cream. In this chapter you'll find infusions of fresh herbs, teas, citrus zest, spices, and flowers. As you start to experiment with your own sherbets, search your cupboards and spice drawers for friends for the fruits you are using.

While you're looking through your cupboards, you might come across one of my secret weapons for enhancing fruit sherbets: almond extract. The flavor is extracted from the kernel inside a bitter almond, but you'll find a similar kernel at the heart of every stone fruit. A hint of almond extract has a way of making fruits taste fruitier.

I also call for an ingredient called malic or citric acid. These are powdered acids that allow you to brighten your fruit sherbets with the flavor of lemon without introducing water from the lemon juice. Malic acid, which comes from apples, has a neutral, clean flavor. Citric acid, derived from citrus, also works well and is often sold in grocery stores for jam and jelly making. If you don't have either, no worries! While the powdered acids will truly make your sherbets pop, you can also use lemon juice to taste, or nothing at all.

One last thing, for the truly curious. Fruits have varying amounts of sugar, and you might wonder if adjustments should be made to account for this fact. In a professional kitchen, I measure the sugar in each sherbet base with a refractometer, a funny little telescope-like device that reveals the exact amount of sugar in the mixture, thereby telling me if I need to make an adjustment. If you work professionally, or simply geek out on things like this and want to use this tool, the ideal measurement for sherbet is 34° brix. I admit I don't bring my refractometer home, though, and I think my homemade sherbets are still pretty delicious.

Blank Slate Sherbet

Makes between 1 and 1½ quarts sherbet

Fruit puree (25%)
250g | 1¼ cups (pages 216–219)

Buttermilk (10%)
100g | ½ cup

Malic or citric acid
5g | 1 teaspoon (optional, or lemon juice to taste)

Milk (30%)
300g | 1½ cups

Cream (10%)
100g | ½ cup

Sugar (15%)
150g | ¾ cup

Glucose (10%)
100g | ½ cup

Texture agent of your choice
(see below)

This recipe is a blank slate, created for you to adapt to any fruit flavor you like. The recipes in this chapter are all based on this formula, with adjustments made to both the ingredients and the techniques. Armed with this basic recipe, you can invent any fruity flavor of sherbet you like—it literally works with any fruit flavor. You can stick with classic flavors we all know and love, like strawberry, raspberry, and orange, or you can stretch people's ideas about sherbet with more exciting fruits that are special to your region.

Make the fruit mixture.
Whisk together the fruit puree, buttermilk, and malic acid in a small bowl. Set in the refrigerator.

Boil the dairy. Place the milk, cream, sugar ①, and glucose in a medium heavy-bottomed saucepan over medium-high heat. Cook, whisking occasionally to discourage the milk from scorching. When the dairy comes to a full rolling boil, reduce the heat to a low simmer for 2 minutes ④. Remove the pot from heat ③.

Chill. Immediately pour the dairy into a shallow metal or glass bowl. Working quickly, fill a large bowl two-thirds of the way with very icy ice water. Nest the hot bowl into this ice bath, stirring occasionally until it cools down.

Mix the base with the fruit mixture. When the base is cool to the touch (50°F or below) ②, remove the bowl from the ice bath and add the reserved fruit mixture, whisking until evenly combined.

Strain. Strain the sherbet through a fine-mesh sieve to remove the particles of fruit that may remain intact. (This step is optional, but will help ensure the smoothest sherbet possible.)

Cure. Transfer the sherbet base to the refrigerator to cure for 4 hours, or preferably overnight. (This step is also optional, but the texture will be much improved with it.)

Churn. When you are ready to churn your sherbet, place it into the bowl of an ice cream maker and churn according to the manufacturer's instructions. The sherbet is finished churning when it thickens into the texture of soft-serve ice cream and holds its shape, typically 20 to 30 minutes.

Harden. To freeze your sherbet in the American hard-pack style, immediately transfer your finished sherbet to a container with an airtight lid. Press plastic wrap on the surface of the sherbet to prevent ice crystals from forming, cover, and store it in your freezer until it hardens completely, between 4 and 12 hours. Or, feel free to enjoy your sherbet immediately; the texture will be similar to soft-serve.

TEXTURE AGENTS

① **Best texture**
Commercial stabilizer
3g | 1 teaspoon mixed with the sugar before it is added to the dairy.

② **Least icy**
Guar or xanthan gum
1g | ¼ teaspoon whirled in a blender with the sherbet base after it is chilled in the ice bath.

③ **Easiest to use**
Tapioca starch
5g | 2 teaspoons mixed with 20g | 2 tablespoons of cold water, whisked into the dairy after it is finished cooking.

④ **Most accessible**
Cornstarch
10g | 1 tablespoon plus 1 teaspoon, mixed with 20g | 2 tablespoons of cold water, whisked into the simmering dairy, then cooked for 1 minute.

fig. 1

fig. 2

fig. 3

fig. 4

fig. 1: Boil the dairy.

fig. 2: Chill the base.

fig. 3: Add the fruit puree mixture.

fig. 4: Combine the fruit puree mixture and the base.

Blood Orange Sherbet

Makes between 1 and 1½ quarts sherbet

Blood orange juice (25%)
250g | 1¼ cups

Buttermilk (10%)
100g | ½ cup

Malic or citric acid
5g | 1 teaspoon (optional, or lemon juice to taste)

Milk (30%)
300g | 1½ cups

Cream (10%)
100g | ½ cup

Sugar (15%)
150g | ¾ cup

Glucose (10%)
100g | ½ cup

Grated blood orange zest
10g | 1 tablespoon, packed

Texture agent of your choice
(see below)

TEXTURE AGENTS

① Best texture
Commercial stabilizer
3g | 1 teaspoon mixed with the sugar before it is added to the dairy.

② Least icy
Guar or xanthan gum
1g | ¼ teaspoon whirled in a blender with the sherbet base after it is chilled in the ice bath.

③ Easiest to use
Tapioca starch
5g | 2 teaspoons mixed with 20g | 2 tablespoons of cold water, whisked into the dairy after it is finished cooking.

④ Most accessible
Cornstarch
10g | 1 tablespoon plus 1 teaspoon, mixed with 20g | 2 tablespoons of cold water, whisked into the simmering dairy, then cooked for 1 minute.

As a child, those little cups of orange sherbet swirled with vanilla ice cream were a must for me, chewing the spoon after the ice cream was gone to get every last drop of flavor out. Re-creating this flavor became my white whale. With a vanilla ice cream recipe under my belt, I started chasing the perfect orange flavor to swirl in.

I used oranges time and time again, but something never sat right with me. While the flavor tasted amazing, the color of the orange sherbet was so pale when churned that it was almost indistinguishable from the vanilla it was swirled into. Rather than resort to food coloring, I employed blood oranges. The red tint in their flesh gave them a beautiful sunset-orange color. Blood oranges also have a secondary, deeper flavor that I associate with raspberries. And I've become such a fan of blood oranges in my sherbet that this recipe features them. However, go ahead and use any delicious orange-like citrus you can get your hands on, like tangerines, navel oranges, clementines, or cara cara oranges. And if you'd like, check out "The Color of Flavor" on page 40 to help you tint your orange sherbet just the right shade.

Make the orange mixture.
Whisk together the orange juice, buttermilk, and malic acid in a small bowl. Set in the refrigerator.

Boil the dairy. Place the milk, cream, sugar ①, and glucose in a medium heavy-bottomed saucepan over medium-high heat. Cook, whisking occasionally to discourage the milk from scorching. When the dairy comes to a full rolling boil, reduce the heat to a low simmer for 2 minutes ④. Remove the pot from heat ③.

Infuse. Stir the zest into the base, and allow it to infuse for 30 minutes.

Strain and chill. Strain the infused sherbet base through a fine-mesh sieve, into a shallow metal or glass bowl, discarding the zest. Fill a large bowl two-thirds of the way with a lot of ice and a little water. Nest the hot bowl into this ice bath, stirring occasionally until it cools down.

Mix the base with the orange mixture. When the base is cool to the touch (50°F or below), remove the bowl from the ice bath ②.

Add the reserved orange mixture to the base, whisking until evenly combined.

Cure. Transfer the sherbet base to the refrigerator to cure for 4 hours, or preferably overnight. (This step is optional, but the texture will be much improved with it.)

Churn. When you are ready to churn your sherbet, place it into the bowl of an ice cream maker and churn according to the manufacturer's instructions. The sherbet is finished churning when it thickens into the texture of soft-serve ice cream and holds its shape, typically 20 to 30 minutes.

Harden. To freeze your sherbet in the American hard-pack style, immediately transfer your finished sherbet to a container with an airtight lid. Press plastic wrap on the surface of the sherbet to prevent ice crystals from forming, cover, and store it in your freezer until it hardens completely, between 4 and 12 hours. Or, feel free to enjoy your sherbet immediately; the texture will be similar to soft-serve.

Black Raspberry Sherbet

Makes between 1 and 1½ quarts sherbet

Black Raspberry Puree (25%)
250g | 1¼ cups (page 216)

Buttermilk (10%)
100g | ½ cup

Malic or citric acid
5g | 1 teaspoon (optional, or lemon juice to taste)

Milk (30%)
300g | 2½ cups

Cream (10%)
100g | ½ cup

Sugar (15%)
150g | ¾ cup

Glucose (10%)
100g | ½ cup

Texture agent of your choice
(see below)

TEXTURE AGENTS

① Best texture
Commercial stabilizer
3g | 1 teaspoon mixed with the sugar before it is added to the ice cream base.

② Least icy
Guar or xanthan gum
1g | ¼ teaspoon whirled in a blender with the ice cream base after it is chilled in the ice bath.

③ Easiest to use
Tapioca starch
5g | 2 teaspoons mixed with 20g | 2 tablespoons of cold water, whisked into the ice cream base after it is finished cooking.

④ Most accessible
Cornstarch
10g | 1 tablespoon plus 1 teaspoon, mixed with 20g | 2 tablespoons of cold water, whisked into the simmering ice cream base, then cooked for 1 minute.

As a recent transplant to the Midwest, I was eager to try a local specialty, and summer's first crop of black raspberries found its way into my pastry kitchen at Blackbird restaurant. Without any knowledge of the fruit, I followed orders, throwing the berries in a large pot to cook them. I almost fainted at the rich, perfumed aroma that filled the room.

Black raspberries don't yield their flavor willingly. Once picked from the thorny vines, they require simmering, spitting out specks of highly staining purple liquid from the pot onto anything and everything within in a five-foot radius. While the seeds are tiny, they are mammoth in number, rendering the puree inedible without straining them out. But the work is worth it, I tell you. If you live in a region without black raspberries, as I have for most of my life, you can look online for a frozen source. Or, you can encourage your midwestern friends to make a batch of this sherbet and pay them a long overdue visit.

I strongly suggest folding in Classic Chocolate Chunks (page 156) for a truly spectacular take on black raspberry chip ice cream.

Make the black raspberry mixture. Whisk together the puree, buttermilk, and malic acid in a small bowl. Set in the refrigerator.

Boil the dairy. Place the milk, cream, sugar ①, and glucose in a medium heavy-bottomed saucepan over medium-high heat. Cook, whisking occasionally to discourage the milk from scorching. When the dairy comes to a full rolling boil, reduce the heat to a low simmer for 2 minutes ④. Remove the pot from heat ③.

Chill. Immediately pour the sherbet base into a shallow metal or glass bowl. Working quickly, fill a large bowl two-thirds of the way with very icy ice water. Nest the hot bowl into this ice bath, stirring occasionally until it cools down.

Mix the base with the black raspberry mixture. When the base is cool to the touch (50°F or below), remove the bowl from the ice bath ②. Add the black raspberry mixture to the base, whisking until evenly combined.

Strain. Strain the sherbet through a fine-mesh sieve to remove the particles of fruit that may remain intact. (This step is optional, but will help ensure the smoothest sherbet possible.)

Cure. Transfer the sherbet base to the refrigerator to cure for 4 hours, or preferably overnight. (This step is also optional, but the texture will be much improved with it.)

Churn. When you are ready to churn your sherbet, place it into the bowl of an ice cream maker and churn according to the manufacturer's instructions. The sherbet is finished churning when it thickens into the texture of soft-serve ice cream and holds its shape, typically 20 to 30 minutes.

Harden. To freeze your sherbet in the American hard-pack style, immediately transfer your finished sherbet to a container with an airtight lid. Press plastic wrap on the surface of the sherbet to prevent ice crystals from forming, cover, and store it in your freezer until it hardens completely, between 4 and 12 hours. Or, feel free to enjoy your sherbet immediately; the texture will be similar to soft-serve.

Peach-Sweet Tea Sherbet

Makes between 1 and 1½ quarts sherbet

Peach Puree (25%)
250g | 1¼ cups (page 217)

Buttermilk (10%)
100g | ½ cup

Almond extract
2g | ¼ teaspoon

Malic or citric acid
5g | 1 teaspoon (optional, or lemon juice to taste)

Milk (30%)
300g | 1½ cups

Cream (10%)
100g | ½ cup

Sugar (15%)
150g | ¾ cup

Glucose (10%)
100g | ½ cup

Black tea
10g | 3 tablespoons

Texture agent of your choice
(see below)

Peaches and sweet tea are summer delights that are better in each other's company. I like to splurge on a good loose-leaf black tea when I make this, either a Darjeeling or English breakfast, then infuse it in the milk and cream before finishing the sherbet. However, any black tea you enjoy will do.

Ripe peaches are soft and supple like no other fruit. For this sherbet, I like to cook them until they become translucent and fragrant before I puree them. It's an extra step, and you certainly can blend your peaches fresh. But I think the flavor of cooked peaches is unbeatable. That said, this recipe can be made with canned peaches as well; just make sure to rinse them of their syrup before you puree them.

Finally, if you crack open the center of a peach pit, you'll find a small nut that looks like an almond. And indeed, the peach and the almond are members of the same family. This peach kernel has the aroma of almond extract, and a small addition of this flavor brings the peaches to life. (The almond extract can be omitted, but I never leave it out if I can help it.)

Make the peach mixture.
Whisk together the peach puree, buttermilk, almond extract, and malic acid in a small bowl. Set in the refrigerator.

Boil the dairy. Place the milk, cream, sugar ①, and glucose in a medium heavy-bottomed saucepan over medium-high heat. Cook, whisking occasionally to discourage the milk from scorching. When the dairy comes to a full rolling boil, reduce the heat to a low simmer for 2 minutes ④. Remove the pot from heat ③.

Infuse. Stir the tea into the sherbet base, and allow it to infuse for 5 minutes. Any longer and the black tea will start to impart a bitterness.

Strain and chill. Strain the infused sherbet base through a fine-mesh sieve, into a shallow metal or glass bowl, discarding the tea. Fill a large bowl two-thirds of the way with a lot of ice and a little water. Nest the hot bowl into this ice bath, stirring occasionally until it cools down.

Mix the base with the peach mixture. When the base is cool to the touch (50°F or below), remove the bowl from the ice bath ②. Add the reserved peach mixture to the base, whisking until evenly combined.

Strain. Strain the sherbet through a fine-mesh sieve to remove the particles of fruit that may remain

---

TEXTURE AGENTS

① Best texture
Commercial stabilizer
3g | 1 teaspoon mixed with the sugar before it is added to the dairy.

② Least icy
Guar or xanthan gum
1g | ¼ teaspoon whirled in a blender with the sherbet base after it is chilled in the ice bath.

③ Easiest to use
Tapioca starch
5g | 2 teaspoons mixed with 20g | 2 tablespoons of cold water, whisked into the dairy after it is finished cooking.

④ Most accessible
Cornstarch
10g | 1 tablespoon plus 1 teaspoon, mixed with 20g | 2 tablespoons of cold water, whisked into the simmering dairy, then cooked for 1 minute.

intact. (This step is optional, but will help ensure the smoothest sherbet possible.)

Cure. Transfer the sherbet base to the refrigerator to cure for 4 hours, or preferably overnight. (This step is also optional, but the texture will be much improved with it.)

Churn. When you are ready to churn your sherbet, place it into the bowl of an ice cream maker and churn according to the manufacturer's instructions. The sherbet is finished churning when it thickens into the texture of soft-serve ice cream and holds its shape, typically 20 to 30 minutes.

Harden. To freeze your sherbet in the American hard-pack style, immediately transfer your finished sherbet to a container with an airtight lid. Press plastic wrap on the surface of the sherbet to prevent ice crystals from forming, cover, and store it in your freezer until it hardens completely, between 4 and 12 hours. Or, feel free to enjoy your sherbet immediately; the texture will be similar to soft-serve.

Pineapple Jasmine Sherbet

Makes between 1 and 1½ quarts sherbet

Pineapple juice (35%)
950g | 1 quart (from about
2 pineapples)

Buttermilk (10%)
100g | ½ cup

Malic or citric acid
5g | 1 teaspoon (optional, or
lemon juice to taste)

Sugar (15%)
150g | ¾ cup

Milk powder (3%)
30g | ¼ cup

Milk (17%)
170g | 1 cup

Cream (10%)
100g | ½ cup

Glucose (10%)
100g | ¼ cup

Jasmine green tea pearls
10g | 2 teaspoons (or
10 tea bags)

Grated lime zest
3g | 1 teaspoon, packed

Texture agent of your choice
(see below)

A mission to re-create the rainbow sherbet scoops of my childhood led me to this pineapple sherbet. I originally made it as one of the rainbow swirled-flavors, but it's amazing on its own. Here, the flavor of pineapple intertwines with the floral perfume of jasmine in a way that makes me want to say silly things about soft breezes in lush tropical climates.

If you live in a pineapple-growing region, like Hawaii, you are among the lucky few who have access to ripe and ready pineapples. For the rest of us, the pineapples we get in the grocery store require a little time to bring out their ripest flavors—around a week to truly bring a pineapple to life. I cut the entire top off my pineapple like a post-punk kid discarding his Mohawk, shaving it flat but not cutting so deeply the flesh is exposed. I then turn the flat-top pineapple upside down on a plate, and tuck the plate someplace out of the way. The pineapple then becomes fragrant and sweet, and when it smells good I bring it down. For this recipe, pass the pineapple flesh through a juicer, and strain the juice through a fine-mesh strainer. If you have to choose between juicing an unripe pineapple and using store-bought pineapple juice, buy the pineapple juice.

Jasmine pearls are made by drying tea leaves and jasmine flowers on alternating racks. Once the tea is perfumed with the white blossom, the leaves are hand-rolled into pearls and dried. If you can't find jasmine pearls, you can use tea bags, which are likely made by adding jasmine essence to cut green tea in the tea factory. It takes about 10 teabags to equal the flavor of the jasmine pearls called for in this recipe.

You can certainly leave the jasmine tea and lime out of this recipe if you'd prefer, or if you're making it as part of the Rainbow Sherbet composed scoop (page 182).

TEXTURE AGENTS

(1) Best texture
Commercial stabilizer
3g | 1 teaspoon mixed
with the sugar before it
is added to the dairy.

(2) Least icy
Guar or xanthan gum
1g | ¼ teaspoon whirled
in a blender with the
sherbet base after it is
chilled in the ice bath.

(3) Easiest to use
Tapioca starch
5g | 2 teaspoons mixed
with 20g | 2 tablespoons
of cold water, whisked
into the dairy after it is
finished cooking.

(4) Most accessible
Cornstarch
10g | 1 tablespoon plus
1 teaspoon, mixed with
20g | 2 tablespoons of
cold water, whisked into
the simmering dairy,
then cooked for 1 minute.

Reduce the pineapple juice. Place the pineapple juice in a small pot over medium-high heat. Simmer the pineapple juice until it has reduced by roughly two-thirds and you have 350g | 1¾ cups of triple-strength pineapple juice. If you reduce it too much, add water until you have the required amount of reduced juice. Let the pineapple juice cool completely.

Make the pineapple mixture. Whisk together the reduced pineapple juice, buttermilk, and malic acid in a small bowl. Set in the refrigerator.

Mix the sugar and milk powder. Place the sugar ① and milk powder in a small bowl and mix until even.

Boil the dairy. Place the milk, cream, and glucose in a medium heavy-bottomed saucepan. Place the pot over medium-high heat and cook, whisking occasionally to discourage the milk from scorching.

Add the milk powder mixture and cook. When the dairy comes to a full rolling boil, add the milk powder mixture and whisk until even ④. Reduce the heat to a low simmer and continue cooking for 2 minutes, whisking frequently to prevent scorching. Remove the pot from the heat ③.

Infuse. Stir the tea and lime zest into the dairy, and allow it to infuse for 5 minutes. Any longer and the tea will begin to impart a bitter flavor.

Strain and chill. Strain the infused sherbet base through a fine-mesh sieve, into a shallow metal or glass bowl, discarding the tea and zest. Fill a large bowl two-thirds of the way with a lot of ice and a little water. Nest the hot bowl into this ice bath, stirring occasionally until it cools down.

Mix the sherbet base with the pineapple mixture. When the sherbet base is cool to the touch (50°F or below), remove the bowl from the ice bath ②. Add the reserved pineapple mixture to the base, whisking until evenly combined.

Strain. Strain the sherbet through a fine-mesh sieve to remove the particles of fruit that may remain intact. (This step is optional, but will help ensure the smoothest sherbet possible.)

Cure. Transfer the sherbet base to the refrigerator to cure for 4 hours, or preferably overnight. (This step is also optional, but the texture will be much improved with it.)

Churn. When you are ready to churn your sherbet, place it into the bowl of an ice cream maker and churn according to the manufacturer's instructions. The sherbet is finished churning when it thickens into the texture of soft-serve ice cream and holds its shape, typically 20 to 30 minutes.

Harden. To freeze your sherbet in the American hard-pack style, immediately transfer your finished sherbet to a container with an airtight lid. Press plastic wrap on the surface of the sherbet to prevent ice crystals from forming, cover, and store it in your freezer until it hardens completely, between 4 and 12 hours. Or, feel free to enjoy your sherbet immediately; the texture will be similar to soft-serve.

Raspberry-Anise Sherbet

Makes between 1 and 1½ quarts sherbet

Raspberry Puree (25%)
250g | 1¼ cups (page 216)

Buttermilk (10%)
100g | ½ cup

Malic or citric acid
3g | ½ teaspoon (optional, or lemon juice to taste)

Milk (30%)
300g | 1½ cups

Cream (10%)
100g | ½ cup

Sugar (15%)
150g | ¾ cup

Glucose (10%)
100g | ½ cup

Anise hyssop leaves
30g | 1 large handful

Texture agent of your choice
(see below)

At Poppy restaurant, Jerry Traunfeld taught me to work with anise hyssop, a tall purple-blossomed plant that grew in our garden. The leaves are soft like the fuzz on a newborn puppy, and the flavor is the most inviting form of anise I've ever tasted. Anise hyssop lacks the sharp angles of licorice, the twang of star anise pods, or the bright edge of fennel, and the leaves can be eaten fresh like basil, or steeped into panna cotta, whipped cream, and ice cream. I spent each summer at Poppy harvesting these leaves, all the while looking for new and exciting fruits to pair with them. I didn't have to look far. Anise hyssop works with just about everything. Raspberries will forever remain my favorite pairing for it though, and this sherbet captures their flavors perfectly.

When I don't have access to anise hyssop leaves, I use green anise seed. Replace the anise hyssop with 5g | 1 tablespoon of the anise seeds and infuse them in the cream in the same manner as the leaves. You won't be disappointed!

If you want a plain raspberry sherbet, or are making this to use in the Rainbow Sherbet composed scoop (page 182), omit the anise hyssop or seed from this recipe, and you'll find the pink scoops you're looking for!

TEXTURE AGENTS

① Best texture
Commercial stabilizer
3g | 1 teaspoon mixed with the sugar before it is added to the dairy.

② Least icy
Guar or xanthan gum
1g | ¼ teaspoon whirled in a blender with the sherbet base after it is chilled in the ice bath.

③ Easiest to use
Tapioca starch
5g | 2 teaspoons mixed with 20g | 2 tablespoons of cold water, whisked into the dairy after it is finished cooking.

④ Most accessible
Cornstarch
10g | 1 tablespoon plus 1 teaspoon, mixed with 20g | 2 tablespoons of cold water, whisked into the simmering dairy, then cooked for 1 minute.

Make the raspberry mixture.
Whisk together the raspberry puree, buttermilk, and malic acid in a small bowl. Set in the refrigerator.

Boil the dairy. Place the milk, cream, sugar ①, and glucose in a medium heavy-bottomed saucepan over medium-high heat. Cook, whisking occasionally to discourage the milk from scorching. When the dairy comes to a full rolling boil, reduce the heat to a low simmer for 2 minutes ④. Remove the pot from heat ③.

Infuse. Stir the anise hyssop into the dairy, and allow to infuse for 30 minutes.

Strain and chill. Strain the infused sherbet base through a fine-mesh sieve, into a shallow metal or glass bowl, discarding the leaves. Fill a large bowl two-thirds of the way with a lot of ice and a little water. Nest the hot bowl into this ice bath, stirring occasionally until it cools down.

Mix the sherbet base with the raspberry mixture. When the sherbet base is cool to the touch (50°F or below), remove the bowl from the ice bath ②. Add the raspberry mixture to the base, whisking until evenly combined.

Strain. Strain the sherbet through a fine-mesh sieve to remove the particles of fruit that may remain intact. (This step is optional, but will help ensure the smoothest sherbet possible.)

Cure. Transfer the sherbet base to the refrigerator to cure for 4 hours, or preferably overnight. (This step is also optional, but the texture will be much improved with it.)

Churn. When you are ready to churn your sherbet, place it into the bowl of an ice cream maker and churn according to the manufacturer's instructions. The sherbet is finished churning when it thickens into the texture of soft-serve ice cream and holds its shape, typically 20 to 30 minutes.

Harden. To freeze your sherbet in the American hard-pack style, immediately transfer your finished sherbet to a container with an airtight lid. Press plastic wrap on the surface of the sherbet to prevent ice crystals from forming, cover, and store it in your freezer until it hardens completely, between 4 and 12 hours. Or, feel free to enjoy your sherbet immediately; the texture will be similar to soft-serve.

Huckleberry Lemon Sherbet

Makes between 1 and 1½ quarts sherbet

Huckleberry Puree (20%)
200g | 1 cup (page 216)

Buttermilk (10%)
100g | ½ cup

Lemon juice (5%)
50g | ¼ cup

Milk (30%)
300g | 1½ cups

Cream (10%)
100g | ½ cup

Sugar (15%)
150g | ¾ cup

Glucose (10%)
100g | ½ cup

Grated lemon zest
3g | 1 teaspoon, packed

Texture agent of your choice
(see below)

A true mountain huckleberry is one of Mother Earth's greatest gifts. It's unmistakable, with the bright acidity of a raspberry, the round sweetness of a blueberry, and a flavor entirely its own. As a child, my life was filled with huckleberries. My father's side of the family would set up camp in the foothills of Washington state's Mount Adams each summer, horses and all. Our campsite was at the base of a little mound of earth called Potato Hill, but it could have just as easily been called Huckleberry Hill, based on the berry-bearing bushes that covered it. When fall approached, we would pick as many huckleberries as we could manage, eating huckleberry pancakes griddled over the fire and storing the rest in the freezer.

If you get your hands on some huckleberries, put this recipe on the top of your to-do list. In the Pacific Northwest, you can find huckleberries at farmers' markets as well as specialty shops, or if you're near Trout Lake, check for them at the general store. And you can always order frozen huckleberries online.

Huckleberries should be cooked before using them to make sherbet. Until the heat softens their flavor, they are quite tart and a touch tannic. Once simmered, the berries become rich, fragrant, and their astringency mellows.

This recipe also works wonderfully with the huckleberry's gentle cousin, the blueberry, and the two can be used interchangeably. Not all blueberries are created equal, and if you plan to make this flavor outside of blueberry season, grab a bag of frozen blueberries from the freezer section—and if you see wild blueberries, use them!

TEXTURE AGENTS

① **Best texture**
Commercial stabilizer
3g | 1 teaspoon mixed with the sugar before it is added to the dairy.

② **Least icy**
Guar or xanthan gum
1g | ¼ teaspoon whirled in a blender with the sherbet base after it is chilled in the ice bath.

③ **Easiest to use**
Tapioca starch
5g | 2 teaspoons mixed with 20g | 2 tablespoons of cold water, whisked into the dairy after it is finished cooking.

④ **Most accessible**
Cornstarch
10g | 1 tablespoon plus 1 teaspoon, mixed with 20g | 2 tablespoons of cold water, whisked into the simmering dairy, then cooked for 1 minute.

Make the huckleberry mixture. Whisk the huckleberry puree, buttermilk, and lemon juice in a small bowl. Set in the refrigerator.

Boil the dairy. Place the milk, cream, sugar ①, and glucose in a medium heavy-bottomed saucepan over medium-high heat. Cook, whisking occasionally to discourage the milk from scorching. When the dairy comes to a full rolling boil, reduce the heat to a low simmer for 2 minutes ④. Remove the pot from heat ③.

Infuse. Stir the lemon zest into the dairy, and allow it to infuse for 30 minutes.

Strain and chill. Strain the infused sherbet base through a fine-mesh sieve, into a shallow metal or glass bowl, discarding zest. Fill a large bowl two-thirds of the way with a lot of ice and a little water. Nest the hot bowl into this ice bath, stirring occasionally until it cools down.

Mix the base with the huckleberry mixture. When the base is cool to the touch (50°F or below), remove the bowl from the ice bath ②. Add the huckleberry mixture to the base, whisking until evenly combined.

Strain. Strain the sherbet through a fine-mesh sieve to remove the particles of fruit that may remain intact. (This step is optional, but will help ensure the smoothest sherbet possible.)

Cure. Transfer the sherbet base to the refrigerator to cure for 4 hours, or preferably overnight. (This step is also optional, but the texture will be much improved with it.)

Churn. When you are ready to churn your sherbet, place it into the bowl of an ice cream maker and churn according to the manufacturer's instructions. The sherbet is finished churning when it thickens into the texture of soft-serve ice cream and holds its shape, typically 20 to 30 minutes.

Harden. To freeze your sherbet in the American hard-pack style, immediately transfer your finished sherbet to a container with an airtight lid. Press plastic wrap on the surface of the sherbet to prevent ice crystals from forming, cover, and store it in your freezer until it hardens completely, between 4 and 12 hours. Or, feel free to enjoy your sherbet immediately; the texture will be similar to soft-serve.

Concord Grape and Rosemary Sherbet

Makes between 1 and 1½ quarts sherbet

Concord Grape Puree (25%)
250g | 1¼ cups (page 217)

Buttermilk (10%)
100g | ½ cup

Malic or citric acid
5g | 1 teaspoon (optional; or lemon juice to taste)

Milk (30%)
300g | 1½ cups

Cream (10%)
100g | ½ cup

Sugar (15%)
150g | ¾ cup

Glucose (10%)
100g | ½ cup

Fresh rosemary
1 5-inch sprig

Texture agent of your choice
(see below)

TEXTURE AGENTS

① Best texture
Commercial stabilizer
3g | 1 teaspoon mixed with the sugar before it is added to the ice cream base.

② Least icy
Guar or xanthan gum
1g | ¼ teaspoon whirled in a blender with the ice cream base after it is chilled in the ice bath.

③ Easiest to use
Tapioca starch
5g | 2 teaspoons mixed with 20g | 2 tablespoons of cold water, whisked into the ice cream base after it is finished cooking.

④ Most accessible
Cornstarch
10g | 1 tablespoon plus 1 teaspoon, mixed with 20g | 2 tablespoons of cold water, whisked into the simmering ice cream base, then cooked for 1 minute.

When I first tasted a concord grape, I was shocked. I couldn't believe there were real grapes that tasted like "grape"! The rosemary lends a woodsy, robust quality, elevating this beyond the childhood flavor of grape juice. Jerry Traunfeld introduced me to this flavor combination when I worked at Poppy, using it to flavor an elegant sorbet. Of course, you can also leave the rosemary out of this recipe.

Bluish, frosted concord grapes now pass through my Chicago kitchen every season, as they grow abundantly across the lake in Michigan. Any that I don't eat out of hand go directly into a pot to be simmered for this sherbet.

In a pinch, 100% Concord grape juice can be a good alternative. However, these are balanced as a beverage, not as a flavoring for ice cream. To substitute Concord grape juice for the cooked grape puree, use 500g | 2½ cups and simmer the juice over low heat until it is reduced by half before adding it to the sherbet.

Make the grape mixture. Whisk the grape puree, buttermilk, and malic acid in a small bowl. Set in the refrigerator.

Boil the dairy. Place the milk, cream, sugar ①, and glucose in a medium heavy-bottomed saucepan over medium-high heat. Cook, whisking occasionally to discourage the milk from scorching. When the dairy comes to a full rolling boil, reduce the heat to a low simmer for 2 minutes ④. Remove the pot from heat ③.

Infuse. Stir the rosemary sprig into the dairy, and allow it to infuse for 10 minutes.

Strain and chill. Strain the infused sherbet base through a fine-mesh sieve, into a shallow metal or glass bowl, discarding the rosemary. Fill a large bowl two-thirds of the way with a lot of ice and a little water. Nest the hot bowl into this ice bath, stirring occasionally until it cools down.

Mix the base with the grape mixture. When the base is cool to the touch (50°F or below), remove the bowl from the ice bath ②. Add the grape mixture to the base, whisking until evenly combined.

Strain. Strain the sherbet through a fine-mesh sieve to remove the particles of fruit that may remain intact. (This step is optional, but will help ensure the smoothest sherbet possible.)

Cure. Transfer the sherbet base to the refrigerator to cure for 4 hours, or preferably overnight. (This step is also optional, but the texture will be much improved with it.)

Churn. When you are ready to churn your sherbet, place it into the bowl of an ice cream maker and churn according to the manufacturer's instructions. The sherbet is finished churning when it thickens into the texture of soft-serve ice cream and holds its shape, typically 20 to 30 minutes.

Harden. To freeze your sherbet in the American hard-pack style, immediately transfer your finished sherbet to a container with an airtight lid. Press plastic wrap on the surface of the sherbet to prevent ice crystals from forming, cover, and store it in your freezer until it hardens completely, between 4 and 12 hours. Or, feel free to enjoy your sherbet immediately; the texture will be similar to soft-serve.

Avocado-Grapefruit Sherbet

Makes between 1 and 1½ quarts sherbet

Milk (25%)
250g | 1¼ cups

Cream (10%)
100g | ½ cup

Sugar (15%)
150g | ¾ cup

Glucose (10%)
100g | ½ cup

Grated grapefruit zest
3g | 1 teaspoon, packed

Grapefruit juice (10%)
100g | ½ cup

Avocado flesh (30%)
300g | 1½ packed cups (from
2 large avocados or 3 small)

Kosher or sea salt
4g | 1 teaspoon

Texture agent of your choice
(see below)

TEXTURE AGENTS

① Best texture
Commercial stabilizer
3g | 1 teaspoon mixed with the
sugar before it is added to the
dairy.

② Least icy
Guar or xanthan gum
1g | ¼ teaspoon whirled in a
blender with the sherbet base
after it is chilled in the ice bath.

③ Easiest to use
Tapioca starch
5g | 2 teaspoons mixed with 20g |
2 tablespoons of cold water,
whisked into the dairy after it is
finished cooking.

④ Most accessible
Cornstarch
10g | 1 tablespoon plus 1 teaspoon,
mixed with 20g | 2 tablespoons
of cold water, whisked into the
simmering dairy, then cooked for
1 minute.

I first encountered avocado sherbet when my Hawaiian-born friend and sous chef Krystal Swendson suggested it. She knew well that Hawaiians, along with many cultures throughout the world, relish the luxurious texture and nutty flavor of avocado as a dessert.

When selecting your avocados for sherbet, you want them a touch on the greener side of ripe. If you have access to avocado leaves, infuse a few of them in the milk to reveal their fruity flavor.

The texture of avocado sherbet is so luxurious, you might start to ask what other flavors you can pair with this green fruit. I'll give you a couple hints: coffee and avocado are quite distinguished, and chocolate and avocado are earthy and unforgettable. You can also exchange some of the milk for coconut milk, or infuse fresh mint into the milk and cream instead of the grapefruit zest. If you omit the grapefruit juice, simply replace it with buttermilk.

Boil the dairy. Place the milk, cream, sugar ①, and glucose in a medium heavy-bottomed saucepan over medium-high heat. Cook, whisking occasionally to discourage the milk from scorching. When the dairy comes to a full roiling boil, reduce the heat to a low simmer for 2 minutes ④. Remove the pot from heat ③.

Infuse. Stir the grapefruit zest into the dairy, and allow it to infuse for 30 minutes.

Strain and chill. Strain the infused sherbet base through a fine-mesh sieve into a shallow metal or glass bowl, discarding zest. Fill a large bowl two-thirds of the way with a lot of ice and a little water. Nest the hot bowl into this ice bath, stirring occasionally until it cools down.

Mix the base with the grapefruit juice. When the base is cool to the touch (50°F or below), remove the bowl from the ice bath ②. Add the grapefruit juice to the base, whisking until evenly combined.

Cure. Transfer the sherbet base to the refrigerator to cure for 4 hours, or preferably overnight. (This step is optional, but the texture will be much improved with it.)

Blend the base with the avocado. Just before churning your sherbet, peel and pit the avocados. Measure the avocados and transfer them to a blender with the salt. Add one-third of the sherbet base and blend on medium speed, pausing to scrape as necessary, until smooth. Add the remaining base and blend on low just until smooth.

Strain. Strain the sherbet through a fine-mesh sieve to remove any particles of fruit. (This step is optional, but will help ensure the smoothest sherbet possible.)

Churn. When you are ready to churn your sherbet, place it into the bowl of an ice cream maker and churn according to the manufacturer's instructions. The sherbet is finished churning when it thickens into the texture of soft-serve ice cream and holds its shape, typically 20 to 30 minutes.

Harden. To freeze your sherbet, immediately transfer the finished sherbet to a container with an airtight lid. Press plastic wrap on the surface of the sherbet, cover, and store it in your freezer for 4 to 12 hours. Or enjoy your sherbet immediately; the texture will be similar to soft-serve.

Strawberry Sherbet

Makes between 1 and 1½ quarts sherbet

Strawberry Puree (25%)
250g | 1¼ cups (page 216)

Buttermilk (10%)
100g | ½ cup

Malic or citric acid
3g | ½ teaspoon (optional, or lemon juice to taste)

Milk (30%)
300g | 1½ cups

Cream (10%)
100g | ½ cup

Sugar (15%)
150g | ¾ cup

Glucose (10%)
100g | ½ cup

Texture agent of your choice
(see below)

While this is a textbook sherbet, I don't always label it as such when I pack it into pints or list it on a menu. Most of the time I call it "Strawberry-Buttermilk Ice Cream" because it's the only strawberry ice cream I make. It's bursting with more strawberry flavor than any ice cream you've tasted.

I love this sherbet at the peak of strawberry season, when the local berries are so red they stain your face and so flavorful you just don't care. Even in season, though, I prefer to make the puree from frozen berries, so I tuck those field-fresh strawberries into the freezer overnight.

As they freeze, the water inside the strawberries turns into sharp ice crystals that puncture the cell walls of the berries. A key part of strawberry flavor comes from an enzymatic reaction that occurs only when the cell walls break, so thawed frozen strawberries taste *more* like strawberries. And if you puree your strawberries when they are only half thawed, the bright red pigment of the fruit is preserved, making for the prettiest purees around.

If putting your strawberries through a freeze-thaw cycle isn't in your time line, go ahead and puree fresh berries. But if it isn't strawberry season, promise me you'll skip the plastic box of strawberries with the same texture as packing peanuts, and grab a bag of frozen berries instead.

TEXTURE AGENTS

① **Best texture**
Commercial stabilizer
3g | 1 teaspoon mixed with the sugar before it is added to the dairy.

② **Least icy**
Guar or xanthan gum
1g | ¼ teaspoon whirled in a blender with the sherbet base after it is chilled in the ice bath.

③ **Easiest to use**
Tapioca starch
5g | 2 teaspoons mixed with 20g | 2 tablespoons of cold water, whisked into the dairy after it is finished cooking.

④ **Most accessible**
Cornstarch
10g | 1 tablespoon plus 1 teaspoon, mixed with 20g | 2 tablespoons of cold water, whisked into the simmering dairy, then cooked for 1 minute.

Make the strawberry mixture.
Whisk together the puree, buttermilk, and malic acid in a small bowl. Set in the refrigerator.

Boil the dairy. Place the milk, cream, sugar ①, and glucose in a medium heavy-bottomed saucepan over medium-high heat. Cook, whisking occasionally to discourage the milk from scorching. When the dairy comes to a full rolling boil, reduce the heat to a low simmer for 2 minutes ④. Remove the pot from heat ③.

Chill. Immediately pour the sherbet base into a shallow metal or glass bowl. Working quickly, fill a large bowl two-thirds of the way with very icy ice water. Nest the hot bowl into this ice bath, stirring occasionally until it cools down.

Mix the base with the strawberry mixture. When the base is cool to the touch (50°F or below), remove the bowl from the ice bath ②. Add the strawberry mixture to the base, whisking until evenly combined.

Strain. Strain the sherbet through a fine-mesh sieve to remove the particles of strawberry that may remain intact. (This step is optional, but will help ensure the smoothest sherbet possible.)

Cure. Transfer the sherbet base to the refrigerator to cure for 4 hours, or preferably overnight. (This step is also optional, but the texture will be much improved with it.)

Churn. When you are ready to churn your sherbet, place it into the bowl of an ice cream maker and churn according to the manufacturer's instructions. The sherbet is finished churning when it thickens into the texture of soft-serve ice cream and holds its shape, typically 20 to 30 minutes.

Harden. To freeze your sherbet in the American hard-pack style, immediately transfer your finished sherbet to a container with an airtight lid. Press plastic wrap on the surface of the sherbet to prevent ice crystals from forming, cover, and store it in your freezer until it hardens completely, between 4 and 12 hours. Or, feel free to enjoy your sherbet immediately; the texture will be similar to soft-serve.

Apricot Rooibos Sherbet

Makes between 1 and 1½ quarts sherbet

Apricot Puree (25%)
250g | 1¼ cups (page 217)

Buttermilk (10%)
100g | ½ cup

Almond extract
2g | ¼ teaspoon

Malic or citric acid
3g | ½ teaspoon (optional, or
lemon juice to taste)

Milk (30%)
300g | 1½ cups

Cream (10%)
100g | ½ cup

Sugar (15%)
150g | ¾ cup

Glucose (10%)
100g | ½ cup

Rooibos tea
10g | 1 tablespoon

Texture agent of your choice
(see below)

TEXTURE AGENTS

① Best texture
Commercial stabilizer
3g | 1 teaspoon mixed with the sugar
before it is added to the dairy.

② Least icy
Guar or xanthan gum
1g | ¼ teaspoon whirled in a blender
with the sherbet base after it is
chilled in the ice bath.

③ Easiest to use
Tapioca starch
5g | 2 teaspoons mixed with 20g |
2 tablespoons of cold water,
whisked into the dairy after it is
finished cooking.

④ Most accessible
Cornstarch
10g | 1 tablespoon plus 1 teaspoon,
mixed with 20g | 2 tablespoons
of cold water, whisked into the
simmering dairy, then cooked for
1 minute.

My grandma Eva canned fruit every year, carried from the eastern half of Washington state to Seattle, over the Cascade Mountains. I would stand in her basement storeroom, my back to the wall of toys preserved from my father's childhood, and stare in awe at the jars lining the shelves as if they contained glistening jewels. I always requested the apricots. Every time I simmer apricots for this sherbet, I am immediately transported to that storeroom, or to her patio where my mom helped me spoon the fruits from the jar without spilling too much syrup.

The golden flavor of apricots, simmered to soft submission, is a perfect match for the African red tea called rooibos. The tea is made of what looks like teeny tiny sticks, and the flavor is warm and luminous like the sun setting over the vast arid plains where this red tea grows. As always, you can omit the rooibos and make a plain apricot sherbet.

Make the apricot mixture. Whisk the apricot puree, buttermilk, almond extract, and malic acid in a small bowl. Set in the refrigerator.

Boil the dairy. Place the milk, cream, sugar ①, and glucose in a medium heavy-bottomed saucepan over medium-high heat. Cook, whisking occasionally to discourage the milk from scorching. When the dairy comes to a full rolling boil, reduce the heat to a low simmer for 2 minutes ④. Remove the pot from heat ③.

Infuse. Stir the rooibos into the dairy, and allow it to infuse for 30 minutes.

Strain and chill. Strain the infused sherbet base through a fine-mesh sieve, into a shallow metal or glass bowl, discarding the rooibos. Fill a large bowl two-thirds of the way with a lot of ice and a little water. Nest the hot bowl into this ice bath, stirring occasionally until it cools down.

Mix the base with the apricot mixture. When the base is cool to the touch (50°F or below), remove the bowl from the ice bath ②. Add the reserved apricot mixture to the base, whisking until evenly combined.

Strain. Strain the sherbet through a fine-mesh sieve to remove the particles of fruit that may remain intact. (This step is optional, but will help ensure the smoothest sherbet possible.)

Cure. Transfer the sherbet base to the refrigerator to cure for 4 hours, or preferably overnight. (This step is also optional, but the texture will be much improved with it.)

Churn. When you are ready to churn your sherbet, place it into the bowl of an ice cream maker and churn according to the manufacturer's instructions. The sherbet is finished churning when it thickens into the texture of soft-serve ice cream and holds its shape, typically 20 to 30 minutes.

Harden. To freeze your sherbet in the American hard-pack style, immediately transfer your finished sherbet to a container with an airtight lid. Press plastic wrap on the surface of the sherbet to prevent ice crystals from forming, cover, and store it in your freezer until it hardens completely, between 4 and 12 hours. Or, feel free to enjoy your sherbet immediately; the texture will be similar to soft-serve.

Pichet and the Starchy Fruits

Sherbet is a style of ice cream I am very attached to. So much so that I got into a public argument about it with my friend Pichet Ong. We were in class at the Penn State Ice Cream Short Course, a week-long immersion offered by the university's dairy science program. (Ice Cream College!)

As the instructor was describing the legal requirements of sherbet—no less than 2% butterfat, no more than 4% milk solids, yada-yada, department of weights and measures, blah blah blah—Pichet, a seasoned pastry chef, started whispering in my ear: "Ask them about sherbets made with starchy fruits." I looked at him, confused. "Ask them about sherbets without dairy, the ones that are creamy because they have starchy fruits or fruits cooked with their skins."

"But those aren't sherbets. Those are *sorbets*," I insisted.

"Alice Waters says in her book that sherbets are sorbets made with starchy fruits. Are you saying Alice Waters is wrong? Are you calling Alice Waters a liar?"

I looked him straight in the eye and said, "Yes. She's wrong."

Those were fighting words, and our argument moved from whispers to loud hisses. When we realized the whole class was looking at us, I raised my hand and asked the question. The teacher repeated what he had said before—that legally, sherbets have dairy in them. I felt vindicated. My sherbets have dairy in them, and I was right. But

Pichet wouldn't drop it. The next day at breakfast he told me Alice texted and said she's mad at me for calling her a liar. To this day, I still get pictures of scoops from Pichet with the question, "Is this real or fake sherbet?" I laugh every time.

I don't bring this up to ask you to choose sides, but to shine light on a faction of pastry chefs who replicate the creamy texture of sherbet by making sorbets with specific fruits. If you open up *Chez Panisse Desserts*, for example, you'll see that Lindsey Shere has filled her book with dairy-free sherbets. Pichet, too, has populated his own book, *The Sweet Spot,* with what I've started calling "California sherbet."

The fruits used to make a California sherbet often contain starches, like bananas or mango, or are high in pectin, from fruits that are cooked with their skins. The starch or pectin acts as a foaming agent, much as butterfat does, trapping the air that is whipped into the sherbet while it's churning. The pectin also acts as a stabilizing agent, reducing ice crystallization. California sherbets are soft, scoopable, and opaque—often giving the illusion of creaminess—unlike a sorbet, which is aptly called "water ice" by manufacturers.

If you'd like to try your hand at this, you can turn any of the sherbet recipes in this book into California sherbets. Just replace the buttermilk with more fruit puree, and replace the milk and cream with water. Then, follow the instructions for stabilizing the sherbet with both starch (page 28) and pectin (page 30). The result will be so creamy you'll understand why Pichet and Alice call it sherbet. Even if they're wrong.

Frozen Yogurts

Don't confuse the recipes in this chapter with the low-fat soft-serve you find in top-it-yourself shops. These frozen yogurts are a celebration of the flavor of yogurt, with the dense, chewy texture of a scoop of American hard-pack ice cream.

These recipes call for Greek yogurt, which is widely available in grocery stores. Because the watery whey is strained out, Greek yogurt is ideal for frozen yogurt, as there is less water to form ice crystals when the base is churned. Resist the urge to reach for the fat-free versions, though. They may belong on your breakfast table, but they will become chalky and brittle when frozen. And if you'd like to strain your own yogurt, see page 215.

When thinking about flavors for your frozen yogurt, consider that the acidity of yogurt makes it a natural mate for fruits; you can replace some of the milk in these recipes with an equal amount of fruit puree, stirring it in before freezing the mixture. And because the frozen yogurt base begins by cooking the milk and cream, you can add complementary flavors by infusing spices, teas, citrus zests, and herbs into the hot dairy.

Don't stop with fruit when creating your own frozen yogurt flavors, though; take a quick walk down the yogurt aisle of the grocery store, and you'll see flavors that reach far beyond simple fruits.

The milk called for in these recipes is a pivotal ingredient, as it can be replaced with any kind of water-based liquid to offer more flavor options, like the aforementioned fruit puree. For example, you can replace the milk with water to infuse dairy-curdling ingredients like hibiscus flowers, fresh ginger, or brown sugar. Better yet, you can replace the milk with another flavorful liquid like lemon juice or espresso. If the build-it-yourself frozen yogurt bars have taught us anything, with their dozens and dozens of toppings, it's that frozen yogurt is an anything-goes frozen dessert. So, let your heart be free when making frozen yogurt, and break every rule.

Blank Slate Frozen Yogurt

Makes between 1 and 1½ quarts sherbet

Full-fat Greek yogurt (40%)
400g | 2 cups

Cream (20%)
200g | 1 cup

Milk or water (15%)
150g | ¾ cup

Sugar (20%)
200g | 1 cup

Glucose (5%)
50g | ¼ cup

Texture agent of your choice
(see below)

This recipe is a blank slate, intentionally created for you to adapt in any way you like. All the recipes in this chapter stem from this basic formula, with adjustments made to both the ingredients and the technique. Armed with this recipe, you can invent any flavor of frozen yogurt you like.

Mix the yogurt. Place the yogurt in a small bowl and whisk until smooth and even, then set aside in the refrigerator.

Boil the dairy. Place the cream, milk (or water), sugar ①, and glucose in a medium heavy-bottomed saucepan over medium-high heat, and cook, whisking occasionally to discourage scorching, until it comes to a full rolling boil ④. Reduce the heat to a low simmer and cook the dairy mixture for 2 minutes. Remove the pot from heat ③.

Chill. Immediately pour the dairy base into a shallow metal or glass bowl. Working quickly, fill a large bowl two-thirds of the way with very icy ice water. Nest the hot bowl into this ice bath, stirring occasionally until it cools down. It will be quite thick.

Mix the base with the yogurt. When the base is cool to the touch (50°F or below), remove the bowl from the ice bath ②. Add the reserved yogurt to the base, whisking until evenly combined.

Strain. Strain the base through a fine-mesh sieve to remove any particles that may be present. (This step is optional, but will help ensure the smoothest frozen yogurt possible.)

Cure. Transfer the base to the refrigerator to cure for 4 hours, or preferably overnight. (This step is also optional, but the texture will be much improved with it.)

Churn. Place the base into the bowl of an ice cream maker and churn according to the manufacturer's instructions. The frozen yogurt is ready when it thickens into the texture of soft-serve ice cream and holds its shape, typically 20 to 30 minutes.

Harden. To freeze your frozen yogurt in the American hard-pack style, immediately transfer it to a container with an airtight lid. Press plastic wrap directly on the surface of the yogurt to prevent ice crystals from forming, cover, and store it in your freezer until it hardens completely, between 4 and 12 hours. Or, feel free to enjoy your yogurt immediately; the texture will be similar to soft-serve.

TEXTURE AGENTS

① **Best texture**
Commercial stabilizer
3g | 1 teaspoon mixed with the sugar before it is added to the dairy.

② **Least icy**
Guar or xanthan gum
1g | ¼ teaspoon whirled in a blender with the frozen yogurt base after it is chilled in the ice bath.

③ **Easiest to use**
Tapioca starch
5g | 2 teaspoons mixed with 20g | 2 tablespoons of cold milk or water, whisked into the dairy after it is finished cooking.

④ **Most accessible**
Cornstarch
10g | 1 tablespoon plus 1 teaspoon, mixed with 20g | 2 tablespoons of cold milk, whisked into the simmering dairy, then cooked for 1 minute.

fig. 1

fig. 2

fig. 3

fig. 4

fig. 1: Boil the dairy.

fig. 2: Chill the base.

fig. 3: Add the yogurt to the base.

fig. 4: Combine the yogurt and the base.

Fresh Ginger Frozen Yogurt

Makes between 1 and 1½ quarts frozen yogurt

Full-fat Greek yogurt (40%)
400g | 2 cups

Cream (20%)
200g | 1 cup

Honey (5%)
50g | ¼ cup

Fresh ginger
50g | about 3 inches, peeled

Water (15%)
150g | ¾ cup

Sugar (15%)
150g | ¾ cup

Glucose (5%)
50g | ¼ cup

Texture agent of your choice
(see below)

Ginger is a wonderful flavor, but there is an enzyme in fresh ginger that has the ability to cut the protein in milk the same way rennet does. If you add raw ginger juice to milk and cream to make ice cream, or in this case frozen yogurt, you will curdle the milk. (People in China have been using this property of ginger to make a milk pudding for a long time.) This is why you have to cook the ginger first, before adding it to the dairy.

Here's another thing about fresh ginger: it's incredibly fibrous. Traditional Japanese cooks have used ceramic ginger graters that tear apart the fibers of ginger, giving a kind of ginger mash. Today, we can use a Microplane. But I take a cue from the great Indian cookbook writer Madhur Jaffrey, who makes quick work of it in a blender.

Make the yogurt mixture. Whisk the yogurt, cream, and honey in a small bowl. Set it in the refrigerator.

Puree the ginger. Chop the ginger into pea-sized pieces, place them in a blender, and add the water. Blend on high until the ginger is completely broken down, then transfer it to a small saucepan.

Cook the ginger syrup, then strain. Add the sugar ① and glucose to the ginger and place over medium-high heat. Cook, whisking occasionally. When the syrup comes to a full rolling boil, remove the pot, reduce the heat to a simmer, and cook for 1 minute. Set aside and let the ginger infuse into the syrup for 30 minutes. Strain the syrup through a fine-mesh sieve ③,④ into a shallow metal or glass bowl.

Chill. Fill a large bowl two-thirds of the way with very icy ice water. Nest the syrup bowl into this ice bath, stirring occasionally until it cools down. It will be quite thick.

Mix the syrup with the yogurt mixture. When the ginger syrup is cool to the touch (50°F or below), remove the bowl from the ice bath ②. Add the reserved yogurt mixture to the base, whisking until evenly combined.

Strain. Strain the base through a fine-mesh sieve to remove any particles that may be present. (This step is optional, but will help ensure the smoothest frozen yogurt possible.)

Cure. Transfer the base to the refrigerator to cure for 4 hours, or preferably overnight. (This step is also optional, but the texture will be much improved with it.)

TEXTURE AGENTS

① **Best texture**
Commercial stabilizer
3g | 1 teaspoon mixed with the sugar before it is added to ginger syrup.

② **Least icy**
Guar or xanthan gum
1g | ¼ teaspoon whirled in a blender with the frozen yogurt base after it is chilled in the ice bath.

③ **Easiest to use**
Tapioca starch
5g | 2 teaspoons mixed with 20g | 2 tablespoons of cold water, whisked into the strained ginger syrup, then whisked over low heat until thickened.

④ **Most accessible**
Cornstarch
10g | 1 tablespoon plus 1 teaspoon, mixed with 20g | 2 tablespoons of cold water, whisked into the strained ginger syrup, then brought to a simmer for 1 minute.

Churn. Place the base into the bowl of an ice cream maker and churn according to the manufacturer's instructions. The frozen yogurt is ready when it thickens into the texture of soft-serve ice cream and holds its shape, typically 20 to 30 minutes.

Harden. To freeze your frozen yogurt in the American hard-pack style, immediately transfer it to a container with an airtight lid. Press plastic wrap directly on the surface of the yogurt to prevent ice crystals from forming, cover, and store it in your freezer until it hardens completely, between 4 and 12 hours. Or, feel free to enjoy your yogurt immediately; the texture will be similar to soft-serve.

Spiced Cane Syrup Frozen Yogurt

Makes between 1 and 1½ quarts frozen yogurt

Full-fat Greek yogurt (40%)
400g | 2 cups

Cane syrup (preferably Steens) (35%)
350g | 1¾ cups

Cream (15%)
150g | ¾ cup

Glucose (10%)
100g | ½ cup

Cinnamon stick
2 pieces, about 3 inches long

Texture agent of your choice
(see below)

TEXTURE AGENTS

① **Best texture**
Commercial stabilizer
3g | 1 teaspoon mixed with 5g | 1 teaspoon of sugar and added to the cream.

② **Least icy**
Guar or xanthan gum
1g | ¼ teaspoon whirled in a blender with the frozen yogurt base after it is chilled in the ice bath.

③ **Easiest to use**
Tapioca starch
5g | 2 teaspoons mixed with 20g | 2 tablespoons of cold milk, whisked into the cream after it is finished cooking.

④ **Most accessible**
Cornstarch
10g | 1 tablespoon plus 1 teaspoon, mixed with 20g | 2 tablespoons of cold milk, whisked into the simmering cream, then cooked for 1 minute.

Cane syrup is wonderful, and why it's not widely celebrated is beyond me. It's made by simply boiling the juice extracted from sugarcane in open kettles. The resulting syrup has the texture of pancake syrup, a hint of earthy molasses, and the flavor of brown sugar. Brown sugar is a frequent bedfellow of cinnamon, a comforting pair that you'll find quite at home in frozen yogurt.

I prefer a brand called Steens Cane Syrup, and it's readily available online. If you're using another brand, there may be subtle variations in water content. Don't hesitate to use it, but cross your fingers and hope for the best! Even if the texture isn't quite perfect, the frozen yogurt will still taste amazing. If you simply can't find cane syrup, you can nearly replicate it at home: mix 2 parts dark brown sugar with 1 part water, and stir over medium-high heat until the sugar syrup is clear.

Make the yogurt mixture. Whisk the yogurt and cane syrup in a small bowl. Set in the refrigerator.

Boil the cream. Place the cream ① and glucose in a medium heavy-bottomed pot over medium-high heat. Cook, whisking occasionally to discourage scorching. When the cream comes to a full rolling boil ④, reduce the heat to a low simmer and cook for 2 minutes. Remove the pot from heat ③.

Infuse. Stir the cinnamon sticks into the cream, and infuse for 30 minutes.

Strain and chill. Strain the infused frozen yogurt base through a fine-mesh sieve, into a shallow metal or glass bowl, discarding cinnamon sticks. Fill a large bowl two-thirds of the way with a lot of ice and a little water. Nest the hot bowl into this ice bath, stirring occasionally until it cools down.

Mix the base with the yogurt mixture. When the base is cool to the touch (50°F or below), remove the bowl from the ice bath ②. Add the reserved yogurt mixture to the base, whisking until evenly combined.

Strain. Strain the base through a fine-mesh sieve to remove any particles that may be present. (This step is optional, but will help ensure the smoothest frozen yogurt possible.)

Cure. Transfer the base to the refrigerator to cure for 4 hours, or preferably overnight. (This step is also optional, but the texture will be much improved with it.)

Churn. Place the base into the bowl of an ice cream maker and churn according to the manufacturer's instructions. The frozen yogurt is ready when it thickens into the texture of soft-serve ice cream and holds its shape, typically 20 to 30 minutes.

Harden. To freeze your frozen yogurt in the American hard-pack style, immediately transfer it to a container with an airtight lid. Press plastic wrap directly on the surface of the yogurt to prevent ice crystals from forming, cover, and store it in your freezer until it hardens completely, between 4 and 12 hours. Or, feel free to enjoy your yogurt immediately; the texture will be similar to soft-serve.

Meyer Lemon Frozen Yogurt

Makes between 1 and 1½ quarts frozen yogurt

Full-fat Greek yogurt (40%)
400g | 2 cups

Meyer lemon juice (15%)
150g | ¾ cup (from about
6 Meyer lemons)

Cream (20%)
200g | 1 cup

Sugar (20%)
200g | 1 cup

Glucose (5%)
50g | ¼ cup

Grated Meyer lemon zest
6g | 1 tablespoon, packed
(from about 6 Meyer lemons)

Texture agent of your choice
(see below)

TEXTURE AGENTS

① Best texture
Commercial stabilizer
3g | 1 teaspoon mixed with the
sugar before it is added to the
dairy.

② Least icy
Guar or xanthan gum
1g | ¼ teaspoon whirled in a
blender with the frozen yogurt
base after it is chilled in the ice
bath.

③ Easiest to use
Tapioca starch
5g | 2 teaspoons mixed with 20g |
2 tablespoons of cold milk or
water, whisked into the dairy after
it is finished cooking.

④ Most accessible
Cornstarch
10g | 1 tablespoon plus 1 teaspoon,
mixed with 20g | 2 tablespoons
of cold milk, whisked into the
simmering dairy, then cooked for
1 minute.

As a young child, I knew three things about my Uncle Tom. One, he had a dog named Fang who won the "ugliest dog" pageant. Two, he wore a sharkskin suit to middle school, in Trenton, New Jersey. And three, he had a lemon tree in his backyard in Santa Cruz, California.

Back home in Seattle, the only things on the trees in my yard were pine cones, sour apples, and gnarly quince. I heard my father say time and time again that although store-bought lemons are sour, if you pick them from a tree they are sweet. I visited Uncle Tom many times over the years and always paid a visit to that tree, but after I started working as a pastry chef I realized it was a Meyer lemon tree! The myth of the tree-sweet lemons was busted. Meyer lemons are sweeter because they're a hybrid of a mandarin orange and a lemon. But with that truth came something better—we could now find these sweet lemons in our own grocery stores during their winter season, since we knew what to look for.

This recipe is wonderful with any lemons, Meyer or not.

Make the yogurt mixture. Whisk the yogurt and lemon juice in a small bowl and set in the refrigerator.

Boil the cream. Place the cream, sugar ①, and glucose in a medium heavy-bottomed saucepan over medium-high heat, and cook, whisking occasionally to discourage scorching, until it comes to a full rolling boil ④. Reduce the heat to a low simmer and cook for 2 minutes. Remove the pot from heat ③.

Infuse. Stir the zest into the cream, and infuse for 30 minutes.

Strain and chill. Strain the infused frozen yogurt base through a fine-mesh sieve, into a shallow metal or glass bowl, discarding zest. Fill a large bowl two-thirds of the way with a lot of ice and a little water. Nest the hot bowl into this ice bath, stirring occasionally until it cools down.

Mix the base with the yogurt. When the base is cool to the touch (50°F or below), remove the bowl from the ice bath ②. Add the reserved yogurt to the base, whisking until evenly combined.

Strain. Strain the base through a fine-mesh sieve to remove any particles that may be present. (This step is optional, but will help ensure the smoothest frozen yogurt possible.)

Cure. Transfer the base to the refrigerator to cure for 4 hours, or preferably overnight. (This step is also optional, but the texture will be much improved with it.)

Churn. Place the base into the bowl of an ice cream maker and churn according to the manufacturer's instructions. The frozen yogurt is ready when it thickens into the texture of soft-serve ice cream and holds its shape, typically 20 to 30 minutes.

Harden. To freeze your frozen yogurt in the American hard-pack style, immediately transfer it to a container with an airtight lid. Press plastic wrap directly on the surface of the yogurt to prevent ice crystals from forming, cover, and store it in your freezer until it hardens completely, between 4 and 12 hours. Or, feel free to enjoy your yogurt immediately; the texture will be similar to soft-serve.

Milk Chocolate Frozen Yogurt

Makes between 1 and 1½ quarts frozen yogurt

Full-fat Greek yogurt (30%)
300g | 1½ cups

Salt
5g | 1 teaspoon

Milk chocolate (20%)
200g | 8 ounces

Cream (15%)
150 | ¾ cup

Milk (15%)
150g | ¾ cup

Sugar (15%)
150g | ¾ cup

Glucose (5%)
50g | ¼ cup

Texture agent of your choice
(see below)

It took years of adulthood before I found a place in my heart for dark, sultry, bitter chocolates, but once they captivated me, milk chocolate became cloyingly sweet and a real snooze. It wasn't until I was in England, staging at The Fat Duck, that milk chocolate came back into my life. The rigor of our long work days left me desperate for calories every night, and I found my solution in bars of Cadbury Dairy Milk and Galaxy chocolate. No one does milk chocolate quite like the British, and thanks to them, I fell back in love with it. I've vowed never to turn my back on it again, and I love adding sweet milk chocolate to frozen yogurt, finding a delicious synergy in their sweet and sour natures.

I recommend buying the nicest milk chocolate you can find, so check the label. Many candy bars, especially the ones meant to melt in your mouth, not in your hand, contain tropical oils and stabilizers that prevent them from mixing smoothly with the other ingredients. So, leave those bars for your s'mores, and the chocolate chips and kisses for your cookies!

TEXTURE AGENTS

① Best texture
Commercial stabilizer
3g | 1 teaspoon mixed with the sugar before it is added to the dairy.

② Least icy
Guar or xanthan gum
1g | ¼ teaspoon whirled in a blender with the frozen yogurt base after it is chilled in the ice bath.

③ Easiest to use
Tapioca starch
5g | 2 teaspoons mixed with 20g | 2 tablespoons of cold milk or water, whisked into the dairy after it is finished cooking.

④ Most accessible
Cornstarch
10g | 1 tablespoon plus 1 teaspoon, mixed with 20g | 2 tablespoons of cold milk, whisked into the simmering dairy, then cooked for 1 minute.

Mix the yogurt. Whisk the yogurt and salt in a small bowl until smooth. Set in the refrigerator.

Chop the chocolate. Chop the chocolate into ¼- or ½-inch pieces. I find this easiest to do with a serrated knife. Place the chocolate pieces in a metal bowl.

Boil the dairy. Place the cream, milk, sugar ①, and glucose in a medium heavy-bottomed saucepan over medium-high heat, and cook, whisking occasionally to discourage scorching, until it comes to a full rolling boil ④. Reduce the heat to a low simmer and cook for 2 minutes. Remove the pot from heat ③.

Mix the dairy and the chocolate. Immediately pour the hot dairy over the chopped chocolate. Allow it to sit undisturbed for 1 minute, then whisk the mixture until smooth and even.

Chill. Immediately pour the chocolate mixture into a shallow metal or glass bowl. Working quickly, fill a large bowl two-thirds of the way with very icy ice water. Nest the hot bowl into this ice bath, stirring occasionally until it cools down.

Mix the base with the yogurt. When the base is cool to the touch (50°F or below), remove the bowl from the ice bath ②. Add the reserved yogurt mixture to the base, whisking until evenly combined.

Strain. Strain the base through a fine-mesh sieve to remove any particles that may be present. (This step is optional, but will help ensure the smoothest frozen yogurt possible.)

Cure. Transfer the base to the refrigerator to cure for 4 hours, or preferably overnight. (This step is also optional, but the texture will be much improved with it.)

Churn. Place the base into the bowl of an ice cream maker and churn according to the manufacturer's instructions. The frozen yogurt is ready when it thickens into the texture of soft-serve ice cream and holds its shape, typically 20 to 30 minutes.

Harden. To freeze your frozen yogurt in the American hard-pack style, immediately transfer it to a container with an airtight lid. Press plastic wrap directly on the surface of the yogurt to prevent ice crystals from forming, cover, and store it in your freezer until it hardens completely, between 4 and 12 hours. Or, feel free to enjoy your yogurt immediately; the texture will be similar to soft-serve.

Key Lime Pie Frozen Yogurt

Makes between 1 and 1½ quarts frozen yogurt

Full-fat Greek yogurt (40%)
400g | 2 cups

Grated lime zest
5g | 1 tablespoon, packed (from about 3 limes)

Lime juice (15%)
150g | ¾ cup (about 1 pound Key limes, or 6 limes)

Egg yolks (5%)
50g | 3 large

Sweetened condensed milk (40%)
400g | 2 cups

Texture agent
(see below)

TEXTURE AGENT

(1) **Best and only option**
Guar or xantham gum
1g | ¼ teaspoon whirled in a blender with the frozen yogurt base.

Like Mighty Mouse, little Key limes pack far more punch than their much larger cousins. It is this punch, which comes from the Key lime's powerful acidity, that enables traditional Key lime pie to set without heat. Because acid can denature protein the same way heat does, we can add lime juice to "cook" fish when we make ceviche. Likewise, we can "cook" the eggs in a Key lime pie with Key lime juice.

This frozen yogurt recipe may be the only one you ever come across that asks you to add eggs. I've tried it without, and it just doesn't live up to the flavor of Key lime pie. In keeping with the pie's tradition, you don't cook the eggs with heat, as is done for a custard ice cream. Instead, lime's acid "cooks" the eggs, left alone to work its magic in the refrigerator for a few hours before adding the custard-like mixture to the frozen yogurt. While Key limes are the ideal choice for this recipe, they aren't always available. Feel free to use any limes you can find, but skip bottled Key lime juice; it pales in comparison to fresh juice, Key lime or otherwise.

Mix the lime zest and yogurt.
Whisk the yogurt and lime zest in a small bowl. Set in the refrigerator.

Make the lime-yolk mixture.
Whisk the lime juice, egg yolks, and condensed milk in a bowl. Place the bowl in the refrigerator for 2 to 3 hours, until the acid "cooks" the yolks and you can see that the mixture has set.

Mix and strain. Whisk together the lime-yolk mixture and the lime-yogurt mixture (1). Strain through a fine-mesh sieve to remove the lime zest.

Cure. Transfer the base to the refrigerator to cure for 4 hours, or preferably overnight. (This step is optional, but the texture will be much improved with it.)

Churn. Place the base into the bowl of an ice cream maker and churn according to the manufacturer's instructions. The frozen yogurt is ready when it thickens into the texture of soft-serve ice cream and holds its shape, typically 20 to 30 minutes.

Harden. To freeze your frozen yogurt in the American hard-pack style, immediately transfer it to a container with an airtight lid. Press plastic wrap directly on the surface of the yogurt to prevent ice crystals from forming, cover, and store it in your freezer until it hardens completely, between 4 and 12 hours. Or, feel free to enjoy your yogurt immediately; the texture will be similar to soft-serve.

Hibiscus Frozen Yogurt

Makes between 1 and 1½ quarts frozen yogurt

Full-fat Greek yogurt (40%)
400g | 2 cups

Cream (20%)
200g | 1 cup

Water (15%)
150g | ¾ cup

Sugar (20%)
200g | 1 cup

Glucose (5%)
50g | ¼ cup

Dried hibiscus flowers
25g | ¼ cup

Texture agent of your choice
(see below)

TEXTURE AGENTS

(1) Best texture
Commercial stabilizer
3g | 1 teaspoon mixed with the sugar before it is added to hibiscus syrup.

(2) Least icy
Guar or xanthan gum
1g | ¼ teaspoon whirled in a blender with the frozen yogurt base after it is chilled in the ice bath.

(3) Easiest to use
Tapioca starch
5g | 2 teaspoons mixed with 20g | 2 tablespoons of cold water, whisked into the strained hibiscus syrup, then whisked over low heat until thickened.

(4) Most accessible
Cornstarch
10g | 1 tablespoon plus 1 teaspoon, mixed with 20g | 2 tablespoons of cold water, whisked into the strained hibiscus syrup, then brought to a simmer for 1 minute.

Red hibiscus flowers have a surprisingly tart, fruity flavor and enough pigment in a single blossom to dye a bedsheet. In Mexico, hibiscus flowers are used to make a bright red beverage called jamaica. It's delicious, albeit usually heavily sweetened, and if your local taco shop sells it, grab a cup with your next order of carnitas. Or, you might recognize it from Starbucks's Passion Tango tea. Thinking in shades of pink, I created a hibiscus yogurt for a spring rhubarb dessert at Blackbird. That dessert is long gone, but I've come back to the fruity and floral hibiscus frozen yogurt over and over, delighting in the beautiful color that hibiscus brings the scoops. Look for hibiscus in specialty spice shops, from tea vendors, or in Mexican grocery stores.

On a technical note, the petals of the flower are acidic, and so if you add them to milk while it's hot, it will curdle. For this recipe, I've replaced the milk with water to make a hibiscus syrup. Once cooled, the syrup can be stirred into the cream and yogurt without risk.

Make the yogurt mixture. Whisk the yogurt and cream together in a small bowl. Set aside in the refrigerator.

Make the hibiscus syrup. Place the water, sugar (1), and glucose in a medium pot over medium-high heat. When the syrup comes to a full rolling boil remove the pot from the heat.

Infuse. Stir the hibiscus flowers into the syrup and infuse for 30 minutes.

Strain and chill. Strain the infused syrup through a fine-mesh sieve, into a shallow metal or glass bowl, discarding the flowers (3),(4). Fill a large bowl two-thirds of the way with a lot of ice and a little water. Nest the hot bowl into this ice bath, stirring occasionally until it cools down.

Mix the syrup with the yogurt. When the hibiscus syrup is cool to the touch (50°F or below), remove the bowl from the ice bath (2). Add the reserved yogurt and cream mixture to the syrup, whisking until evenly combined.

Strain. Strain the base through a fine-mesh sieve to remove any particles that may be present. (This step is optional, but will help ensure the smoothest frozen yogurt possible.)

Cure. Transfer the base to the refrigerator to cure for 4 hours, or preferably overnight. (This step is also optional, but the texture will be much improved with it.)

Churn. Place the base into the bowl of an ice cream maker and churn according to the manufacturer's instructions. The frozen yogurt is ready when it thickens into the texture of soft-serve ice cream and holds its shape, typically 20 to 30 minutes.

Harden. To freeze your frozen yogurt in the American hard-pack style, immediately transfer it to a container with an airtight lid. Press plastic wrap directly on the surface of the yogurt to prevent ice crystals from forming, cover, and store it in your freezer until it hardens completely, between 4 and 12 hours. Or, feel free to enjoy your yogurt immediately; the texture will be similar to soft-serve.

Mango Lassi Frozen Yogurt

Makes between 1 and 1½ quarts frozen yogurt

Full-fat Greek yogurt (40%)
400g | 2 cups

Mango Puree (10%)
100g | ½ cup (page 218)

Buttermilk (5%)
50g | ¼ cup

Orange flower water
5g | 1 teaspoon

Kosher or sea salt
3g | ½ teaspoon

Cream (20%)
200g | 1 cup

Sugar (20%)
200g | 1 cup

Glucose (5%)
50g | ¼ cup

Texture agent of your choice
(see below)

Lassis are refreshing beverages from India. They come in many flavors, some sweet, some salty, but they are all made with yogurt. My favorite version is laced with fresh mango, fragrant orange blossom water, and a touch of salt. It was a no-brainer to create a scoop of frozen yogurt to capture everything wonderful about this drink.

The light touch of salt and the candy-like perfume of orange flower water elevate the simple mango frozen yogurt. Find it in Indian or South Asian grocery stores, or online. If you can't find it, though, you can use orange zest or extract to taste. It's by no means the same, but it'll add a lovely aroma.

I've also included buttermilk in this frozen yogurt. The lassis sold in India are made with dairy products cultured differently from the yogurts we get here. I've never been to India, but I developed this recipe for the Indian-influenced Poppy restaurant, a concept born while the owner Jerry Traunfeld was in the vast country researching spices. It was his recommendation to add buttermilk, bringing this flavor in line with the lassis he sipped abroad. If you find yourself without it, you can replace it with milk.

Make the yogurt mixture.
Whisk the yogurt, mango puree, buttermilk, orange flower water, and salt in a small bowl. Set in the refrigerator.

Boil the cream. Place the cream, sugar ①, and glucose in a medium heavy-bottomed saucepan over medium-high heat and cook, whisking occasionally to discourage scorching, until it comes to a full rolling boil ④. Reduce the heat to a low simmer and cook for 2 minutes. Remove the pot from heat ③.

Chill. Immediately pour the base into a shallow metal or glass bowl. Working quickly, fill a large bowl two-thirds of the way with very icy ice water. Nest the hot bowl into this ice bath, stirring occasionally until it cools down. It will be quite thick.

Mix the base with the yogurt.
When the base is cool to the touch (50°F or below), remove the bowl from the ice bath ②. Add the mango mixture to the base, whisking until evenly combined.

Strain. Strain the base through a fine-mesh sieve to remove any particles that may be present. (This step is optional, but will help ensure the smoothest frozen yogurt possible.)

Cure. Transfer the base to the refrigerator to cure for 4 hours, or preferably overnight. (This step is also optional, but the texture will be much improved with it.)

TEXTURE AGENTS

① **Best texture**
Commercial stabilizer
3g | 1 teaspoon mixed with the sugar before it is added to the cream.

② **Least icy**
Guar or xanthan gum
1g | ¼ teaspoon whirled in a blender with the frozen yogurt base after it is chilled in the ice bath.

③ **Easiest to use**
Tapioca starch
5g | 2 teaspoons mixed with 20g | 2 tablespoons of cold milk or water, whisked into the cream after it is finished cooking.

④ **Most accessible**
Cornstarch
10g | 1 tablespoon plus 1 teaspoon, mixed with 20g | 2 tablespoons of cold milk, whisked into the simmering cream, then cooked for 1 minute.

Churn. Place the base into the bowl of an ice cream maker and churn according to the manufacturer's instructions. The frozen yogurt is ready when it thickens into the texture of soft-serve ice cream and holds its shape, typically 20 to 30 minutes.

Harden. To freeze your frozen yogurt in the American hard-pack style, immediately transfer it to a container with an airtight lid. Press plastic wrap directly on the surface of the yogurt to prevent ice crystals from forming, cover, and store it in your freezer until it hardens completely, between 4 and 12 hours. Or, feel free to enjoy your yogurt immediately; the texture will be similar to soft-serve.

Blueberry Lavender Frozen Yogurt

Makes between 1 and 1½ quarts frozen yogurt

Full-fat Greek yogurt (40%)
400g | 2 cups

Blueberry Puree (10%)
100g | ½ cup (page 216)

Cream (20%)
200g | 1 cup

Milk (5%)
50g | ¼ cup

Sugar (20%)
200g | 1 cup

Glucose (5%)
50g | ¼ cup

Dried lavender buds
5g | 1 tablespoon

Texture agent of your choice
(see below)

TEXTURE AGENTS

① Best texture
Commercial stabilizer
3g | 1 teaspoon mixed with the sugar before it is added to the dairy.

② Least icy
Guar or xanthan gum
1g | ¼ teaspoon whirled in a blender with the frozen yogurt base after it is chilled in the ice bath.

③ Easiest to use
Tapioca starch
5g | 2 teaspoons mixed with 20g | 2 tablespoons of cold milk or water, whisked into the dairy after it is finished cooking.

④ Most accessible
Cornstarch
10g | 1 tablespoon plus 1 teaspoon, mixed with 20g | 2 tablespoons of cold milk, whisked into the simmering dairy, then cooked for 1 minute.

There is a softer side to blueberries that is often overlooked. When simmered, blueberries are demure, a quality I attribute to lavender as well. Together, blueberry and lavender quietly ignite, their reserved flavors losing inhibition like two shy lovers emerging only in each other's presence.

If you think lavender tastes like soap, you're not alone. It's a lovely flavor, but can easily become intrusive if left unchecked. And dried lavender buds range in flavor drastically, some so faint they are hardly noticeable and some so intense you think you've just eaten the sachet your grandmother keeps in her unmentionables drawer. To combat this, I recommend tasting your lavender infusion frequently and straining the buds from the milk when the flavor is pleasant, but not overwhelming. I admit that I've been caught off guard by potent lavender, and if you find yourself with a soapy-tasting infusion, I recommend beginning again.

If you are in the tart-tastic lemon-blueberry fan club, then by all means, add some lemon! Replace 50g | ¼ cup of the yogurt (5% of the recipe) with lemon juice, and swap lemon zest for the lavender.

Make the yogurt mixture. Whisk the yogurt and blueberry puree in a small bowl. Set aside in the refrigerator.

Boil the dairy. Place the cream, milk, sugar ①, and glucose in a heavy-bottomed saucepan over medium-high heat. Cook, whisking to discourage scorching, until it comes to a full boil ④. Reduce the heat to a low simmer and cook for 2 minutes. Remove the pot from heat ③.

Infuse. Stir the lavender into the dairy and infuse for 10 to 20 minutes, tasting every 5 minutes, until the base is fragrant, but not soapy and overpowering.

Strain and chill. Strain the infused frozen yogurt base through a fine-mesh sieve, into a shallow metal or glass bowl, discarding lavender. Fill a large bowl two-thirds of the way with a lot of ice and a little water. Nest the hot bowl into this ice bath, stirring occasionally until it cools down.

Mix the base with the yogurt. When the base is cool to the touch (50°F or below), remove the bowl from the ice bath ②. Add the yogurt-blueberry mixture to the base, whisking until evenly combined.

Strain. Strain the base through a fine-mesh sieve to remove any particles that may be present. (This step is optional, but will help ensure the smoothest frozen yogurt possible.)

Cure. Transfer the base to the refrigerator to cure for 4 hours, or preferably overnight. (This step is also optional, but the texture will be much improved with it.)

Churn. Place the base into the bowl of an ice cream maker and churn according to the manufacturer's instructions. The frozen yogurt is ready when it thickens into the texture of soft-serve ice cream and holds its shape, typically 20 to 30 minutes.

Harden. To freeze your frozen yogurt in the American hard-pack style, immediately transfer it to a container with an airtight lid. Press plastic wrap directly on the surface of the yogurt to prevent ice crystals from forming, cover, and store it in your freezer until it hardens completely, between 4 and 12 hours. Or, feel free to enjoy your yogurt immediately; the texture will be similar to soft-serve.

Orange Rhubarb Frozen Yogurt

Makes between 1 and 1½ quarts frozen yogurt

Full-fat Greek yogurt (40%)
400g | 2 cups

Rhubarb Puree (10%)
100g | ½ cups (page 219)

Rhubarb juice (5%)
50g | ¼ cup

Cream (20%)
200g | 1 cup

Sugar (20%)
200g | 1 cup

Glucose (5%)
50g | ¼ cup

Grated orange zest
3g | 1 teaspoon, packed

Texture agent of your choice
(see below)

TEXTURE AGENTS

① Best texture
Commercial stabilizer
3g | 1 teaspoon mixed with the sugar before it is added to the cream.

② Least icy
Guar or xanthan gum
1g | ¼ teaspoon whirled in a blender with the frozen yogurt base after it is chilled in the ice bath.

③ Easiest to use
Tapioca starch
5g | 2 teaspoons mixed with 20g | 2 tablespoons of cold milk or water, whisked into the cream after it is finished cooking.

④ Most accessible
Cornstarch
10g | 1 tablespoon plus 1 teaspoon, mixed with 20g | 2 tablespoons of cold milk, whisked into the simmering cream, then cooked for 1 minute.

Rhubarb is the first dessert-worthy flavor to arrive every year, popping out of the ground moments after the frost melts. As rhubarb comes into season, oranges begin to make their way out, but not before the two cross paths. I'm so glad they do, because rhubarb and orange together is beyond delicious. In fact, I pair the two so often that I sometimes forget what rhubarb tastes like on its own. I make an orange-rhubarb compote every spring that has gained a tiny legion of faithful fans, and my friends Lorie and Matthew stir it into yogurt for breakfast. I know this because Iris, their daughter, told me. When Iris talks, I listen, and from her cue I adapted the compote to make this frozen yogurt.

For this frozen yogurt I also like to add a little bit of fresh rhubarb juice. It contributes a vegetal, earthy quality, but if you can't juice a stalk or two of rhubarb, no worries! Simply replace the rhubarb juice with more rhubarb puree, or better yet, with orange juice.

Make the yogurt mixture. Whisk the yogurt, rhubarb puree, and rhubarb juice in a small bowl. Set aside in the refrigerator.

Boil the cream. Place the cream, sugar ①, and glucose in a medium heavy-bottomed saucepan over medium-high heat, and cook, whisking occasionally to discourage scorching, until it comes to a full rolling boil ④. Reduce the heat to a low simmer and cook for 2 minutes. Remove the pot from heat ③.

Infuse. Stir the orange zest into the cream, and infuse for 30 minutes.

Strain and chill. Strain the base through a fine-mesh sieve, into a shallow metal or glass bowl, discarding zest. Fill a large bowl two-thirds of the way with a lot of ice and a little water. Nest the hot bowl into this ice bath, stirring occasionally until it cools down.

Mix the base with the yogurt. When the base is cool to the touch (50°F or below), remove the bowl from the ice bath ②. Add the reserved yogurt-rhubarb mixture to the base, whisking until evenly combined.

Strain. Strain the base through a fine-mesh sieve to remove any particles that may be present. (This step is optional, but will help ensure the smoothest frozen yogurt possible.)

Cure. Transfer the base to the refrigerator to cure for 4 hours, or preferably overnight. (This step is also optional, but the texture will be much improved with it.)

Churn. Place the base into the bowl of an ice cream maker and churn according to the manufacturer's instructions. The frozen yogurt is ready when it thickens into the texture of soft-serve ice cream and holds its shape, typically 20 to 30 minutes.

Harden. To freeze your frozen yogurt in the American hard-pack style, immediately transfer it to a container with an airtight lid. Press plastic wrap directly on the surface of the yogurt to prevent ice crystals from forming, cover, and store it in your freezer until it hardens completely, between 4 and 12 hours. Or, feel free to enjoy your yogurt immediately; the texture will be similar to soft-serve.

Peach Jalapeño Frozen Yogurt

Makes between 1 and 1½ quarts frozen yogurt

Full-fat Greek yogurt (40%)
400g | 2 cups

Peach Puree (10%)
100g | ½ cup (page 217)

Almond extract
2g | ¼ teaspoon

Cream (20%)
200g | 1 cup

Milk (5%)
50g | ¼ cup

Sugar (20%)
200g | 1 cup

Glucose (5%)
50g | ¼ cup

Jalapeño pepper
1, sliced into ¼-inch coins

Texture agent of your choice
(see below)

The flavor of jalapeño, when infused in dairy, is nothing like the hot chiles themselves. The milk neutralizes the capsaicin that is responsible for the heat, and you are left with a nutty, peppery flavor that is insanely delicious. I absolutely love pairing the flavor of jalapeño with fruit—in particular, the supple richness of peaches. I like it so much, I might never pair jalapeño frozen yogurt with any other fruit if peaches didn't go out of season. But since they do, I've enjoyed this frozen yogurt with strawberries, raspberries, nectarines, and mango as well.

TEXTURE AGENTS

① **Best texture**
Commercial stabilizer
3g | 1 teaspoon mixed with the sugar before it is added to the dairy.

② **Least icy**
Guar or xanthan gum
1g | ¼ teaspoon whirled in a blender with the frozen yogurt base after it is chilled in the ice bath.

③ **Easiest to use**
Tapioca starch
5g | 2 teaspoons mixed with 20g | 2 tablespoons of cold milk or water, whisked into the dairy after it is finished cooking.

④ **Most accessible**
Cornstarch
10g | 1 tablespoon plus 1 teaspoon, mixed with 20g | 2 tablespoons of cold milk, whisked into the simmering dairy, then cooked for 1 minute.

Make the yogurt mixture. Whisk the yogurt, peach puree, and almond extract in a small bowl. Set in the refrigerator.

Boil the dairy. Place the cream, milk, sugar ①, and glucose in a medium heavy-bottomed saucepan over medium-high heat, and cook, whisking occasionally to discourage scorching, until it comes to a full rolling boil ④. Reduce the heat to a low simmer and cook for 2 minutes. Remove the pot from heat ③.

Infuse. Stir the jalapeño into the dairy and infuse for 30 minutes.

Strain and chill. Strain the infused frozen yogurt base through a fine-mesh sieve, into a shallow metal or glass bowl, discarding jalapeño. Fill a large bowl two-thirds of the way with a lot of ice and a little water. Nest the hot bowl into this ice bath, stirring occasionally until it cools down.

Mix the base with the yogurt. When the base is cool to the touch (50°F or below), remove the bowl from the ice bath ②. Add the yogurt mixture to the base, whisking until evenly combined.

Strain. Strain the base through a fine-mesh sieve to remove any particles that may be present. (This step is optional, but will help ensure the smoothest frozen yogurt possible.)

Cure. Transfer the base to the refrigerator to cure for 4 hours, or preferably overnight. (This step is also optional, but the texture will be much improved with it.)

Churn. Place the base into the bowl of an ice cream maker and churn according to the manufacturer's instructions. The frozen yogurt is ready when it thickens into the texture of soft-serve ice cream and holds its shape, typically 20 to 30 minutes.

Harden. To freeze your frozen yogurt in the American hard-pack style, immediately transfer it to a container with an airtight lid. Press plastic wrap directly on the surface of the yogurt to prevent ice crystals from forming, cover, and store it in your freezer until it hardens completely, between 4 and 12 hours. Or, feel free to enjoy your yogurt immediately; the texture will be similar to soft-serve.

Honey Chai Frozen Yogurt

Makes between 1 and 1½ quarts frozen yogurt

Full-fat Greek yogurt (40%)
400g | 2 cups

Honey (20%)
200g | 1 cup

Cream (20%)
200g | 1 cup

Milk (15%)
150g | ¾ cup

Glucose (5%)
50g | ¼ cup

Cinnamon stick
1 piece, 3 inches long

Black peppercorns
20

Whole cloves
5

Green cardamom pods, cracked
20

Darjeeling tea leaves
20g | 4 tablespoons (about
12 standard tea bags, or more
as needed)

Texture agent of your choice
(see below)

When tea was first exported from China, the early continental traders who carried the leaves over the mountains adopted the word *cha* from the local dialect. Later, Dutch ships brought tea back to Europe, establishing their trade with the island regions of Southeast Asia, and instead borrowed the provincial word *te*. Today *chai* simply means "tea" in most parts of the world. However, in the United States, the word has come to represent a style of tea from India, called *masala chai*, or "spiced tea," typically blended with an array of whole spices, sweetened, and enriched with milk. Contemporary dictionaries have gone as far as to add *chai* to their pages, defining it as a spiced tea, forever narrowing the scope of the word's meaning in the English language.

I like to use Darjeeling tea leaves, a black tea grown in India, and add whole spices for a simple chai flavor. If you have a chai tea blend you like, use it in place of the Darjeeling tea and omit the whole spices.

Incidentally, if you'd like a plain-honey frozen yogurt, you've come to the right place. Simply omit steeping the tea and spices in the base. Or try infusing lavender or sprigs of thyme into the base instead! There are so many wonderful flavors that pair with honey, and this recipe can accommodate them all.

TEXTURE AGENTS

① **Best texture**
Commercial stabilizer
3g | 1 teaspoon mixed with 5g | 1 teaspoon of sugar and added to the dairy.

② **Least icy**
Guar or xanthan gum
1g | ¼ teaspoon whirled in a blender with the frozen yogurt base after it is chilled in the ice bath.

③ **Easiest to use**
Tapioca starch
5g | 2 teaspoons mixed with 20g | 2 tablespoons of cold milk or water, whisked into the dairy after it is finished cooking.

④ **Most accessible**
Cornstarch
10g | 1 tablespoon plus 1 teaspoon, mixed with 20g | 2 tablespoons of cold milk, whisked into the simmering dairy, then cooked for 1 minute.

Make the yogurt mixture. Whisk the yogurt and honey in a small bowl. Set in the refrigerator.

Boil the dairy. Place the cream, milk, and glucose ①, in a medium heavy-bottomed saucepan over medium-high heat, and cook, whisking occasionally to discourage scorching, until it comes to a full rolling boil ④. Reduce the heat to a low simmer and cook for 2 minutes. Remove the pot from heat ③.

Infuse. Add the cinnamon stick, black peppercorns, cloves, and cardamom to the dairy and infuse for 15 minutes. Place the pot over medium-high heat and bring back to a simmer. Remove the pot from heat and add the Darjeeling tea, and infuse for 5 minutes. Do not be tempted to let the tea steep longer; it will become bitter.

Strain and chill. Strain the infused frozen yogurt base through a fine-mesh sieve, into a shallow metal or glass bowl, discarding tea and spices. Fill a large bowl two-thirds of the way with a lot of ice and a little water. Nest the hot bowl into this ice bath, stirring occasionally until it cools down.

Mix the base with the yogurt. When the base is cool to the touch (50°F or below), remove the bowl from the ice bath ②. Add the reserved yogurt-honey mixture to the base, whisking until evenly combined.

Strain. Strain the base through a fine-mesh sieve to remove any particles that may be present. (This step is optional, but will help ensure the smoothest frozen yogurt possible.)

Cure. Transfer the base to the refrigerator to cure for 4 hours, or preferably overnight. (This step is also optional, but the texture will be much improved with it.)

Churn. Place the base into the bowl of an ice cream maker and churn according to the manufacturer's instructions. The frozen yogurt is ready when it thickens into the texture of soft-serve ice cream and holds its shape, typically 20 to 30 minutes.

Harden. To freeze your frozen yogurt in the American hard-pack style, immediately transfer it to a container with an airtight lid. Press plastic wrap directly on the surface of the yogurt to prevent ice crystals from forming, cover, and store it in your freezer until it hardens completely, between 4 and 12 hours. Or, feel free to enjoy your yogurt immediately; the texture will be similar to soft-serve.

Add-Ins

Once upon a time, ice cream add-ins were limited to a ripple of fruit or a handful of nuts; rocky road, with nuts *and* marshmallows, was as extravagant as it got. Today, though, a scoop of ice cream can be a textural playground, and everything from cookie dough to pretzels is fair game.

This chapter is devoted to the bits and bobs we add to ice creams. Sometimes called mix-ins, or add-ins, these include every cookie, nut, candy, fruit, sauce, ribbon, and sweet brick-a-brack that transforms our ice creams into composed scoops.

The recipes in this chapter can double as sundae toppings, but each has been specifically formulated to be the perfect texture when frozen. The ribbons and ripples include glucose, which depresses their freezing points, keeping them soft in the freezer. Add-ins like chocolate chunks and peanut butter ribbons are made to melt in your mouth, a quality owed to the addition of coconut oil. The brownie is a little underbaked, giving it a nice chew when frozen—and please don't actually try to bake the cookie doughs!

Some of these recipes instruct you to fully prepare the add-ins, then store them in your freezer. Unless the recipe indicates otherwise, be sure to take the time to freeze. Not only will these add-ins need to be frozen when you add them to your freshly churned ice cream, but also many of them will need to be stored in the freezer between batches. Since they are designed for frozen temperatures, if you store them any place warmer, even in a refrigerator, they are at risk of smushing together or absorbing moisture and getting soggy.

Since the quantity of an add-in needed for a quart of ice cream is relatively small, each recipe yields two to three times as much as you need for a batch of ice cream. I hope this encourages you to try your hand at a second ice cream flavor, or to rally the troops and have a sundae party!

Ribbons & Ripples

Fudge Ripple

MAKES JUST OVER 1 PINT

There is nothing more quintessential to an ice cream than a fudge ripple. It took me all of one try to master the perfect fudge ripple for ice cream because I'd already found the perfect hot fudge recipe, a simple version in Alice Medrich's book *Bittersweet*. For truly spectacular fudge, I prefer Cocoa Barry extra brute cocoa powder, or the super-dark and smoky cocoa powder from Valrhona. But feel free to use your favorite brand.

This recipe is designed to be soft and chewy at frozen temperatures. If you want a *hot* fudge recipe, replace the glucose with an equal amount of sugar and double the cream. Finally, finish the sauce by stirring in 25g | 2 tablespoons of butter for a hot fudge you won't likely stray from again.

Cocoa powder	Glucose
75g	1 cup	100g	½ cup
Sugar	**Cream**
50g	¼ cup	200g	1 cup
Salt	
5g	1 teaspoon	

Mix the dry ingredients. Place the cocoa powder, sugar, and salt in a medium bowl and whisk everything until evenly combined.

Heat the wet ingredients. Place the glucose and cream in a medium saucepan and cook over medium-high heat, whisking to dissolve the glucose. When the cream comes to a full rolling boil, remove the pot from heat.

Mix the dry and wet ingredients. Add one-third of the hot cream to the cocoa powder, and whisk to a thick paste. Add the cream in two more additions, whisking between each until smooth.

Cook the fudge. Transfer the fudge back to the pot, scraping the sides of the bowl clean with a rubber spatula. This is important for the final texture; if you leave any fudge behind, your ripple will be too thin. Place the pot over medium-low heat and cook, stirring with a rubber spatula to prevent scorching, until the fudge starts to bubble and is very smooth.

Strain. Pass the fudge through a fine-mesh sieve to catch any lumps of undissolved cocoa powder, then transfer the fudge ripple to an airtight container. Store the fudge in the refrigerator for a week before using, or in the freezer for up to a month.

Creamy Caramel Ribbon

MAKES ABOUT 1 PINT

When it comes to caramel ribbons in ice cream, I want the caramel to be soft enough to dissolve in my mouth, but chewy enough that I can feel it when I bite into a scoop. The ideal texture is found with glucose, which not only reduces the sweetness of the caramel but also helps keep it soft at frozen temperatures.

The most important part of making a caramel sauce is cooking it so the sugars darken into a rich amber, but not so dark that it becomes bitter. Watch the cooking sugar like a hawk, and add the butter to stop the cooking when the perfect color is achieved. Test the color with strips of white paper. (The pot will distort the color of the caramel.) And when making any caramel, keep a bowl of ice water nearby in case of burns.

This recipe will keep in your freezer between batches for up to 3 months, and is as delicious warmed and drizzled over ice cream as it is folded into it.

Cream	Sugar
250g	1¼ cups	250g	1¼ cups
Glucose	**Water**
100g	½ cup	100g	1 cup
Salt	**Vanilla extract**
5g	1 teaspoon	5g	1 teaspoon
Butter	
25g	2 tablespoons	

Heat the cream and glucose. Cook the cream, glucose, and salt in a small pot over medium-high heat until the cream begins to simmer, stirring to dissolve the glucose. Remove the cream from the heat and set aside in a warm place. Place the butter near the stove.

Caramelize the sugar. Place the sugar and water in a small heavy-bottomed saucepan, and stir gently.

Place the pot over medium-high heat, and use a moist pastry brush dipped in clean water to wash down stray sugar crystals so they dissolve in the boiling sugar. Continue cooking, washing down any crystals, until the sugar reaches a medium amber. Dip a piece of white paper in the caramel to test the color.

Mix the cream into the caramel. When you have reached caramel color, immediately remove the pot from heat, and stir in the butter to stop the cooking. Add the warm cream bit by bit, being careful as it will sputter. Add the vanilla and stir. If there are any lumps of unmelted caramel, continue cooking the sauce at a low simmer until smooth and even.

Prepare the caramel sauce as an add-in. Strain the caramel sauce through a fine-mesh sieve, then transfer the warm caramel to a container and let it cool in the refrigerator. Once cool, cover tightly. This will keep for 2 weeks in the refrigerator. To add the caramel to ice cream, stir it vigorously until it is fluid enough to drizzle into freshly churned ice cream.

Peanut Butter Ribbon

MAKES 1¼ CUPS

One of my favorite store-bought ice creams is Häagen-Dazs's Chocolate Peanut Butter Ice Cream. Inside are sheets of firm peanut butter that run through the ice cream like a seam of coal. It takes some pressure for the spoon to shatter the hard peanut butter, but the salty chunks dissolve in your mouth.

That melt-in-your-mouth, not-in-your-pint texture comes from coconut oil. Look for extra-virgin coconut oil, or expeller pressed, which has been deodorized and doesn't taste like coconut. Or, you can add regular coconut oil and enjoy its natural flavor! If you can't find coconut oil, substitute canola oil; you won't get quite the same texture, but I'd hate for you to miss out on this amazing peanut butter ribbon just because of some coconut oil.

Use any nut butter you like for this recipe. As an added bonus, because of the coconut oil you can use this peanut butter ribbon like Magic Shell, pouring it over scoops of ice cream and watching it solidify.

Creamy peanut butter	Kosher or sea salt
250g | 1 cup	5g | 1 teaspoon

Coconut oil
45g \| ¼ cup

Melt the ingredients. Place the peanut butter, coconut oil, and salt in a medium heatproof bowl. Find a pot with a mouth a few inches smaller than the bowl, and fill it with 2 inches of water. Place the pot over high heat and cook until it comes to a boil, then reduce the heat to a simmer. Nestle the bowl of peanut butter over the pot of simmering water, and melt the peanut butter and coconut oil over this water bath; mix.

Store the ribbon. Remove the bowl from the double boiler, and let it cool to room temperature. Store the peanut butter ribbon in an airtight container in your cupboard.

Prepare the ribbon as an add-in. To use the peanut butter ribbon in your ice cream, heat it just enough that it is fluid but not hot. This should be about 60°F. Pour the fluid peanut butter ribbon over freshly churned ice cream, let it harden, then continue to layer ice cream and peanut butter ribbon.

Pink Peppercorn Caramel

MAKES A LITTLE OVER 1 PINT

Pink peppercorns share nothing more than a name with the black peppercorns we grind over our food. Pink peppercorns are actually a spicy little berry, which explains their fruity, aromatic quality. They make a lovely piquant addition to the sweetness of a caramel. By infusing the whole peppercorns, you can capture more of their intoxicating fragrance. I find their flavor is best when they are cracked very roughly in a blender just before infusing.

Water	Pink peppercorns (roughly cracked)
300g | 1½ cups (divided)	30g | ¼ cup

Glucose	**Sugar**
100g | ½ cup	250g | 1¼ cups

Salt	**Butter**
5g | 1 teaspoon	25g | 2 tablespoons

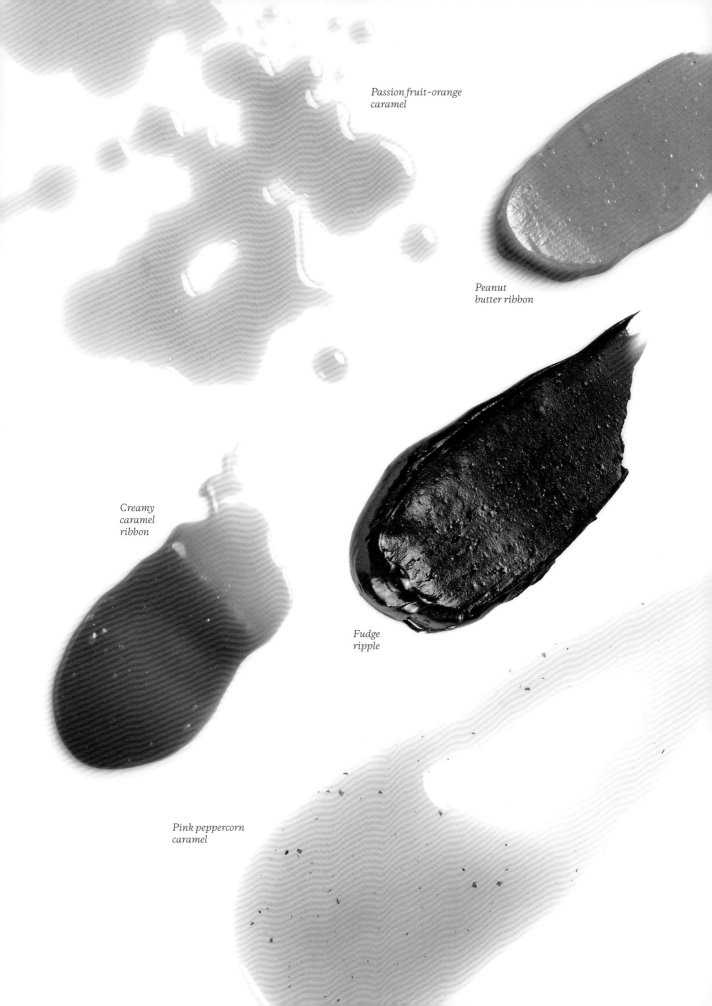

Passion fruit–orange caramel

Peanut butter ribbon

Creamy caramel ribbon

Fudge ripple

Pink peppercorn caramel

Make the pink peppercorn "tea." Put 200g | 1 cup water, the glucose, and salt in a small saucepan and place it over medium-high heat until the water comes to a boil, stirring to dissolve the glucose. Remove the pot from heat, stir in the pink peppercorns, and set aside in a warm place to infuse for 30 minutes. Strain the tea and reserve in a warm place.

Cook the caramel. Place the remaining 100g | ½ cup water and the sugar in a small heavy-bottomed saucepan, and stir gently. Place the pot over medium-high heat, and use a moist pastry brush dipped in clean water to wash down any stray sugar crystals so they dissolve in the boiling sugar. Continue cooking, washing down any sugar crystals, until the sugar reaches a light amber. Dip a piece of white paper in the caramel to test the color.

Mix the caramel with the butter and tea. Immediately remove the pot from heat, and stir in the butter to stop the cooking. Add the warm pink peppercorn tea bit by bit, being careful as it may sputter.

Prepare the caramel as an add-in. Transfer the warm caramel to a container and let it cool in the refrigerator. Once cool, cover tightly. The caramel will keep for 2 weeks in the refrigerator. To add the caramel to ice cream, stir it vigorously until it is fluid enough to drizzle into freshly churned ice cream.

Warm the juice. Place the passion fruit juice, orange juice, and glucose in a small saucepan over medium-high heat. Cook, stirring occasionally, until the glucose is dissolved and the juice is bubbling. Remove from the heat and set aside in a warm place.

Caramelize the sugar. Place the water and sugar in a medium heavy-bottomed saucepan, and stir gently. Cook over medium-high heat, and use a moist pastry brush dipped in clean water to wash down any stray sugar crystals so they dissolve in the boiling sugar. Continue cooking, washing down any sugar crystals, until the sugar reaches a medium amber. Dip a piece of white paper in the caramel to test the color.

Mix the juice with the caramel. Immediately remove the pot from heat, and add one-fourth of the reserved passion fruit juice, being careful to avoid any sputtering. Stir the caramel until the passion fruit juice is evenly incorporated. Continue adding the remainder of the passion fruit juice, bit by bit, stirring between additions.

Prepare the caramel as an add-in. Transfer the warm caramel to a container and let it cool in the refrigerator. When the caramel is cool, cover it tightly and store it in the refrigerator for 2 weeks, or up to 3 months in the freezer. To add the caramel to ice cream, thaw (if necessary) and stir it vigorously until it is fluid enough to drizzle into freshly churned ice cream.

Passion Fruit–Orange Caramel

MAKES ABOUT 1 PINT

Passion fruit has a vibrant flavor—tangy like lemon with the tropical fruitiness of a pineapple. Unless you live in the tropics, you'll only occasionally see the unassuming fruit in your grocery store, so it's more likely that you'll use a frozen passion fruit juice. If you do see the fruit, however, remember that it's ripe when brown and wrinkled.

This recipe is also great if you just replace the passion fruit with more orange or tangerine juice.

Passion Fruit Juice (page 219) 100g	½ cup	**Glucose** 50g	⅓ cup
Orange juice 100g	½ cup	**Water** 50g	¼ cup
	Sugar 100g	½ cup

Plum Caramel

MAKES ABOUT 1 PINT

Plum caramel was included in the first dessert I ever put on a menu as a pastry chef. I had taken the pastry chef job at Eva Restaurant in Seattle, sight unseen. When I arrived, Amy, the chef, had buckets of plums from her backyard. I dug up a recipe for plum caramel from the Chez Panisse dessert book, and almost shrieked with delight when I tasted the finished product. The acidity of the plums made the brightest caramel sauce I had ever tasted, and the caramelized sugar melded with the musky quality of the ripe plums into something much larger than the sum of its parts. I've modified the recipe since then, and the flavor never fails to surprise me.

I've also had amazing results making this recipe with apricots instead of plums, and I would think almost any bright acidic fruit puree will shine.

Plum Puree (page 217)	Sugar
250g | 1¼ cups	150g | ¾ cup
Glucose	**Water**
50g | ¼ cup	50g | ¼ cup

Heat the puree. Place the puree and glucose in a small saucepan over medium-high heat. Cook, stirring occasionally, until the glucose is dissolved and the puree is bubbling. Set aside in a warm place.

Caramelize the sugar. Place the sugar and water in a medium heavy-bottomed saucepan, and stir gently. Place the pot over medium-high heat, and use a moist pastry brush dipped in clean water to wash down any stray sugar crystals so they dissolve in the boiling sugar. Continue cooking, washing down any sugar crystals, until the sugar reaches a medium amber. Dip a piece of white paper in the caramel to test the color.

Mix the puree into the caramel. Immediately remove the pot from heat, and add one-fourth of the reserved plum puree, being careful to avoid any sputtering. Stir the caramel until the plum puree is evenly incorporated. Continue adding the remainder of the plum puree, bit by bit, stirring between additions.

Prepare the caramel as an add-in. Transfer the warm plum caramel to a container and let it cool in the refrigerator. When the caramel is cool, cover it tightly and store it in the refrigerator for 2 weeks, or up to 3 months in the freezer. To add the caramel to ice cream, thaw (if necessary) and stir it vigorously until it is fluid enough to drizzle into freshly churned ice cream.

Milk Jam

MAKES ABOUT 1 PINT

If you boil milk with a little sugar, it will eventually become golden brown and transform into a spreadable jam. You might know it as dulce de leche. Unlike caramel, which gets its deep golden brown flavor from the breakdown of sugars, milk jam gets its flavor from the Maillard reaction, which involves the browning of proteins. You might find yourself spooning milk jam on everything, from cookies to toast, and even into your morning coffee—hint, hint.

Most grocery store milk is high-heat pasteurized, which cooks the milk protein in advance, reducing its ability to join forces and gel your jam.

To counter this, the recipe uses a bit of baking soda to transform the milk, and the result is more like a sauce than a spreadable jam. But if you find a lovely vat-pasteurized milk from a local dairy, omit the baking soda and prepare to be wowed by how rich and thick the milk gets.

Milk	Baking soda
1000g | 1 quart	1g | ¼ teaspoon
Sugar	**Salt**
250g | 1¼ cups	3g | ½ teaspoon
Glucose	**Vanilla bean**
125g | ½ cup	1 bean (or 5g | 1 teaspoon vanilla extract, added after the jam has cooked)

Combine the ingredients. Place the milk, sugar, glucose, baking soda, and salt in a medium heavy-bottomed saucepan. Split the vanilla bean in half lengthwise, and use the tip of your knife to scrape the seeds from the vanilla bean. Place the seeds in the pot, and reserve the pod for another use.

Cook the milk jam. Set the pot over medium-high heat and cook, stirring frequently, until the milk comes to a boil. Reduce the heat as low as you can get it while maintaining a simmer. Continue cooking, stirring occasionally, until the milk jam takes on a tawny hue, like the color of a fawn, and becomes thick. This will take anywhere from 60 to 90 minutes. The lower and slower you can cook your milk jam, the deeper the flavor will be.

Blend the milk jam. After the milk jam reaches the desired tawny color and gravy-like thickness, immediately transfer it to a blender and blend on high for 1 minute.

Cool and store. Transfer the milk jam to a container and let it cool in the refrigerator. Once cool, cover the container tightly and store in the refrigerator for up to 4 weeks, or the freezer for up to 3 months. To add the milk jam to ice cream, thaw (if necessary) and stir it vigorously until it is fluid enough to drizzle.

Butterscotch Ripple

MAKES ABOUT 3 CUPS

I developed this butterscotch to drown a date cake as a riff on sticky toffee pudding, a British dessert which is neither toffee flavored nor a pudding. It is sticky, however, thanks to this butterscotch sauce, which I've since modified to work as a ripple in ice cream. There seems to be no standard for what butterscotch is these days, with chips, candies, and sauces all flavored so differently. In this recipe you'll find a brown sugar caramel, a little rum, and the most important part, butter. The butterscotch teeters on the edge of too much, but a little bright lemon flavor keeps it from falling into an abyss of richness.

Cream 450g | 2¼ cups (divided)	**Glucose** 100g | ½ cup
Salt 3g | ½ teaspoon	**Dark brown sugar** 200g | 1 cup
Vanilla extract 5g | 1 teaspoon	**Grated lemon zest** 3g | 1 teaspoon, packed
Dark rum 25g | 2 tablespoons	**Butter** 50g | ¼ cup
Lemon juice 15g | 1 tablespoon	

Prepare the rum cream. Whisk 250g | 1¼ cups cream, the salt, vanilla, rum, and lemon juice in a small bowl. Set aside.

Cook the caramel. Place the glucose, brown sugar, lemon zest, butter, and remaining 200g | 1 cup cream in a medium heavy-bottomed saucepan over medium-high heat. Cook, stirring occasionally, until boiling. Reduce the heat to medium to quiet the sputtering, and insert a kitchen thermometer. Cook the butterscotch to 240°F, stirring occasionally to prevent scorching on the bottom of the pan.

Add the rum cream. When the butterscotch reaches 240°F, remove the pot from the heat. Carefully stir in the rum cream.

Strain the butterscotch. Strain the warm butterscotch through a fine-mesh strainer, and transfer the sauce to a container to cool in the refrigerator.

Prepare the butterscotch as an ice cream add-in. Once the butterscotch is cool, place it in an airtight container and store it in your refrigerator for 2 weeks, or your freezer for up to 3 months.

Sorghum Ribbon

MAKES ABOUT 1 PINT

Sorghum syrup is a deeply American flavor at risk of being lost. Because it can only be harvested once a year, sorghum was overtaken by its more productive cousin, sugarcane. But sorghum syrup is spectacular. The flavor is more brash than molasses, with a nuanced quality I can only call "farmy." If you live in the South, you're more likely to have seen this thick brown syrup, as this crop favors warm humid climates. It's available by mail order for the rest of us, and I urge you to get your hands on some lest this distinctly American product disappears entirely.

You can drizzle sorghum syrup straight into your ice cream if you like and skip this recipe all together. However, I find the flavor can be a little overpowering when eaten straight from the bottle, and I have created this recipe to provide a milder sorghum ribbon.

Sorghum syrup 300g | 1½ cups	**Salt** 2g | ⅓ teaspoon
Hot water 50g | ¼ cup	**Glucose** 50g | ¼ cup

Mix the syrup. Whisk the sorghum syrup, hot water, salt, and glucose in a medium bowl. If you find your ingredients aren't blending together, carefully warm the syrup in the microwave or on the stovetop until you can whisk it easily.

Cool and store. Transfer the sorghum ribbon to a container and cover it tightly. The sorghum ribbon will keep in the refrigerator for 2 weeks or the freezer for 3 months. To add the sorghum ribbon to ice cream, thaw (if necessary) and stir it vigorously until it is fluid enough to drizzle.

Fruit Compotes

Friends often ask me what a compote is, as they have come across a wide variety of recipes using this moniker. To me, compote is a thick fruit mess, somewhere between a sauce and a jam, with all the chunks left intact. I like to use fruit compotes in ice cream to show off the flavor and texture of fruits that shine when cooked, like cranberries and blueberries. By cooking out the water and adding enough sugar, the iciness common with fresh fruit is eliminated and the fruit delivers intense flavor. The right amount of sugar (or glucose) gives it a perfect texture when frozen.

You can adjust the ratio of sugar to glucose in accordance with each fruit's innate sweetness—more glucose if the fruit is already sweet, and more sugar if the fruit is tart. Just remember that the ratio of sugar to fruit must remain as written—so you'd need to decrease the glucose if you're using more sugar and vice versa—to keep your compotes soft when frozen inside an ice cream.

Cranberry-vanilla compote

Blueberry-basil compote

Blueberry-Basil Compote

MAKES ABOUT 3 CUPS

Blueberries
450g | 1 pound

Lemon juice
15g | 1 tablespoon

Sugar
150g | ¾ cup

Glucose
100g | ⅔ cup

Basil leaves
10 fresh

Cook the compote. Place the blueberries, lemon juice, sugar, and glucose in a medium saucepan over medium heat. Cook, stirring occasionally, so the blueberries begin to give off their juices. When the liquid starts to bubble and the blueberries look soupy, add the basil and reduce the heat to medium low. Cook until the mixture looks jammy, 20 to 30 minutes. If you want to test the texture of your compote, freeze a plate, and drop small spoonfuls of the compote onto the plate. After a minute in the freezer, you'll know if your compote is too runny or is nice and jammy.

Cool and store. Transfer your compote to a container, remove the basil, and let it cool in the refrigerator. Once cool, cover tightly and store in your refrigerator for 2 weeks, or the freezer for up to 3 months. To add the compote to ice cream, thaw (if necessary) and stir it vigorously until it is fluid enough to drizzle.

Cranberry-Vanilla Compote

MAKES ABOUT 3 CUPS

Cranberries
450g | 1 pound

Sugar
200g | 1 cup

Glucose
50g | ⅓ cup

Vanilla bean
1 whole

Cook the compote. Place the cranberries, sugar, and glucose in a medium saucepan over medium heat. Cook, stirring occasionally, so the cranberries begin to give off their juices. When the liquid starts to bubble and the cranberries look soupy, split the vanilla bean in half lengthwise, scrape the seeds from the pod with the tip of a paring knife, and add both the seeds and the pod. Reduce the heat to medium low and cook until the mixture looks jammy, 10 to 15 minutes. If you want to test the texture of your compote, freeze a plate, and drop small spoonfuls of the compote onto the plate. After a minute in the freezer, you'll know if your compote is too runny or is nice and jammy.

Cool and store. Transfer your compote to a container and let it cool in the refrigerator. Once cool, cover tightly and store in your refrigerator for 2 weeks, or the freezer for up to 3 months. To add the compote to ice cream, thaw (if necessary) and stir it vigorously until it is fluid enough to drizzle.

Rhubarb-Orange Compote

MAKES ABOUT 3 CUPS

Rhubarb
450g | 1 pound, in ½-inch pieces

Sugar
200g | 1 cup

Glucose
100g | ⅔ cup

Grated orange zest
10g | 1 tablespoon, packed

Orange-flavored liqueur
50g | ¼ cup

Butter
25g | 2 tablespoons

Cook the compote. Place the rhubarb in a medium heavy-bottomed saucepan with the sugar, glucose, and orange zest over medium heat. Cook, stirring occasionally, as the chunks of rhubarb begin to give off their juices and appear to melt. When the liquefied rhubarb starts to bubble, stir in the orange liqueur and butter. Continue to cook, stirring occasionally, until the compote looks jammy, 20 to 30 minutes. If you want to test the texture of your compote, freeze a plate, and drop small spoonfuls of the compote onto the plate. After a minute in the freezer, you'll know if your compote is too runny or is nice and jammy.

Cool and store. Transfer your rhubarb-orange compote to a container and let it cool in the refrigerator. Once cool, cover tightly and store in your refrigerator for 2 weeks, or the freezer for up to 3 months. To add the compote to ice cream, thaw (if necessary) and stir it vigorously until it is fluid enough to drizzle.

Fruit Ripples

Adding ribbons of fruit to your ice cream is the best way to express fruit flavor in a scoop. At least that's what the professors at the Penn State ice cream science program told me. Adding fresh fruit to ice cream forces us to deal with their high water content, and to avoid that, most fruit-flavored ice creams are scented with an artificial flavor and enhanced with a few pieces of real fruit. While I've created an entire section of very fruity sherbets, I took the professionals' advice and started adding fruit ripples as well.

By combining fruit puree with glucose and sugar, you can create ribbons of intense fruit flavor that stay soft in the freezer. The fruit purees themselves are easy to make provided you have a blender, and you can find recipes for them on pages 216-19. For fruits that are best left uncooked, like strawberries and red raspberries, the sugar is dissolved in a syrup before being stirred in, whereas fruits that can handle heat are cooked directly with the sugars. To show how a fruit puree is made into a ripple, I give strawberry and black raspberry as examples, but you can apply whichever technique suits the fruit you have chosen. Often, too, it's just a matter of preference.

Strawberry Ripple (Uncooked Ripple Method)

MAKES JUST OVER 1 PINT

Sugar
100g | ½ cup

Glucose
100g | ½ cup

Water
25g | 2 tablespoons

Strawberry Puree (page 216)
300g | 1½ cups

Malic acid
3g | ½ teaspoon (optional)

Cook the sugar syrup. Place the sugar, glucose, and water in a small saucepan over medium heat. Stir frequently and cook until the syrup is clear and the sugar has dissolved.

Add the puree. Remove the syrup from heat and let it cool to room temperature. Stir in the strawberry puree and malic acid.

Cool and store. Transfer the ripple to a container. Cover tightly and store it in the refrigerator for 2 weeks or up to 3 months in the freezer.

Black Raspberry Ripple (Cooked Ripple Method)

MAKES JUST OVER 1 PINT

Black Raspberry Puree (page 216)
400g | 2¼ cups

Sugar
100g | 1½ cups

Glucose
100g | ⅔ cup

Malic acid
3g | ½ teaspoon

Cook the ripple. Place the black raspberry puree, sugar, glucose, and malic acid in a medium saucepan over medium heat. Cook, stirring frequently, until the fruit begins to bubble. Continue simmering for 10 minutes, until the ribbon is thick and jammy.

Cool and store. Transfer the black raspberry ripple to a container and let it cool in the refrigerator. Once cool, cover the container tightly and store it in the refrigerator for 2 weeks or up to 3 months in the freezer.

Winter Strawberry Ripple

MAKES JUST OVER 1 PINT

I call this a winter strawberry ripple because I developed it to make use of the out-of-season strawberries available in clam shells year-round. (Waiting ten months between strawberry seasons is just too long!) These strawberries aren't as flavorful, and at times are quite crunchy. But you can harness their berry flavor by roasting them with a tart syrup. You can most certainly make this ripple with summer berries, too, but I was surprised when the summer berries took twice as long to cook! It turns out the ripe berries released extra juices that took longer to cook off.

Sugar	**Water**
100g | ½ cup	50g | ¼ cup
Dried hibiscus flowers	**Strawberries**
10g | 3 tablespoons	450g | 1 pound
Glucose	**Vanilla extract**
100g | ½ cup	3g | ½ teaspoon

Preheat the oven and prepare the syrup. Preheat the oven to 350°F. Place the sugar, hibiscus, glucose, and water in a medium saucepan over medium-high heat, and bring to a simmer. Remove the pot from the heat, let the hibiscus steep for 10 minutes, then strain the hibiscus from the syrup.

Prepare the strawberries. Cut the tops off the strawberries and slice them ¼ inch thick. Place the strawberries in a 9 by 13-inch baking dish, and stir in the hibiscus syrup.

Roast the strawberries. Roast the strawberries. Stir them every 10 minutes or so to encourage even cooking. After 45 minutes, the berries should be thick and bubbly, but if they are still soupy, continue cooking, checking every 5 minutes, until they look jammy.

Puree the strawberries. Transfer the hot berries to the bowl of a food processor and add the vanilla. Process the berries until they are pureed, then transfer them to an airtight container with a lid.

Cool and store. Let the ripple cool completely in the refrigerator, then cover. The ripple will keep for 2 weeks in the refrigerator or in the freezer for 3 months.

Lemon Curd

MAKES ABOUT 1 PINT

Lemon curd is essentially a custardy lemon pudding, usually used in tarts or as a spread. It's also highly prized by pastry chefs as a vehicle for lemon flavor, as the juice of the citrus is too acidic to present on its own.

To make lemon curd as an ice cream add-in, you need to use more sugar than most lemon curd recipes to ensure it's soft at frozen temperatures. In this recipe I call for glucose, which isn't as sweet as granulated sugar. If you aren't using the glucose, replace it with an equal amount of corn syrup or granulated sugar. The texture is like a pudding pop! Any extra lemon curd can be spooned over pancakes or other baked treats, or stored in your freezer for another ice cream adventure.

Eggs	**Grated lemon zest**
40g | 2 large	5g | 2 teaspoons, packed (from 1 large or 2 small lemons)
Sugar	
200g | 1 cup	
Glucose	**Lemon juice**
100g | ½ cup	100g | ½ cup (from 2 large or 4 small lemons)
	Butter
	160g | ¾ cup

Prepare a double boiler. Whisk the eggs, sugar, glucose, and lemon zest in a large metal mixing bowl. Find a pot with an opening a few inches smaller than the bowl you've chosen, fill it with 2 inches of water, and set it over medium-high heat. When the water begins to simmer, reduce the heat to medium low and nest the bowl of eggs and sugar over it.

Cook the lemon curd. Whisk the curd until the mixture becomes homogenous. Add the lemon juice. Cook and whisk the lemon mixture until it becomes thick and foamy, and the eggs cook enough so that when ribbons of the mixture are drizzled back into the bowl, they form small peaks before disappearing into the mix. If you check the temperature with a thermometer, it should read between 170° and 180°F. This will take just a little longer than your arms want it to; switch arms if they get exhausted.

*Lemon
curd*

*Strawberry
ripple*

*Red raspberry
ripple*

Mix in the butter, cool the curd, and store. When the curd has thickened, remove the pot from heat, and add the butter, one or two lumps at a time, whisking it in completely between additions. When all the butter has been added, transfer the lemon curd to a container and press plastic wrap directly on the surface to cool. But before you do, taste the warm lemon curd—it's one of life's secret pleasures, something only the chef can know. The lemon curd will keep in your refrigerator for 1 week or in the freezer for 3 months.

Soft Almond Meringue

MAKES ABOUT 1 QUART

Meringue is a simple mixture of egg whites and sugar, whipped until fluffy and light. The meringue can be baked crisp (see page 150), then folded into an ice cream. Soft meringues can also be spread between layers of freshly churned ice cream, where it will form creamy pockets inside firm ice cream.

In either case, meringue is best when it is made slow, slow, slow. It's tempting to turn the mixer to high, shortening the time between liquid egg white and fluffy meringue. Resist this urge! You'll get a more stable meringue if you whip slow and low.

You can add extracts to the meringue as long as they aren't oil based. Vanilla is classic, but I am a sucker for an almond meringue. The cream of tartar is optional, but it helps ensure the meringue whips properly.

To add soft meringue to your ice cream, it must be made moments before your ice cream finishes churning, or it will deflate. Start whipping your meringue as soon as the ice cream starts churning; they will be finished at almost the same time.

Prepare the egg whites. Place the egg whites in the very clean bowl of a stand mixer, and fit the mixer with a very clean whip attachment. Add the almond extract, salt, and cream of tartar, if using, and set aside.

Make the syrup. Place the sugar and water in a small saucepan over medium-high heat. Cook, stirring occasionally. When the syrup comes to a boil, reduce the heat to medium and cook until it reaches 240°F.

Simultaneously, whip the egg whites. As soon as the sugar starts to boil, turn the mixer on to medium-low speed. Your goal is to have the egg whites just start to hold medium peaks the moment the boiling syrup reaches 240°F. If your whites hold peaks early, turn the mixer to low, but never stop it! If you stop the motion, the egg whites will seize.

Add the syrup to the whites. When the syrup reaches 240°F, remove the pot from heat and make sure the mixer speed is at medium low. Drizzle the syrup in, being very careful the whip doesn't spit the hot syrup back at you. Aim the stream for the space between where the whip and the bowl come closest to each other. (If your whites aren't quite at medium peaks yet, hold the syrup off the stove until they are.)

Finish the whipping and use the meringue. When all the syrup has been added, turn the mixer to high and whip until the meringue is cool, about 5 minutes. Immediately add the soft meringue to freshly churned ice cream, layering it carefully with the soft ice cream in a freezer-proof container.

Egg whites
100g | ½ cup (from about 3 large eggs)

Almond extract
3g | ½ teaspoon

Salt
1g | ¼ teaspoon

Cream of tartar (optional)
2g | ¼ teaspoon

Sugar
150g | ¾ cup

Water
50g | ¼ cup

Bits and Bobs

Roasted-Vanilla Meringue Bits

MAKES A LITTLE OVER 1 QUART
MERINGUE PIECES

While Soft Almond Meringue (page 149) is wonderful inside a scoop of ice cream, meringue can also be baked into the lightest, crispiest ice cream add-in. For this recipe I toast the vanilla beans, which adds a flavor similar to a toasted marshmallow! Once roasted and crisp, the vanilla beans can be ground in a blender, a coffee grinder, or with a mortar and pestle if you have the patience. This roasted vanilla powder might become one of your favorite flavors once you have it around, and it can live in your cupboard indefinitely.

Vanilla beans
2

Egg whites
100g | ½ cup (from about 5 large eggs)

Salt
2g | ¼ teaspoon

Cream of tartar (optional)
2g | ¼ teaspoon

Sugar
150g | ¾ cup

Vanilla extract
5g | 1 teaspoon

Prepare the vanilla. Preheat the oven to 200°F. Split the vanilla beans down the center lengthwise with a sharp knife to expose the seeds, and place the beans in a small baking dish. Bake the beans for 30 minutes, until they are crisp and fragrant. Remove the beans from the oven, let them cool completely at room temperature, then grind them in a spice grinder or mortar and pestle until they are powdered. Sift the roasted vanilla powder through a fine-mesh sieve and discard any large pieces. Store the roasted vanilla powder in an airtight container at room temperature until you are ready to use it.

Preheat the oven and prepare the pans. Preheat the oven to 200°F or the lowest setting it has. Lightly grease two sheet pans and line them with parchment paper.

Whip the whites. Place the egg whites, salt, and cream of tartar, if using, in the very clean bowl of a stand mixer fitted with a very clean whip attachment. Turn the mixer to a medium speed (no. 6 on a Kitchen-Aid), and whip until the egg whites begin to hold their shape and form soft peaks.

Add the sugar and vanilla. Begin adding the sugar 1 tablespoon at a time. It's important that you add small amounts of sugar at a time, and whip for a minute between additions, allowing the sugar time to dissolve into the meringue before the next addition. If you short-cut this step, the whole granules of sugar will become pockets of moisture after baking. When all the sugar has been added, add the vanilla extract and 5g | 1 teaspoon of roasted vanilla powder, and whip the meringue for another 2 minutes.

Bake the meringue. Transfer the meringue to the prepared pans and spread to the edges in a single layer. Bake the meringue for 2 to 3 hours, until the meringue is dry all the way through. Alternatively, you can pipe the meringue into kisses, or any other shape you desire, but if the shape is large, the baking time may need to be extended.

Prepare the meringue as an add-in. Remove the meringue from the oven, let it cool on the pan, then break it up into shards and place them in an airtight container. Store the crisp meringues for 3 days at room temperature.

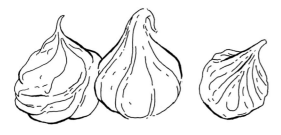

Candied Citrus Bits

MAKES ABOUT ½ CUP

Candying citrus creates translucent, chewy, intensely fragrant fruit that look a little like Neo coming out of the primordial ooze that the *Matrix* machines had kept him in. These candied citrus fruits stay good in their syrup tucked away in your refrigerator for up to 6 months, until you are ready to dice them and add them to ice cream.

I have tried this technique with every citrus I've ever gotten my hands on. My favorite is grapefruit, whose abrasive flavor becomes soft and obliging. You need to choose citrus varieties with a thick skin that adheres to the flesh, avoiding easy-to-peel fruits like satsumas, which fall apart when boiled.

This recipe differs from many similar ones you may come across, as I keep the citrus flesh attached to the rind as it cooks. I find this gives a much tastier and fruitier flavor than simply simmering citrus peel in syrup alone. The most time-consuming part is blanching the whole fruit. Trust me, this blanching and cooling process is necessary; my attempts to shortcut this have always given me the same bitter, unpleasant results. To lessen the time a bit, you can set three pots of water to boil at the same time. Thank goodness the candied citrus lasts so long—you can make enough to justify the time it takes. Note: If you can find kumquats, their cooking time is much shorter and they don't require blanching.

Citrus fruits	Sugar
1 grapefruit, 2 oranges, 3 lemons, 5 tangerines, or 1 pound of kumquats	700g | 3 cups
	Water
	700g | 3 cups

Blanch the citrus. Fill a medium pot with about 8 cups of water and bring to a boil. Dunk the citrus fruits in the boiling water for 15 seconds, rinse with cold water, and repeat two more times with fresh boiling water each time. (You can boil three pots of water at once to save time.) Skip this blanching step if you are using kumquats.

Make the syrup. Place the sugar and water in a large saucepan over high heat. Cook the syrup until it comes to a boil, stirring to dissolve the sugar, then reduce the heat to a low simmer.

Prep and cook the citrus. Cut the citrus into 4 wedges each, slicing from stem to tip. If using kumquats, cut them into ¼-inch-thick slices and seed them. Place the citrus wedges in the pot of simmering syrup and cook for 3 to 4 hours, until the fruit sinks to the bottom and has absorbed enough sugar that it's translucent. During the cooking, the water will boil away and the syrup will condense; you will need to keep an eye on this, and add warm water periodically, usually ½ cup every 30 minutes, to maintain the syrup consistency. (If you don't, the water will all evaporate, the sugar will caramelize, and your painstakingly blanched citrus will burn. Trust me, it's a sad sight.)

Cool and store. When the citrus is translucent, remove the pot from the stove and let the citrus cool in the syrup. Transfer the fruit and syrup to a container, cover tightly, and store in the refrigerator for up to 6 months.

Prepare the fruit as an add-in. Remove a wedge of citrus from the syrup and rinse it under cold water until it is no longer dripping syrup. Peel the flesh from the pith, and discard the flesh. Dice the candied peel into ¼-inch cubes, and transfer to a container temporarily, until you are ready to scatter them into your freshly churned ice cream. Or, let the candied citrus dry at room temperature until they are tacky, then toss in granulated sugar.

Cookie
butter

Marshmallows

Candied
kumquats

Buttered pecans

*Candied lemon
bits (dried)*

*Roasted-vanilla
meringue bits*

Cookie Butter Bits

MAKES 3 CUPS

If you've never seen cookie butter, it's like peanut butter in color and texture, but is made of *ground cookies*. Whoever invented it deserves a genius award. It's really easy to make with a food processor; simply place cookies in the food processor and grind them into oblivion. Just as with peanuts, the fat from the cookies begins to render as it is ground finer and finer, and eventually you have cookie butter. Adding a little coconut oil makes it melt in your mouth, even when frozen.

As long as the cookie is rich in butter, it will turn into cookie butter. This recipe uses Graham Crackers (page 168), but you could easily use the Chocolate Wafers (page 165). (Do *not* attempt this with graham crackers from the store, though. They simply won't work because they are too lean.) Once the cookies are pureed, the cookie butter can be spread out thin and frozen, then chopped into bits to be folded into your ice cream. If you have any cookie butter left over, leave it at room temperature and spread it on your toast!

Graham Crackers
(must be from recipe on page 168) or other butter-rich cookies
400g | 3 cups, crushed

Coconut oil
25g | 2 tablespoons, melted

Salt
2g | ¼ teaspoon

Grind the cookies. Place the crushed crackers, coconut oil, and salt in the bowl of a food processor. Process the cookies until they are finely ground. If they begin to stick to the walls of the bowl, stop the food processor, scrape the walls clean, and turn the machine back on. Continue processing until the cookie butter is smooth and fluid, up to 10 minutes.

Freeze the cookie butter. Line a sheet pan with parchment paper, and transfer the cookie butter to the pan. Spread it out to a ¼-inch thickness, then transfer the pan to the freezer and freeze for 1 hour, or until solid.

Break up the cookie butter. Invert the sheet pan onto a cutting board. Carefully peel back the parchment paper and discard it. Break the cookie butter into a few large pieces. Leave one piece on the cutting board, and immediately place the remaining pieces back in the freezer.

Chop and store. Chop the cookie butter into bite-size pieces using a serrated knife, then immediately place in a container in the freezer. Continue chopping the cookie butter, one piece at a time. Store in an airtight container in the freezer for up to 1 month.

Buttered Pecans

MAKES ABOUT 3 CUPS

Buttered pecans are one of the most classic ice cream add-ins, and are surprisingly simple to prepare; you just roast pecans in a puddle of melting butter. The butter browns as the nuts toast, adding even more nutty flavor to the pecans; once out of the oven, the pecans soak up the browned butter that floats around them as they cool.

I once asked around about the flavor of the ice cream in a typical butter pecan ice cream. Ryan Pfeiffer, my friend and the chef at Blackbird restaurant, hit the nail on the head when he said, "Those old man candies"—Werther's Originals, the buttery toffee-like candies rich with brown sugar popular with grandpas everywhere. You'll find my take on this combination in the Bourbon Butterscotch Ice Cream (page 54), which was invented to house these nuts. But don't stop there! Buttered pecans have a broader ice cream destiny in store, and I leave it to you to find it for them.

Pecan pieces
225g | ½ pound

Butter
50g | ¼ cup

Salt
5g | 1 teaspoon

Prepare the pecans. Preheat the oven to 350°F. Spread the pecans in a single layer on a sheet pan and dot the butter all over the top. Season with the salt.

Roast. Roast the pecans for 8 to 10 minutes, stirring every 2 minutes. When the nuts have taken on a darker shade and the butter has browned, transfer the pan to a wire rack to cool at room temperature.

Store. Store the pecans in an airtight container in the freezer for up to 1 month.

Marshmallows

MAKES ABOUT 6 CUPS

Marshmallows are one of the world's best ice cream add-ins. They stay fluffy and soft in the freezer, and offer sweet little pockets to chew on as the ice cream melts in your mouth. Marshmallows are compatible with literally every flavor of ice cream. I particularly love the way the chewy marshmallows hint at the texture of bubblegum when tucked inside Strawberry Bubblemallow (page 204).

You'll find homemade marshmallows a far cry from those sold in bags at the grocery store. They take six hours or more to set up, but even if you didn't plan ahead, skip buying those marshmallows from the store. Instead, smear just-made marshmallow between layers of freshly churned ice cream and let it set up in the freezer.

Neutral oil (such as canola)	**Salt** 2g | ¼ teaspoon
Cold water 100g | ½ cup	**Water** 100g | ½ cup
Unflavored gelatin 10g | 1 tablespoon	**Vanilla extract** 10g | 2 teaspoons
Granulated sugar 250g | 1¼ cups	**Confectioners' sugar** 150g | 1¼ cups
Glucose 100g | ½ cup	**Cornstarch** 20g | 2 tablespoons

Prepare the pan. Lightly oil a 9 by 13-inch baking dish with a neutral oil, like canola, and set it aside.

Bloom the gelatin. Place the cold water in a small bowl and sprinkle the gelatin over it. Let sit at room temperature for 10 minutes, until it's softened and translucent. Transfer the bloomed gelatin and water to a small saucepan set over medium-low heat, and cook, stirring constantly, until the gelatin melts. Pour it into the bowl of a stand mixer fit with the whip attachment.

Cook the syrup. Place the granulated sugar, glucose, salt, and water in a small saucepan over medium-high heat. Cook, stirring occasionally, until the syrup starts to boil. Reduce the heat to medium, and cook until it reaches 250°F on a kitchen thermometer.

Whip the syrup with the gelatin. Pour the syrup into the bowl with the gelatin. Turn the mixer on high speed and whip the syrup for 10 to 15 minutes. It is helpful to cover the mixer with a dishtowel to prevent small splatters of syrup from spraying everything in a two-foot radius. The marshmallow is just about done when you can hear the mixer slow down, and the mixture is fluffy and stiff like whipped cream.

Add the vanilla. Turn the mixer to medium speed and add the vanilla. The mixer will speed back up momentarily, then slow back down as the vanilla mixes in completely.

Cast the marshmallow. Transfer the fluffy marshmallow to the oiled pan and spread it out with a rubber spatula. Lightly oil your hands and gently rub the surface of the marshmallow with a light coating of oil. Place a piece of plastic wrap directly on the surface and press it down. Let set at room temperature for 6 hours, and preferably overnight.

Prepare the marshmallows as an add-in. Sift the confectioners' sugar and cornstarch together into a large mixing bowl to make the marshmallow coating, and use it to generously dust a large cutting board. Remove the plastic wrap from the marshmallow layer, and transfer the layer to the dusted board. Dust the surface with marshmallow coating; then, using a long knife, cut the marshmallow into 1-inch strips, dusting each strip in marshmallow coating as you cut it. Line up three or four strips and then cut crosswise into 1-inch pieces, transferring the cut marshmallows to the bowl with the coating as you cut them. Toss to coat the marshmallows well. Shake the excess coating off the marshmallows, then transfer them to a 1-gallon zippered plastic bag.

Store. Store the marshmallows in the sealed bag at room temperature for 3 days, or in the freezer for up to 1 month.

Chunks & Crunches

Classic Chocolate Chunks

MAKES ABOUT 3 CUPS

You know the slogan "Melts in your mouth, not in your hand"? This is great for eating a piece of room-temperature chocolate; your mouth warms the chocolate to melting temperatures quickly. However, if chocolate is frozen, your mouth takes much longer to warm the chocolate enough to melt. If you've ever eaten an ice cream with chocolate chunks that feel waxy and don't melt, it's not because the chocolate is cheap. It's because that chocolate is meant to be eaten at room temperature.

Ice cream manufacturers figured this out a long time ago, and have the chocolate chips in their ice cream specially made to melt rapidly when frozen. They do this by replacing some of the cocoa butter with soft tropical oils. The Italians have another trick. They drizzle melted chocolate directly into their gelato as it finishes churning. They call it stracciatella, and it has the most wonderful tiny flecks of chocolate that melt in your mouth.

For the rest of us, there is this recipe! Chocolate is melted first like the Italians do, and a little coconut oil is added, like the pros do. Seek out expeller-pressed coconut oil, which is free of coconut flavor. You can use any chocolate you like for this recipe—dark, milk, or even white. And feel free to add flavored oils as well, like peppermint oil! One of my go-to variations trades the dark chocolate for milk chocolate along with 3g | 1 teaspoon of toasted sesame oil.

Chocolate, finely chopped	Salt
450g	1 pound	3g	½ teaspoon

Coconut oil
50g | ¼ cup

Melt the chocolate. Combine all the ingredients in a medium metal or glass bowl. Find a pot with a mouth a few inches smaller than the bowl, and fill it with 2 inches of water. Bring the water to a boil over high heat. Reduce the heat to maintain a simmer. Nest the bowl of chocolate into the double boiler. Stir occasionally, until the chocolate mixture is smooth.

Freeze the chocolate. Transfer the chocolate to an 8 by 10-inch pan, and place the pan in the freezer. Freeze for 2 hours, or up to 24 hours.

Unmold the chocolate. Remove the pan from the freezer, and turn it upside down onto a cutting board. Tap the pan to help free up the chocolate, which will have contracted just enough in the freezer to pull itself off the sides and bottom of the pan.

Break up the chocolate. Break the chocolate into a few large pieces. Leave one piece on the cutting board, and place the remaining pieces back in the pan, and put immediately in the freezer.

Prepare the chocolate chunks as an add-in. Chop the chocolate into bite-size pieces, using a serrated knife if you have one. Gather up the pieces quickly, as they may melt, and immediately place them in an airtight container in the freezer. Chop the rest in this fashion, with only one piece of chocolate out of the freezer at a time. Store the chocolate in the freezer for up to 1 month.

Pretzel Toffee Chunks
(or Buttercrunch Toffee Chunks)

MAKES ABOUT 1 QUART PRETZEL TOFFEE
CHUNKS OR ABOUT 2 CUPS BUTTERCRUNCH
TOFFEE CHUNKS

The idea of something as luxurious as butter in crunch form seems impossible—and charmed. It's magic to watch butter and sugar bubble and boil until golden brown, and once cooled, the molten mixture hardens to a texture that can only be called one thing: buttercrunch.

If you work quickly, you can often scatter any of several things across the surface of the molten toffee and they will stick to the surface, partially embedded in the candy. I've used pink peppercorns, sesame seeds, peanuts, and even popcorn! For large chunks, like the pretzels for Ricky's Coffee Pretzel Toffee (page 211), cover the bottom of the pan with pretzels, then pour the hot toffee over, ensuring the pretzels are hugged tightly by the toffee.

There is a small bit of water used in this recipe; it lightens the texture a touch and is a great place to introduce flavor; feel free to replace the water with bourbon or espresso. To prevent them from getting sticky, keep the chopped bits of buttercrunch toffee or pretzel toffee in the freezer until you're ready to scatter them into a freshly churned ice cream.

Mini pretzels
100g | about 2 cups (optional)

Butter
120g | ½ cup

Sugar
150g | ¾ cup

Glucose
50g | ¼ cup

Water
25g | 2 tablespoons

Salt
3g | ½ teaspoon

Vanilla extract
5g | 1 teaspoon

Dark chocolate, finely chopped
100g | 3½ ounces

Prepare the pan. Line a sheet pan with a silicone baking mat or grease it lightly. If you are preparing pretzel toffee, place the pretzels on the pan and arrange them in a single layer, making sure they lay flat, shoulder to shoulder. Set the pan close by; you'll need it the moment the toffee is finished cooking.

Cook the toffee. Melt the butter in a medium heavy-bottomed saucepan over medium heat. Add the sugar, glucose, water, salt, and vanilla. Turn the heat up to medium high, and cook, stirring frequently with a heatproof spatula to prevent scorching, until the toffee is 300°F on a kitchen thermometer. (If you don't have a thermometer, cook it to a rich golden brown, or until your brain says, "That's the color of toffee.") Remove the pan from heat. On occasion, the toffee can look a little broken when the cooking is finished. To remedy this, continue stirring the cooked toffee away from the heat; as it drops in temperature, it will come back together.

Cast the toffee. Pour the molten toffee into the prepared pan (over the pretzels, if using), and quickly assist the hot oozing toffee with a spatula to spread into an even layer about ¼ inch thick.

Cover the toffee with chocolate. Immediately scatter the dark chocolate over the hot toffee, and let it sit undisturbed for 2 minutes. When all the chocolate has melted, spread it evenly over the surface of the toffee. Let the toffee cool completely at room temperature, about 30 minutes.

Prepare the toffee as an add-in. If the chocolate isn't completely set but the toffee is cool, place it in the freezer for 5 minutes to finish hardening the chocolate. Remove the toffee from the pan and chop it into bite-size chunks. Transfer the toffee chunks to an airtight container and store it in the freezer for up to 1 month.

Nutterbuddy Crunch

MAKES A LITTLE OVER 1 QUART,
LOOSELY PACKED

This is one of the most addicting, snackable, impress-your-friends recipes in my repertoire: melted milk chocolate and peanut butter coat crispy flakes and cacao nibs, making a salty, crunchy, peanut-buttery crunch.

The hardest ingredient to find for this recipe is fuilletine, which looks like crushed corn flakes, but has the flavor of an ice cream cone. Fuilletine stays crisp when added to confections, and it crackles between your teeth. You can substitute Rice Krispies, and I wouldn't shame you, but you'll be greatly rewarded if you special-order fuilletine from an internet supplier or harass a local pastry chef for some of the good stuff. Once your ingredients are in hand, I promise this comes together in a jiffy.

When you finish making this peanut crunch, be sure to keep it frozen at all times; it will melt at room temperature.

Creamy peanut butter	**Fuilletine**
150g | ½ cup	200g | 2 cups
Milk chocolate, chopped	**Cacao nibs**
75g | 3 ounces	100g | ¾ cup
Coconut oil	**Salt**
(preferably expeller-pressed)	5g | 1 teaspoon
25g | 2 tablespoons	

Melt the peanut butter, chocolate, and oil. Place the peanut butter, milk chocolate, and coconut oil in a large mixing bowl. Find a pot with a mouth a few inches smaller than the bowl, fill it with 2 inches of water, and bring it to a boil over medium-high heat. Reduce the heat to a simmer, then set the mixing bowl on top. Melt the peanut butter mixture, stirring occasionally, until evenly mixed.

Mix in the solids. Set the mixing bowl on a towel to wipe away any moisture from the bottom. Stir in the fuilletine, cacao nibs, and salt.

Chill the mixture. Line a sheet pan with parchment paper, and scatter the peanut butter mixture in an even layer. Place in the refrigerator for 10 to 15 minutes, until it is semi-firm. Break up the mixture into individual bites by tossing it with your hands.

Freeze and store. Transfer the pan to the freezer for 1 hour, or up to 24 hours. When the crumbled Nutterbuddy Crunch is completely frozen, loosely pack it into an airtight container to keep for up to 3 months in the freezer.

Cinnamon–Brown Sugar Streusel

MAKES ABOUT 3 CUPS STREUSEL CHUNKS

Streusel is the topping on a fruit crumble or coffee cake, but did you ever think to bake the crumble on its own? It's an amazing topping for sundaes, and it is even better when folded into a scoop of ice cream.

This recipe is versatile and open to adaptation. Try substituting up to 50 percent of the wheat flour for something more flavorful, like buckwheat flour. If you want to make it completely wheat free, that's cool, too—just add 8g \| 1 tablespoon cornstarch to your choice of alternative flour. You can add any dried spices you like, and I also recommend adding whole grains, such as rolled oats or kasha. Additionally, you can use an oil instead of the butter, such as hazelnut oil or olive oil. If you stick with butter, though, you can brown it or infuse it with whole herbs or spices; or, melt the butter with some coffee beans to infuse (and strain out). And of course, chopped nuts always make a great addition to a streusel—just throw a handful in along with the flour!

Butter	**Ground cinnamon**
110g | ½ cup	5g | 2 teaspoons
Vanilla extract	**Salt**
5g | 1 teaspoon	3g | ½ teaspoon
Flour	**Brown sugar (light or dark)**
150g | 1 cup plus 2 tablespoons	75g | ⅓ cup, tightly packed
Baking powder	**Granulated sugar**
1g | ¼ teaspoon	75g | ⅓ cup

Preheat the oven and prepare the pan. Preheat the oven to 350°F and line a sheet pan with parchment paper.

Melt the butter. Melt the butter in a small saucepan over medium heat. Remove from heat and add the vanilla. Let cool; the butter should be cool but still fluid when you add it to the remaining streusel ingredients.

Mix the dry ingredients and add the butter. Whisk the flour, baking powder, cinnamon, and salt in a large bowl. Whisk in the brown sugar and granulated sugar until blended. Pour in the melted butter, and use your hands to quickly toss the ingredients together, breaking up the clumps as they form. Continue tossing until the little nuggets of streusel are between ¼ inch and ¾ inch in size.

Bake the streusel. Transfer the streusel to the sheet pan, spread it out, and bake it for 10 minutes. Remove the pan from the oven, and stir the streusel, pulling the sides into the center and redistributing the center to the edges. Break up any large clumps that have started to come together. Bake for an additional 5 minutes, until the streusel is golden brown and cooked through.

Cool and store. Transfer the pan to a wire rack to cool, then store the streusel in an airtight container in the freezer for up to 1 month.

Almond-Browned Butter Streusel

MAKES ABOUT 3 CUPS STREUSEL CHUNKS

Butter 125g | ½ cup plus 1 tablespoon	**Baking powder** 1g | ¼ teaspoon
Almond extract 5g | 1 teaspoon	**Salt** 3g | ½ teaspoon
Flour 150g | 1 cup plus 2 tablespoons	**Chopped almonds** 100g | ⅔ cup, toasted
	Granulated sugar 150g | ¾ cup

Preheat the oven and prepare the pan. Preheat the oven to 350°F. Line the bottoms of two sheet pans with parchment paper.

Melt the butter. Melt the butter in a small saucepan over medium heat until all the water has boiled out and the milk solids are starting to brown and become fragrant. Strain the butter into a clean bowl. Add the almond extract and set aside to cool; the browned butter should be cool but still fluid when you add it to the remaining streusel ingredients.

Mix the dry ingredients and add the butter. Whisk together the flour, baking powder, and salt in a large bowl, then stir in the almonds. Add the granulated sugar and continue whisking, breaking up any lumps as necessary. Pour in the melted butter, and use your hands to quickly toss the ingredients together, breaking up the clumps as they form. Continue tossing until the little nuggets of streusel are between ¼ and ¾ inch in size.

Bake the streusel. Transfer the streusel to the sheet pans and bake for 10 minutes. Remove the pans from the oven, and stir the streusel, pulling the sides into the center and redistributing the center to the edges. Break up any large clumps of streusel that have started to come together. Bake for an additional 10 to 15 minutes, until the streusel is golden brown and cooked through.

Cool and store. Transfer the pans to a wire rack to cool, then store the streusel in an airtight container in the freezer for up to 1 month.

Toffee

*Caramelized
Rice Krispies*

Pretzel toffee

*Cinnamon-brown
sugar streusel*

Almond-browned
butter streusel

Nutterbuddy
crunch

Caramel
popcorn

Caramelized Rice Krispies

MAKES 1 QUART

This technique comes from the French pastry chef Pierre Herme. He cooks Rice Krispies in a sugar syrup until they are encased in a nubby white coating like Frosted Flakes. Then he adds them to a hot, clean pan where they caramelize on contact. A few turns of a spoon, and the fragile bits of rice cereal are wrapped in the thinnest coating of caramel. It's brilliant.

You can apply this technique to all manner of pantry items. Cereals? Check. Seeds? Check. Nuts? You better believe it. If you apply this technique to nuts, use the volume measurement as your guide—that is, 3¼ cups of nuts—rather than weight. The surface area of Rice Krispies and nuts is similar, but the weight is not.

Sugar
100g | ½ cup

Salt
5g | 1 teaspoon

Water
25g | 2 tablespoons

Rice Krispies
100g | 3¼ cups

Cook the syrup. Place the sugar, water, and salt in a large saucepan, about 3 times as big as the quantity of cereal, to allow for proper stirring. Cook over medium-high heat, stirring until the sugar crystals dissolve.

Frost the Rice Krispies. As soon as the bubbles slow down in the syrup and it reaches 240°F on a kitchen thermometer, remove it from heat and add the Rice Krispies all at once. Stir gently to coat with the syrup. Remove the pan from the heat and continue stirring, until the syrup around the cereal pieces begins to turn white and crystallize.

Preheat a skillet. Place a large skillet over medium heat for 2 minutes. Test the pan to see if it is hot enough by tossing in one or two crystalized Rice Krispies. They should begin to caramelize on contact, picking up color in under 5 seconds. (Give the pan more time if necessary, or if the Krispies start to smoke and burn on contact, let the pan cool down a little.)

Caramelize. Add the Rice Krispies and begin stirring, or flipping the pan if you're comfortable doing so, to cook them evenly, until golden brown.

Cool and break up the Rice Krispies. Pour the Rice Krispies out onto a sheet pan and spread gently with a spatula. Let cool just enough to handle, about a minute or two, then gently start tossing them with your hands to break up any large clumps.

Store. Allow the caramelized Rice Krispies to cool completely, then gather them into an airtight container and store them in the freezer for up to 1 month.

Caramel Popcorn

MAKES 6 CUPS

When my grandmother heard about my deep love for caramel popcorn, she quickly taught me how to prepare it. I'll never forget the image of her kneeling in front of the oven, her head almost inside it, as she stirred the caramel corn. It's something I've continued to do at almost every restaurant I've worked at, whether placing the caramel popcorn over chocolate caramel mousse, scattering it across apple cider sorbet, or just serving it on its own.

When I started making ice creams to pack into pints, the caramel popcorn went right in there, too. The caramel shell protects the popcorn from absorbing moisture in the ice cream, while keeping the popcorn nice and crisp. It *is* a bit of a production, I admit, and you'll want to clear your counters. But it's a labor of love, and I think of Grandma Eva every time I pull a pan of caramel corn out of the oven. This is her recipe, and I've always used corn syrup. If you prefer, use glucose or the inverted sugar syrup on page 214 in its place.

Popped popcorn
40g | 5 cups

Dark brown sugar
200g | ½ cup

Water
75g | ⅓ cup

Light corn syrup
50g | ¼ cup

Butter
50g | ¼ cup

Kosher or sea salt
5g | 1 teaspoon

Warm the popcorn. Preheat the oven to 250°F. Line a sheet pan with a silicone baking mat if you have one; otherwise leave it naked. Place the popped popcorn on the sheet pan and spread it evenly, leaving about 1 inch around the edge of the pan. Warm the popcorn in the oven while you prepare the caramel.

Prepare the caramel. Place the brown sugar, water, corn syrup, butter, and salt in a medium saucepan over medium heat. Cook, stirring occasionally, until the caramel reaches 240°F on a kitchen thermometer, then remove from the heat.

Drizzle the popcorn. Remove the pan from the oven. Drizzle the caramel evenly over the popcorn, then stir gently until the popcorn is evenly coated.

Bake the popcorn. Bake the popcorn for 30 minutes, pulling the pan out to stir every 10 minutes. Test the popcorn for doneness; remove a piece and set it on the countertop. Give it a minute to cool, then test it by biting into it. If it's crisp, it's done. If it's still chewy, continue baking and stirring until finished.

Cool and store. Remove the pan from the oven and place on a wire rack to cool. For the first few minutes, stir the caramel popcorn every minute or so to help break it up. Once the popcorn stops sticking together when it is left undisturbed, let it cool completely. Transfer the cooled popcorn to an airtight container, and store it in the freezer for up to 1 month.

Cakes & Cookies

I will eat any cookie dough stuffed into ice cream (or not)—chocolate chip, peanut butter, oatmeal, gingersnaps, snickerdoodle. But when I started formulating cookie dough to be frozen instead of baked, I realized you don't need the same ingredients. Since the cookies don't rise in the oven, the baking soda or baking powder is unnecessary. Likewise, the moisture provided by the egg could be substituted by any liquid, and the fat doesn't need to be butter—any oil can provide the same fatty goodness. Most important, the flour doesn't need to be wheat flour, since it's not going to stretch and hold a cookie together while it is baked.

So, if you are sensitive to any of these ingredients, then you can substitute them without risk! However, I personally love the quintessential "cookie dough" flavor, so these recipes do contain raw eggs, flour, and butter; the baking soda, however, is gone, so don't make the mistake of trying to bake these cookie doughs.

Chocolate Chip Cookie Dough

MAKES ABOUT 3 CUPS CUBED PIECES

Butter	**Salt**
100g | ½ cup	5g | 1 teaspoon
Brown sugar	**Egg**
75g | ⅓ cup	50g | 1 large
Granulated sugar	**Chocolate Chips**
75g | ⅓ cup	100g | ¾ cup
Vanilla extract	**Flour**
5g | 1 teaspoon	150g | 1¼ cups

Blend the butter and sugars. Place the butter, brown sugar, granulated sugar, vanilla, and salt in the bowl of a stand mixer fitted with the paddle attachment. Mix on medium speed until you have a smooth and even paste.

Mix in the egg, chocolate, and flour. Add the egg and mix until evenly combined. Add the chocolate pieces, and turn the speed to low. When the chocolate is evenly distributed, add the flour and mix until the dough comes together.

Freeze, cut, and store. Transfer the dough to a sheet pan or cake pan, spread it out ½ inch thick, and place in the freezer for 1 hour, or up to 1 day. When it's rock-hard, transfer to a cutting board. Cut the dough into ½-inch cubes. Place the dough back in the freezer, and when it's hardened again, store in an airtight container in the freezer for up to 1 month.

Peanut Butter Cookie Dough

MAKES ABOUT 3 CUPS CUBED PIECES

Butter	**Salt**
50g | ¼ cup	5g | 1 teaspoon
Peanut butter	**Egg**
50g | ¼ cup	50g | 1 large
Brown sugar	**Chopped peanuts**
50g | ¼ cup	50g | ⅓ cup
Granulated sugar	**Flour**
100g | ½ cup	150g | 1¼ cups
Vanilla extract	
5g | 1 teaspoon	

Blend the butter, peanut butter, and sugars. Place the butter, peanut butter, brown sugar, granulated sugar, vanilla, and salt in the bowl of a stand mixer fitted with the paddle attachment. Mix on medium speed until you have a smooth and even paste.

Mix in the egg, peanuts, and flour. Add the egg and mix until evenly combined. Add the peanuts, and turn the speed to low. When the peanuts are evenly distributed, add the flour, and mix until it forms a dough.

Freeze, cut, and store. Transfer the cookie dough to a sheet pan or cake pan, spread it out ½ inch thick for ease of cutting later, and place it in the freezer for 1 hour, or up to 1 day. When it's rock-hard, transfer to a cutting board. Cut the cookie dough into ½-inch cubes. Place the cookie dough back in the freezer, and when it's hardened again, store in an airtight container in the freezer for up to 1 month.

Chocolate Wafers

MAKES 1½ QUARTS CRUSHED COOKIE PIECES

This is the ultimate chocolate wafer for cookies-and-cream ice cream. The flavor is so deep and dark, it puts those black-and-white sandwich-eos to shame. The dough is rolled in logs and chilled before being sliced and baked, allowing you to cook as many or as few cookies as you like. The flavor of this cookie is directly tied to the quality of cocoa powder you use. You can order my personal favorite, Cacao Barry's extra brute cocoa powder, online.

If you want to use these for Cookies, Cookies, and Cream (page 191), leave half of the dough unbaked, and add chopped chunks of the cookie dough along with the crushed baked cookies, for an ice cream like no other.

Flour	**Dark brown sugar**
350g	2¾ cups	300g	1½ cups
Cocoa powder	**Granulated sugar**
50g	⅔ cup	100g	½ cup
Baking soda	**Salt**
5g	1 teaspoon	7g	1½ teaspoons
Butter, softened	
300g	1½ cups	

Mix the dry ingredients together. Sift the flour, cocoa powder, and baking soda together into a bowl, and set aside.

Cream the butter and sugars. Place the butter, brown sugar, granulated sugar, and salt in the bowl of a stand mixer fitted with a paddle attachment, and cream on high speed for 3 minutes. Scrape the paddle and sides of the bowl well.

Add the dry mixture. Add the flour mixture, and mix on low speed until the cookie dough comes together into a tight mass.

Shape the logs. Remove the cookie dough from the bowl, divide it into two pieces, and shape each piece into a log 2 inches in diameter. Wrap each log tightly in plastic wrap, and transfer to the refrigerator for 3 hours, or up to 1 week. (Or, wrap the logs in a double layer of plastic wrap and keep them in the freezer for up to 1 month.)

Preheat the oven and prepare the pans. Preheat the oven to 350°F. Line two sheet pans with parchment.

Slice the dough and bake. Cut the logs into ⅓-inch slices, and place these 1 inch apart on the sheet pans. Bake for 5 minutes, rotate the pans 180 degrees and swap the pans' racks, then bake for an additional 4 to 6 minutes. Because the cookies are so dark, it's hard to tell if they are done just by looking. Press the center of a cookie that is in the middle of the sheet pan; if it feels set, remove the cookies from the oven. If your finger leaves a clear indent, let the cookies bake a little longer.

Cool the cookies. Transfer the sheet pans to a wire rack and let the cookies cool completely on the pans. (If you need the pans to bake more cookies, let the cookies cool until they are firm enough to be lifted without breaking, about 10 minutes, and continue to cool on a wire rack.)

Prepare the cookies as an add-in. Once the cookies are completely cool and crisp, place them in a zippered plastic bag, seal it tightly, and gently tap the cookies with a large spoon, until they are crushed into bite-size pieces. Try to get as much air out of the bag as possible, then transfer the bag to the freezer to store for up to 1 month.

Gooey butter cake

Chocolate chip cookie dough

Chocolate wafers

Peanut butter cookie dough

Graham crackers

Brownie chunks

Graham Crackers

MAKES ABOUT 1 QUART CHOPPED PIECES

How a graham cracker made it in this world without being called a cookie is beyond me. It's all cookie, and it anchors so many of the desserts we know and love.

The flavor of store-bought graham crackers is hard to capture at home, mostly because the formula is proprietary and includes artificial flavors. However, what can be created at home has the depth of whole wheat flour, the richness of honey, a hint of cinnamon, and an excellent bite. The dough is a little sticky, and if you have parchment paper, rolling the dough between two sheets helps you get the dough nice and thin for baking.

All-purpose flour	**Butter, softened**
200g | 1⅔ cups	225g | 1 cup
Whole wheat flour	**Brown sugar**
100g | ¾ cup	60g | ¼ cup, tightly packed
Kosher or sea salt	**Granulated sugar**
7g | 1½ teaspoons	100g | ½ cup
Baking soda	**Honey**
4g | ¾ teaspoon	25g | 2 tablespoons
Ground cinnamon	
5g | 1 teaspoon	

Sift the dry ingredients. Whisk the flours, salt, baking soda, and cinnamon in a medium bowl, then use a fine-mesh sieve or sifter to sift the dry ingredients together.

Cream the butter and sugars. Place butter, brown sugar, granulated sugar, and honey in the bowl of a stand mixer fitted with a paddle attachment. Cream on high speed for 2 minutes, then scrape down the sides of the bowl and mix for an additional 2 minutes.

Mix the wet and dry ingredients. Add the dry ingredients to the mixer bowl and mix on low speed for 1 minute. Stop the mixer, scrape down the sides of the bowl, and mix for an additional 1 minute, or until the dough is uniform.

Roll out the dough. Cut two pieces of parchment paper to the same size as a sheet pan. Transfer the dough to one piece of parchment paper and press it into a rectangle. Place the second piece of parchment paper on top, and roll the dough to a thickness of ¼ inch. You can flip the parchment-wrapped dough over, and peel and replace the pieces of parchment to allow the dough to spread out as necessary. Place the parchment-wrapped dough on the sheet pan and put in the freezer for 1 hour, to freeze solid.

Bake the graham crackers. Preheat the oven to 350°F about 10 minutes before you remove the dough from the freezer. Line two sheet pans with parchment paper. When ready to bake, peel back the top piece of parchment paper. Use a fork to prick the surface, one prick every inch or so. Cut the large sheet of dough into 16 even pieces, then pull them off the bottom piece of parchment. Divide the graham crackers between the sheet pans, spacing them evenly with at least 2 inches between each cracker. Bake the graham crackers for 6 minutes, then rotate the pans and switch their oven racks and bake for an additional 4 to 8 minutes, or until the cookie springs back when touched in the center. Remove the pans from the oven and transfer to a cooling rack, allowing the graham cracker to cool completely on the pans at room temperature.

Chop and store. Chop the graham crackers into ¼- to ½-inch pieces. Transfer the chopped graham crackers to an airtight container or zippered plastic bag and store in the freezer for up to 3 months.

Brownies

MAKES ABOUT 5 CUPS BROWNIE CUBES

I have an on-and-off love affair with brownie sundaes that is almost always on. I'll devour a brownie sundae at Chili's as fast as I will at a boutique scoop shop. I also love the texture of brownie chunks scattered inside an ice cream, like a sundae in a scoop. In this recipe, the brownies are a little underbaked, which increases their chewiness when frozen. I've found great success substituting gluten-free flour blends in this recipe, so those of you with sensitivities need never abandon brownie sundaes again!

Dark chocolate	**Cocoa powder**
225g | 8 ounces	25g | ⅓ cup
Butter	**Sugar**
165g | ¾ cup	150g | ¾ cup

Salt	Flour
3g | ½ teaspoon	125g | 1 cup
Eggs	**Baking powder**
150g | 3 large	3g | ½ teaspoon

Preheat the oven and prepare the pan. Preheat the oven to 325°F. Lightly oil an 8-inch square baking pan, then line the bottom with parchment paper.

Melt the chocolate, butter, and cocoa powder. Place the chocolate, butter, and cocoa powder in a metal bowl. Find a pot with a mouth a few inches smaller than the bowl, and fill it with 2 inches of water. Boil the water over high heat, reduce the heat to a simmer, then nest the metal bowl of chocolate over it. Stir occasionally, until the chocolate and butter are completely smooth, then set aside in a warm place. (Alternatively, you can melt these ingredients in the microwave.)

Whip the sugar and eggs. Place the sugar, salt, and eggs in the bowl of a stand mixer fitted with the whip attachment. Whip on high speed for 5 minutes, until the eggs triple in volume and become the color of butter.

Mix in the chocolate. Stop the mixer and add the chocolate mixture. Mix again on medium speed until the chocolate has been evenly incorporated.

Mix in the flour. Remove the bowl from the mixer, and detach the whip attachment. Scrape the sides of the bowl thoroughly, making sure to reach all the way to the bottom. Add the flour and baking powder to the bowl, and place back on the stand mixer, this time fitted with the paddle attachment. Mix on low speed until the flour has been combined, then increase the mixer to medium speed and mix for 2 minutes more. This extra mixing develops the gluten (in wheat flour) and makes for chewier brownies.

Bake and cool the brownies. Transfer the brownie batter to the pan, and spread evenly. Bake the brownies for 15 minutes, then rotate the pan front to back and bake for another 5 to 10 minutes, just until the edges begin to pull away from the sides of the pan. Remove the brownie from the oven, and transfer to a wire rack to cool. Once cool, transfer the pan with the brownie to the freezer for 2 hours, or up to 1 day.

Cut and store. When the brownie is firm, remove it from the pan, peel off the parchment paper, and transfer to a cutting board. Cut the brownie into ¾-inch cubes. Store in an airtight container in the freezer for up to 1 month.

Gooey Butter Cake

MAKES ABOUT 2 QUARTS CAKE CUBES

I was unaware of gooey butter cake until I moved to the Midwest, but once I heard someone speak those three words together I knew I had to eat it. Gooey butter cake is a St. Louis anomaly, halfway between a cake and a pecanless pecan pie. The cake is prepared in layers—a dense dough is pressed into the bottom of the pan, and a syrupy cream cheese goo is poured over the top. During baking, the two layers transform into a single cake, one that is far greater than the sum of its parts.

I replaced the commonly required corn syrup with glucose, taking advantage of glucose's reduced sweetness. Corn syrup can be used instead, if that's what you have—just get your sweet tooth ready! Cubes of this gooey cake can be added to any ice cream you like, but I find it is happiest in a scoop of Cream Cheese Ice Cream (page 90).

For the butter cake layer	*For the gooey layer*
Flour	**Cream cheese, softened**
250g | 2 cups	225g | 8 ounces
Granulated sugar	**Grated lemon zest**
300g | 1½ cups	2g | 1 teaspoon
Baking powder	**Confectioners' sugar**
10g | 2 teaspoons	300g | 2½ cups
Salt	**Glucose**
3g | ½ teaspoon	150g | ⅔ cup
Egg	**Salt**
50g | 1 large	5g | 1 teaspoon
Butter, melted	**Eggs**
100g | ½ cup	100g | 2 large
	Butter, melted
	100g | ½ cup
	Vanilla extract
	10g | 2 teaspoons
	Almond extract
	1g | ¼ teaspoon

Preheat the oven and prepare the pan. Preheat the oven to 350°F. Lightly oil an 8 by 10-inch baking pan and line the bottom with parchment paper.

Mix the cake dough and press into the pan. Stir together the flour, granulated sugar, baking powder, and salt in the bowl of a stand mixer fitted with the paddle attachment. Add the egg and melted butter at once, and beat on low speed until everything comes together into an even dough. Transfer the dough to the pan and press it into the bottom evenly.

Mix the gooey layer and add it to the pan. Make sure the cream cheese isn't so cold that the food processor will lock up as it tries to blend it. Place the cream cheese, lemon zest, confectioners' sugar, glucose, and salt in the bowl of a food processor, and process until evenly combined. Scrape the sides of the bowl and add the eggs, pulsing until evenly mixed. Add the melted butter, vanilla, and almond extract, and process until the mixture is completely smooth, scraping the sides of the bowl as necessary. Transfer the gooey layer to the pan, and spread it evenly to the edges.

Bake the cake. Bake for 45 minutes. Give the cake a little poke in the center, breaking through the crust to inspect the filling. If it shimmies just a little, like Jell-o, the cake is ready to come out of the oven. If it's still oozy, bake for 10 more minutes. Transfer the pan to a wire rack to cool completely.

Freeze, cut, and store. Carefully loosen the edge of the cake from the pan, and place the pan in the freezer for 2 hours, or up to 24 hours. When the cake is frozen solid, transfer it to a cutting board. Remove the parchment paper, and cut the cake into 1-inch cubes. Place the cubes back in the freezer until frozen solid again, then store in a container, tightly covered, in the freezer for up to 1 month.

Cheesecake

MAKES 1½ QUARTS OF CHEESECAKE PIECES

This is a wonderful cheesecake recipe on its own, one that has served me with equal success both inside a scoop and inside a crumb crust. You will need to make this cake in order to make the Cheesecake Ice Cream on page 91. Luckily, you'll end up with more cheesecake than you need for one batch of ice cream. This cheesecake also makes a great add-in, chopped up and added to fruity sherbets or dark chocolate and coffee ice creams, and the extras can live in your freezer until you settle on another flavor of ice cream to add the chunks to!

Sugar
180g | ¾ cup

Vanilla bean
1 whole (or 10g |
2 teaspoons vanilla extract)

Cream cheese, softened
450g | 1 pound

Salt
2g | ⅓ teaspoon

Crème fraîche
50g | ¼ cup

Milk
50g | ¼ cup

Cornstarch
10g | 2 tablespoons

Eggs
100g | 2 large

Preheat the oven and prepare the pan. Preheat the oven to 300°F. Prepare an 8-inch square cake pan or a 9-inch round cake pan by lightly greasing it and lining the bottom with parchment paper.

Mix the sugar with the vanilla. Place the sugar in a small bowl. Split the vanilla bean lengthwise, and using the tip of your knife, scrape the seeds from the bean. Rub the seeds with the sugar until broken up. Sift the slightly clumpy vanilla sugar into the bowl of a stand mixer. (If using vanilla extract, simply place the sugar and vanilla extract in the bowl of a stand mixer.) Save the empty vanilla pod for another use.

Mix in the cream cheese. Add the cream cheese and salt to the bowl, and fit the mixer with the paddle attachment. Mix on a medium speed for 1 minute, until smooth. Scrape the sides of the bowl, add the crème fraîche, and mix on medium speed for 1 minute.

Add the milk and cornstarch. Stir the milk and cornstarch together in a small bowl to make a slurry. Add it to the cheesecake batter, and mix on medium-low speed until evenly incorporated.

Mix in the eggs. Scrape down the sides of the bowl again, making sure to scrape the bottom as well, and add the eggs one at a time, mixing until evenly mixed in between additions (this is especially important if you increase the batch size of this recipe). Remove the bowl, scrape the sides and bottom of the bowl, and then replace on the mixer and mix on medium-high speed for 1 more minute, until perfectly smooth.

Bake. Transfer the batter to the cake pan. Bake for 12 to 15 minutes, until the cheesecake is set in the center. Transfer the pan to a wire rack and let the cake cool completely at room temperature.

To prepare the cheesecake as an ice cream add-in. Place the cheesecake in the freezer for 2 hours, or up to 1 day. When frozen solid, peel off the parchment paper, and cut the cake into ¾-inch pieces. Store the pieces in an airtight container in the freezer for up to 1 month.

To prepare the cheesecake as a puree. If you're making this for the Cheesecake Ice Cream (page 91), scrape the cheesecake into the bowl of a food processor and puree until smooth. Transfer the puree to an airtight container and store it in the refrigerator for up to 1 week.

Marzipan Cake

MAKES ABOUT 1½ QUARTS OF CAKE PIECES

This is one of my favorite cakes. It's made so many appearances on my menus that it was only a matter of time before I started stuffing it into scoops of ice cream. The cake is made with almond paste, a dense, sweet paste made of almonds and sugar. I came across this amazing cake when working with my friend Jason Stratton, who prepared it for his Italian restaurant Spinasse. His recipe instructed me to cream the butter, sugar, and almond paste for 10 minutes, "so it isn't rubbery and dense like your mom's face." His joke lightened both the mood in the kitchen and the cake itself, drawing everyone's attention to the most crucial detail in the recipe.

My version of this cake is soaked in a syrup made from amaretto immediately after it comes out of the oven, giving it the moistest crumb. The syrup also makes it perfect for freezing, as the sugar keeps the cake soft. If you prefer, replace the amaretto with 20g | 1 tablespoon plus 2 teaspoons water and 5g | 1 teaspoon almond extract.

For the cake

Almond paste	Eggs
200g	7 ounces	150g	3 large
Sugar	**Amaretto**
75g	⅓ cup	25g	2 tablespoons
Honey	**Flour**
25g	2 tablespoons	50g	⅓ cup
Butter	**Salt**
100g	½ cup	3g	½ teaspoon

For the syrup

Sugar	Amaretto
50g	¼ cup	25g	2 tablespoons
Water	
25g	2 tablespoons	

Preheat the oven and prepare the pan. Preheat the oven to 350°F. Lightly oil an 8 by 10-inch cake pan and line it with parchment paper.

Mix the almond paste, sugar, and honey. Place the almond paste, sugar, and honey in the bowl of a stand mixer fitted with the paddle attachment. Mix on medium-low speed until the almond paste is fully broken up; depending on your almond paste, this will vary in appearance from sandy to smooth.

Cream the butter. Add the butter to the bowl, and cream on high speed for 5 minutes. Scrape the paddle and the bowl well, and mix on high again for 5 minutes so it's not dense and rubbery like your mom's face.

Mix in the eggs, liqueur, and flour. With the mixer on medium speed, add the eggs, one at a time, mixing for 1 minute after each addition. Scrape the sides of the bowl, add the amaretto, and mix for 1 more minute. Sift the flour into the bowl, add the salt, and mix on low speed until the cake batter comes together.

Bake. Transfer the batter to the pan and spread it to the edges. Bake for 15 to 20 minutes, until the center of the cake springs back when touched.

Prepare the amaretto syrup. While the cake is baking, place the sugar and water in a small saucepan over medium-high heat. Cook the syrup, stirring, until it is clear. Remove the pot from heat and stir in the amaretto.

Soak, cool, and freeze the cake. When the cake is baked, transfer the pan to a wire rack. Use a pastry brush to carefully brush the syrup over the surface of the hot cake. Leave the cake on the rack to cool, then place the pan in the freezer for 2 hours, or up to 24 hours.

Cut and store. When the cake is frozen solid, remove the parchment paper, and cut the cake into 1-inch cubes. Store in an airtight container in the freezer for up to 1 month.

COMPOSED
SCOOPS

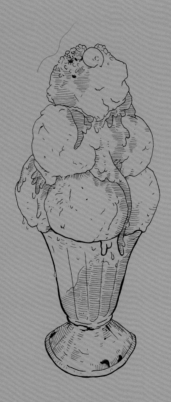

This chapter has the kind of ice creams I most love to eat—complex scoops so packed with different textures and flavors that it's like eating an entire composed dessert in a single bite. I came of age during the reign of Ben and Jerry, who made their mark on the world by packing their pints full of crazy add-ins. At one time, cookie dough ice cream was revolutionary, and these two guys changed the landscape of ice cream for good.

Inspiration for a great scoop can come from anywhere. Some of the flavor and add-in combinations here are spun off from the classic ice creams I grew up on, like Cheesecake Neapolitan (page 196) or Rainbow Sherbet (page 182), made with raspberry, orange, and pineapple. (You'll also learn my technique for combining flavors without them bleeding into each other.)

Some of the scoops are updates of nostalgic Americana, like Chocolate Peanut Butter Brownie Crunch (page 203), which pushes that classic combination over the edge with chunks of brownie, candied Rice Krispies, and a ribbon of peanut butter. Or Strawberry Bubblemallow (page 204), which will capture the heart of anyone who loved bubblegum as a kid, with a ribbon of strawberry and chewy marshmallows packed into a bubblegum ice cream fit for adults.

Some scoops are inspired by the places I've traveled or the people I've met, and many are inspired by desserts from the menus from the restaurants I've worked at. Blueberry-Basil Crumble Ice Cream (page 207) was inspired by the mixed-berry crumbles we served warm at Poppy, with scoops of ice cream infused with the cinnamon basil leaves growing in our garden.

My hope for this chapter is to inspire you. Each of these scoops tells you a little about me, and I know you've got stories to tell, too. Let the people around you, your travels, your childhood memories, the desserts you've eaten, and the flavors you love inspire your own creations. The scoops in this chapter should help you understand how to conceive a composed ice cream, and the recipes in the earlier chapters of this book should help you build any scoop you can dream of.

A couple things, though, before you start. Composed scoops take a little planning on your part, and so I suggest starting these scoops two days before you want to eat these ice creams. It's a long time to wait, I know. But you can make the ice cream base one day, then while it cures in the refrigerator, you can make the add-ins. By the time the ice cream base has cured, the add-ins will be ready, and you can churn your ice cream, layer it, and put it in the freezer to harden. (Note that these scoops require the ice creams to be freshly churned, but not yet frozen solid, to layer in the add-ins. Recipes that swirl two or more flavors together require even more days of planning, churning, and hardening before they are combined.)

You'll see a few recipes with larger yields—specifically, the scoops that swirl more than one flavor of ice cream together. When we tested half-batches of ice creams, we found the slow-churning home machines froze the ice cream before it could be properly whipped, and the results were overly dense and brittle. You'll always get the best results when you fill your ice cream machine with the amount of ice cream recommended by the manufacturer, and for most home machines, this is a quart. For this reason, a few of the recipes make multiple quarts, and I recommend you find a few friends to help you polish off the additional yield. A little extra ice cream rarely goes to waste.

Also, I highly recommend stabilizing your ice cream using one of the "texture agents" for composed scoops. The stabilizer reduces the water activity in the ice cream, which helps keep the add-ins from absorbing the moisture and losing their integrity. This keeps the add-ins fresh inside the ice cream in the freezer for up to two weeks, making the extra effort a more lasting investment.

The Methods

Layering Ribbons or Ripples

Chill the container. Place a storage container in the freezer; you'll want it very cold before you fill it.

Layer the ice cream with the add-ins. Remove the container from the freezer, drizzle a couple spoonfuls of the ribbon over the bottom. Spread one-third of the just-churned ice cream in the container. Drizzle one-third of the ribbon over the ice cream. Repeat this layering two more times. Plunge a spatula through the layers four or five times to distribute the ribbon. (If mixing in multiple ribbons, simply add both or all of the ribbons at the same time, with the same method described above.)

Freeze. Press a piece of plastic wrap directly on the surface of the ice cream, cover the container with a lid, and place it in your freezer for 4 to 12 hours, until completely firm.

Layering Bits

Chill the container. Place a storage container in the freezer; you'll want it very cold before you fill it.

Layer the ice cream with the add-ins. Remove the chilled container from the freezer and scatter a few of the bits on the bottom. Spread one-third of the just-churned ice cream into the container. Sprinkle one-third of the bits over the ice cream. Repeat the layers two more times. Plunge a spatula through the layers four or five times to distribute the bits.

Freeze the ice cream. Press a piece of plastic wrap directly on the surface of the ice cream, cover the container with a lid, and place in the freezer for 4 to 12 hours, until completely firm.

Layering Bits and Ripples

Chill the container. Place a storage container in the freezer; you'll want it very cold before you fill it.

Layer the ice cream with the add-ins. Remove the chilled container from the freezer, drizzle a couple spoonfuls of the ripple, and scatter a few pieces of the bits over the bottom. Spread one-third of the just-churned ice cream into the container. Drizzle one-third of the ripple over the ice cream and sprinkle one-third of the bits over as well. Repeat the layers two more times. Plunge a spatula through the layers four or five times to distribute the add-ins.

Freeze. Press a piece of plastic wrap directly on the surface of the ice cream, cover the container with a lid, and place it in the freezer for 4 to 12 hours, until completely firm.

fig. 1

fig. 2

fig. 3

fig. 4

fig. 1: *Layering bits.*

fig. 2: *Layering in ice cream.*

fig. 3: *Layering in ripples.*

fig. 4: *Layering in more bits.*

Swirling Flavors

Chill the container. Place a large storage container in the freezer; you'll want it very cold before you fill it.

Layer the ingredients. Remove the container from the freezer and place one-third of the freshly churned, soft ice cream into it. Scoop half of the hardened ice cream, in big chunks, into the soft ice cream, floating them like icebergs and spacing them evenly. Cover with half the remaining soft ice cream, making sure to fill in the cracks between the scoops. Add the remaining hardened ice cream in scoops again, then cover with the remaining soft ice cream, making sure every bit of the two flavors is in the container. (If you're swirling 3 flavors, keep one "base" flavor just-churned, and fully harden the other two. Simply add scoops of both frozen flavors, rather than just one, as described above.)

Freeze. Press a piece of plastic wrap directly on the surface of the ice cream, cover the container with a lid, and place it in your freezer for 4 to 12 hours, until completely firm.

fig. 1

fig. 2

fig. 3

fig. 4

fig. 1: *Spreading just-churned ice cream.*

fig. 2: *Adding scoops of hardened ice cream.*

fig. 3: *Covering with soft ice cream.*

fig. 4: *Adding more hardened ice cream.*

Carnival Corn

Makes between 1½ and 2 quarts
ice cream

This flavor is an homage to the shopping
malls of the '80s and '90s, which always
seemed to be anchored on one end by a
caramel popcorn stand, flooding the mall
with its aroma. If you weren't born in the
days of the Mall Rat, then this ice cream
will help transport you to one of the most
(in)glorious eras of indoor shopping in
America's history.

50g | ⅓ cup Buttercrunch Toffee Chunks
(page 157)

50g | 1½ cups Caramel Popcorn
(page 163)

**150g | ¾ cup Creamy Caramel Ribbon,
stirred**
(page 138)

1 batch Popcorn Ice Cream, just churned
(page 92)

*Follow the method for layering bits and ripples on
page 176.*

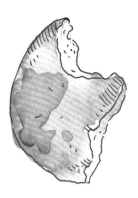

Top-Notch Donut Ice Cream

Makes between 1½ and 2 quarts ice cream

Donut fanatics: this ice cream was created especially for you. Swirling the fudge ripple and sprinkles into this ice cream mimics the chocolate glaze and sprinkles of one of my favorite donuts, but don't stop there! You can replicate any of your favorite donuts by, for example, adding Lemon Curd (page 147) or raspberry jam, or sprinkling in coconut flakes or chocolate jimmies!

150g | ¾ cup Fudge Ripple
(page 138)

15g | 3 tablespoons sprinkles

1 batch Donut Ice Cream, just churned
(page 82)

Follow the method for layering bits and ripples on page 176.

Rainbow Sherbet

Makes between 3 and 3½ quarts
ice cream

This classic flavor takes a few days to make,
particularly if you have a single-use freeze-
the-bowl–style ice cream maker. But you
will be rewarded for your perseverance with
the most delicious rainbow sherbet ever.
Because you need to make three sherbets
for this flavor, you'll find yourself with quite
a bit of Rainbow Sherbet, so plan a party for
all your friends! For plain raspberry sherbet
omit the anise flavors from the Raspberry-
Anise Sherbet (page 106), and for plain
pineapple sherbet, omit the jasmine and
lime from the Pineapple Jasmine Sherbet
(page 104). Don't be tempted to make the
sherbets in half-batches; small batches don't
churn properly in most home machines.

1 batch Blood Orange Sherbet, just churned
(page 100)

1 batch plain raspberry sherbet, hardened
(page 106)

1 batch plain pineapple sherbet, hardened
(page 104)

Follow the method for swirling flavors on page 177.

Bourbon Butter Pecan Supreme

Makes between 1½ and 2 quarts ice cream

When Dove's Luncheonette opened in Chicago, Paul Kahan asked me to make the ice creams for their diner-style dessert menu. I created this riff on the classic American butter pecan, with a boost of flavor from bourbon. I've since added a ribbon of butterscotch, a flavor I know will always win Paul's heart, and I hope yours, too.

200g | 1 cup Butterscotch Ripple
(page 143)

150g | 1 cup Buttered Pecans
(page 154)

1 batch Bourbon Butterscotch Ice Cream, just churned
(page 54)

Follow the method for layering bits and ripples on page 176.

Elementary School Swirl

Makes between 2 and 2½ quarts
ice cream

Those little cups of vanilla and orange
swirls have been upgraded here with a
vanilla custard ice cream and blood orange
sherbet. You can pack this flavor into tiny
cups and serve it with a wooden spoon
if you like, but I find the swirls are too
beautiful to hide.

1 batch Vanilla Ice Cream, just churned
(page 52)

1 batch Blood Orange Sherbet, hardened
(page 100)

Follow the method for swirling flavors on page 177.

Gooey Butter Cake with Candied Lemon

Makes between 1½ and 2 quarts ice cream

The Midwest is home to a special accident called gooey butter cake, which is, as my friend Jane puts it, "like cream cheese frosting baked into the cake." Right she is, and this sticky cake is even better frozen. Here, we've added it to cream cheese ice cream for a bit of tang, and scattered candied lemon bits to brighten the rich scoops.

200g | 1½ cups chunks of Gooey Butter Cake
(page 169)

50g | ⅓ cup Candied Citrus Bits, made with lemon
(page 151) or store bought

1 batch Cream Cheese Ice Cream, just churned
(page 90)

Follow the method for layering bits on page 175.

Mint Chocolate Chip Cookie Dough

Makes between 1 1/2 and 2 quarts
ice cream

My friend Caroline notoriously struggles with making decisions, and thank goodness she does. This mash-up flavor was created in a moment of her indecision when I pressed her for her favorite flavor. "I don't know! Mint Chocolate Chip? Cookie Dough?" she asked me. I simply replied, "Yes," and the two of us have never looked back.

150g | 1 cup Chocolate Chip Cookie Dough pieces
(page 164)

80g | 1/2 cup Classic Chocolate Chunks
(page 156)

1 batch Garden Mint Ice Cream, just churned
(page 84)

Follow the method for layering bits on page 175.

Cookies, Cookies, and Cream

Makes between 1 1/2 and 2 quarts
ice cream

Crushed chocolate cookies are one of the original add-ins, making cookies and cream ice cream. For this variation on the classic, I've used chocolate cookie dough along with bits of deep dark chocolate wafers. It's old-school cookies and cream with new-school cookie dough.

150g | 1 cup diced dough pieces from Chocolate Wafers
(page 165)

150g | 1 cup Chocolate Wafer pieces
(page 165)

1 batch Vanilla Ice Cream, just churned
(page 52)

Follow the method for layering bits on page 175.

Lemony Lemon
Crème Fraîche

Makes between 1 ½ and 2 quarts
ice cream

My Aunt Mary is a bona fide lemon-
head. She will choose a lemon dessert
over all others 100% of the time, and she
is constantly asking me for new lemon
dessert recipes. She even bought herself a
special Microplane just for zesting lemons for making cookies! This ice cream is
for people like Aunt Mary who absolutely
love-love-love lemon. It's puckery enough to
come with a warning label, but for any true
lemon lover, it's a badge of honor.

200g | 1 cup Lemon Curd
(page 147)

**50g | ⅓ cup Candied Citrus Bits,
made with lemon**
(page 151) or store bought

**1 batch Lemon Crème Fraîche Ice Cream,
just churned**
(page 88)

*Follow the method for layering bits and ripples on
page 176.*

Portofino
Cherry Chunk

Makes between 1½ and 2 quarts
ice cream

When I visit my sister Libby in Freiburg,
Germany, we always go to her local shop,
Portofino's, for ice cream. She gets dark
chocolate, and I get "kirsch yogurt," which
is flavored with candied Amarena cherries.
This scoop is like what would happen if we
mashed together our standard orders; I love
the combination of tangy yogurt, bittersweet chocolate, and cherries.

150g | 1 cup Classic Chocolate Chunks
(page 156)

**100g | ½ cup chopped jarred Amarena
cherries, or other candied cherry**

**1 batch Blank Slate Frozen Yogurt,
just churned**
(page 118)

Follow the method for layering bits on page 175.

Cheesecake Neapolitan

Makes between 3 and 3½ quarts ice cream

My friend Jason grew up thinking Neapolitan ice cream was a variety pack, each of his siblings choosing their favorite—chocolate, strawberry, or vanilla—from the carton. Cheesecake Neapolitan swirls the flavors together, replacing the simple vanilla with cheesecake ice cream. With one taste, you'll believe that these three were born to be together.

1 batch Cheesecake Ice Cream, just churned
(page 91)

1 batch Blue Ribbon Chocolate Ice Cream, hardened
(page 78)

1 batch Strawberry Sherbet, hardened
(page 112)

Follow the method for swirling flavors on page 177.

Kid's Play

Makes between 1½ and 2 quarts ice cream

At Avec restaurant, we often served a marzipan cake with fresh raspberries, toasted almonds, and whipped goat cheese. This ice cream perfectly captures that deliciously playful dessert, and the title nods toward the adorable baby goats we would love to feed scoops of this ice cream to.

150g | ¾ cup Strawberry Ripple, made with Raspberry Puree instead
(pages 146, 216)

150g | 1 cup Marzipan Cake cubes
(page 171)

50g | ¼ cup chopped toasted almonds

1 batch Goat Cheese Ice Cream, just churned
(page 83)

Follow the method for layering bits and ripples on page 176.

Cardamom, Plum, and Marzipan

Makes between 1½ and 2 quarts
ice cream

Green Cardamom Ice Cream is the perfect
backdrop for the wonderful flavor of plum
caramel and crumbles of almond-y marzipan cake; the warm spice and sweet almond
intertwine, and the tart caramel brightens it
beautifully. This unique and elegant flavor
came from a summer dessert at Blackbird
restaurant, created when plums were bursting on the local trees, and I've been making
this ice cream since. It's as comfortable on
your back porch as it is at a formal dinner,
and I hope you find the occasion to invite it
into your life.

150g | ¾ cup Plum Caramel
(page 141)

150g | 1½ cups Marzipan Cake cubes
(page 171)

**1 batch Green Cardamom Ice Cream,
just churned**
(page 64)

*Follow the method for layering bits and ripples on
page 176.*

Haystack Ice Cream

Makes between 1½ and 2 quarts
ice cream

My experience with hay-flavored ice cream
in Denmark left an indelible mark on my
palate. I love its toasty, grassy aromas.
Here, the unusual flavor is accompanied
by a ribbon of light summer honey and
blueberry compote. Feel free to substitute
strawberries, blackberries, or raspberries—
they all work wonderfully. For the blueberry
compote, omit the basil from the Blueberry-
Basil Compote on page 145.

150g | ¾ cup light honey

150g | 1 cup plain blueberry compote
(page 145)

**1 batch Toasted Hay Ice Cream,
just churned**
(page 60)

Follow the method for layering ripples on page 175.

Nutterbuddy
Ice Cream

Makes between 1½ and 2 quarts
ice cream

I prepare Nutterbuddies—small crispy
peanut-butter-and-chocolate squares—as
a confection for many of the restaurants
I've worked for, in Seattle and Chicago,
and they've garnered quite a cult following.
This ice cream was created for the legions
of Nutterbuddy fans, and has earned a few
more fans of its own along the way.

**150g | ¾ cup Creamy Caramel Ribbon,
stirred**
(page 138)

200g | 1½ cups Nutterbuddy Crunch
(page 158)

1 batch Vanilla Ice Cream, just churned
(page 52)

*Follow the method for layering bits and ripples on
page 176.*

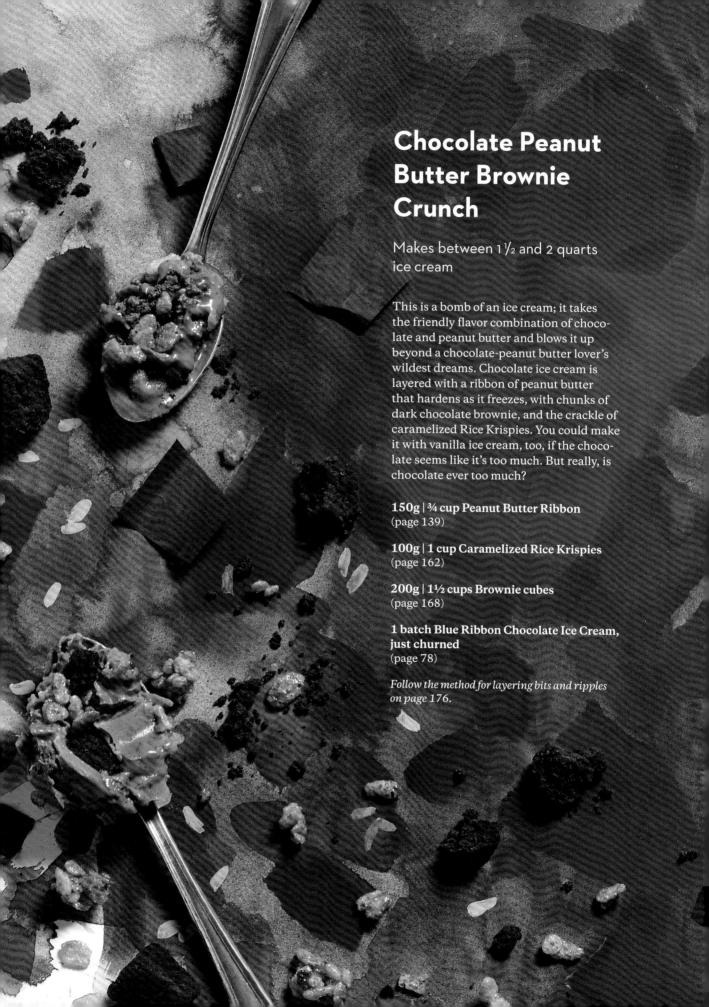

Chocolate Peanut Butter Brownie Crunch

Makes between 1½ and 2 quarts ice cream

This is a bomb of an ice cream; it takes the friendly flavor combination of chocolate and peanut butter and blows it up beyond a chocolate-peanut butter lover's wildest dreams. Chocolate ice cream is layered with a ribbon of peanut butter that hardens as it freezes, with chunks of dark chocolate brownie, and the crackle of caramelized Rice Krispies. You could make it with vanilla ice cream, too, if the chocolate seems like it's too much. But really, is chocolate ever too much?

150g | ¾ cup Peanut Butter Ribbon
(page 139)

100g | 1 cup Caramelized Rice Krispies
(page 162)

200g | 1½ cups Brownie cubes
(page 168)

1 batch Blue Ribbon Chocolate Ice Cream, just churned
(page 78)

Follow the method for layering bits and ripples on page 176.

Strawberry Bubblemallow

Makes between 1½ and 2 quarts ice cream

Bubblegum Ice Cream is the perfect setting for a
ribbon of strawberry and big fluffy pieces of marshmallow. Anyone who loved bubblegum as a kid will
find this suits their inner child and their adult taste
buds at the same time. And it's a perfect ice cream to
make for any little ones running around your life!

150g | ¾ cup Strawberry Ripple
(page 146)

100g | 2 cups Marshmallows
(page 155)

**1 batch Bubblegum Ice Cream,
just churned**
(page 94)

*Follow the method for layering bits and
ripples on page 176.*

Blueberry-Basil Crumble Ice Cream

Makes between 1½ and 2 quarts
ice cream

At Poppy restaurant, we always paired
cinnamon basil ice cream with blueberries, and this ice cream honors that tradition. Blueberry-Basil Compote is rippled
throughout cinnamon basil–scented ice
cream, and the crumble comes from a
handful of crisp hazelnut streusel. It's like
eating blueberry crumble à la mode in each
bite. You could, and should, substitute
any fruit compote for the blueberries and
achieve similar crumble-like results.

200g | 1 cup Blueberry-Basil Compote
(page 145)

**150g | 1 cup Almond-Browned Butter
Streusel, made with hazelnuts instead
of almonds**
(page 159)

**1 batch Cinnamon Basil Ice Cream,
just churned**
(page 80)

*Follow the method for layering bits and ripples on
page 176.*

Tangerine Dreams

Makes between 1½ and 2 quarts
sherbet

This sherbet is perfect for curing the winter
blues. When the holidays are over and
summer is barely a light at the end of the
tunnel, citrus fruits are in the peak of their
season. The Blood Orange Sherbet gets a
facelift by substituting tangy tangerines.
A bright passion fruit caramel winds its
way throughout the ice cream between tiny
wheels of candied kumquats, while crispy
bits of Roasted-Vanilla Meringue offer
sweet refuge from the bright flavors, and a
little texture as well.

**150g | ¾ cup Passion Fruit-Orange
Caramel**
(page 141)

**100g | ½ cup Candied Citrus Bits, made
with kumquat, sliced**
(page 151)

30g | 1 cup Roasted-Vanilla Meringue Bits
(page 150)

**1 batch Blood Orange Sherbet made with
tangerines instead, just churned**
(page 100)

*Follow the method for layering bits and ripples on
page 176.*

That's My Jam

Makes between 1½ and 2 quarts ice cream

Krystle Swendson, a Hawaii native and my former sous chef at Blackbird, is obsessed with milk jam, also known as dulce de leche. She stirs it into her coffee (do it!) and spreads it on toast. She once created a dessert with the flavors of parsnip, milk jam, cranberries, and cookie butter that was so impressive it was quickly turned into an ice cream we all dubbed "That's My Jam." If you are feeling adventurous, you can follow in Krystle's footsteps and infuse a large sliced-up parsnip into the Blank Slate Custard Ice Cream (page 50). You'll find the flavor combination bold and familiar at the same time.

100g | ¾ cup Cookie Butter Bits
(page 154)

150g | ¾ cup Cranberry-Vanilla Compote
(page 145)

100g | ½ cup Milk Jam
(page 142)

1 batch Vanilla Ice Cream, just churned
(page 52)

Follow the method for layering bits and ripples on page 176.

Ricky's Coffee Pretzel Toffee

Makes between 1 ½ and 2 quarts ice cream

Ricky is one of the owners of Blackbird restaurant, as well as my muse. Whenever I need inspiration, I go to Ricky and he says something like "Why don't you add some pretzels, honey bunny? People seem to like those." This ice cream was tailor-made for him, filling his favorite coffee ice cream with pieces of pretzel toffee and big chunks of chocolate. So, here's to Ricky—and here's to you, too. May you have your own Ricky nearby when you are inventing your own ice creams!

150g | ¾ cup Classic Chocolate Chunks
(page 156)

150g | 1½ cups Pretzel Toffee Chunks
(page 157)

1 batch Cold-Press Coffee Ice Cream, just churned
(page 56)

Follow the method for layering bits on page 175.

FRUIT PUREES AND OTHER BASICS

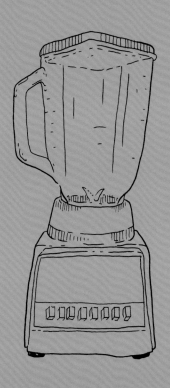

Inverted Sugar Syrup—an alternative to glucose

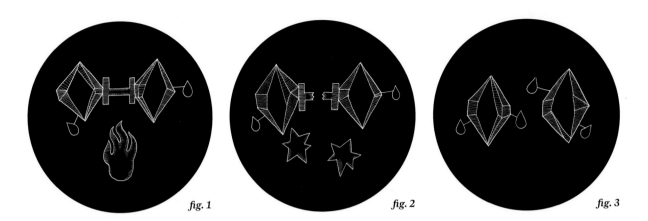

fig. 1
fig. 2
fig. 3

When we tested the recipes in this book, I insisted we shop for ingredients just as most readers would, pushing our carts down the aisles of our neighborhood grocery stores. I know firsthand how hard glucose can be to find, and how expensive it is once you do. You can substitute corn syrup, which is widely available and inexpensive—and a good alternative, in my opinion. In fact, corn syrup is mostly made of glucose! But the corn syrup sold in the grocery store is sweetened with high fructose corn syrup and vanilla flavoring, which deters many people from reaching for it.

There is another option aside from glucose or corn syrup, called inverted sugar syrup, which you can make at home. By boiling granulated sugar with water and an acid, the hydrogen bond that ties the disaccharide together is destroyed, breaking sucrose into two monosaccharides, fructose and glucose; this process is called "inverting the sugar," and the result is called "inverted (or invert) sugar syrup."

Inverted sugar syrup can be exchanged for glucose in any of the recipes in this book, and will keep in your pantry for up to six months. The inverted sugar syrup has the same sweetness as granulated sugar, which is the only drawback to using an inverted sugar syrup instead of the milder glucose. Your ice creams will be sweeter, but the texture will be wonderful!

Inverted Sugar Syrup

MAKES 5 CUPS

Granulated sugar
1000g | 4 cups

Water
500g | 2 cups

Citric or malic acid, or cream of tartar
5g | 1 teaspoon (or 1 tablespoon lemon juice)

Cook the sugar. Place the sugar, water, and acid in a medium pot set over high heat. Cook, stirring to help dissolve the sugar, until the syrup is clear and has come to a boil. Reduce the heat to a simmer, and continue cooking the sugar syrup until a kitchen thermometer reads 245°F.

Cool and store. Remove the pot from heat, and let the syrup cool at room temperature for 1 hour. Transfer it to an airtight container with a lid, and store at room temperature for up to 6 months.

fig. 1: *Applying heat to the disaccharide.*

fig. 2: *Adding acid as well breaks the bond.*

fig. 3: *Split into two monosaccharides, the sugar can now grasp twice the amount of water.*

Dairy at Home

Homemade Greek Yogurt

MAKES 2¼ CUPS

Ten years ago, every frozen yogurt recipe in this book would have started with instructions for draining the watery whey from the yogurt. Thankfully, though, Greek yogurt has flooded the market, already strained for you. However, there are times when you may still want to strain your own yogurt—perhaps if you are culturing it yourself, or are buying it from a local dairy.

Of course, you don't need a recipe to strain yogurt. Just set it in a lined strainer over a container to catch the whey. But for our frozen-yogurt purposes, you want to eliminate a precise amount of the whey. This ensures your strained yogurt has just the right amount of water in it when you turn it into frozen yogurt—you don't want it to freeze too thick or too hard. For the best results, let the yogurt strain overnight, then weigh the yogurt and add enough of the collected whey back in to bring the total weight to the precise number given here.

When you're finished, don't throw the whey down the drain; it is a wonderfully acidic addition to baked goods whenever water is called for, particularly when making sourdough breads.

Yogurt
800g | 4 cups

Strain the yogurt. Line a fine-mesh basket strainer with paper towels, a coffee filter, or cheesecloth. Place the strainer over a bowl, then add the yogurt to the strainer. Cover the bowl and strainer with plastic wrap, and place it in the refrigerator for 8 hours.

Measure and adjust. Transfer the yogurt from the strainer to a clean, medium bowl and stir until it is smooth and even. Measure the yogurt, and add enough of the collected whey to bring the total weight to 450g | 2¼ cups. Stir the yogurt and added whey until smooth, and use it in any of the recipes called for in this book.

Crème Fraîche

MAKES 2 CUPS

Richer and denser than sour cream, crème fraîche's tanginess makes it a favorite ingredient of many pastry chefs. It can be relatively expensive or, for some people, a little tricky to find. Happily, it's easy to make at home.

Heavy cream
440g | 1 pint

Lemon juice
5g | 1 teaspoon

Cultured buttermilk
15g | 1 tablespoon

Heat the cream. Pour the cream into a small saucepan and place it over medium-low heat. Cook the cream, stirring occasionally, until just warm to the touch, 90 to 95°F. Remove the pot from heat, stir in the buttermilk and lemon juice, and pour the cream into an airtight container with a lid.

Culture. Place the container in a warm place in your kitchen, and leave it for 48 hours. During this time the active cultures in the buttermilk will transform your cream into rich, tangy crème fraiche.

Chill and store. Transfer the crème fraîche to the refrigerator, and let it set up for 2 hours before you use it. The crème fraîche will keep for up to 2 weeks in the refrigerator. (Do not freeze; the ice crystals will damage the butterfat and the crème fraîche will split when thawed.)

Fruit Purees

In general, making fruit puree is fairly straight-forward: you cut up fruit, cook it until soft, and then blend in a blender. But I like to vary the technique to highlight the characteristics of each fruit. Sometimes I cook it, sometimes I leave it raw, and in some cases, I freeze the fruit and then thaw it to let ice crystallization help break down the cell walls, releasing the juices.

Each of the following yields about 1 pint of puree, which is enough to make any of the recipes in this book, plus a little extra. You can tuck the leftover fruit puree into lemonades, iced teas, or make ripples with it using the recipes on page 146.

If the fruit you are using is out of season, I recommend that you buy good-quality frozen fruit instead of the relatively flavorless stuff in your produce aisle. These frozen fruits are usually harvested in season, when they are plentiful and flavorful, then tucked away in giant freezers for the remainder of the year.

Strawberry or Raspberry Puree

MAKES ABOUT 2 CUPS

Strawberries or raspberries
450g | 1 pound

Prep and freeze. For strawberries, cut off the hulls or leaves and rinse the berries in cold water. Drain and slice the berries in half, or, if very large, in quarters. For raspberries, carefully rinse in cold water, then drain. Put the strawberries or raspberries on a sheet pan and place in the freezer. Freeze for 4 hours, until completely solid, then remove and place in a blender.

Thaw and blend. Let the fruit thaw in the blender for 30 to 45 minutes, until 75 percent thawed. (If you don't wish to wait, skip the freezing step and blend the raw fruit; but this freeze-thaw technique breaks open the berries' cells for more intense flavor.) Blend the berries on medium speed until they start to break down, then increase the speed to high and liquefy them. Stop the blender to press the fruit to the bottom of the blender, if necessary.

Strain and store. When the puree is smooth, pass it through a fine-mesh sieve to catch as many seeds as possible. Store the puree in an airtight container in the refrigerator for 1 week, or in the freezer for 3 months.

Blackberry, Black Raspberry, Blueberry, or Huckleberry Puree

MAKES ABOUT 2 CUPS

Blackberries, black raspberries, blueberries, or huckleberries
450g | 1 pound

Clean and cook. Remove any leaves from among the berries and rinse the berries in cold water. Place in a medium saucepan set over medium heat. Cook, stirring with a spoon to help mash the berries, until they start to bubble. Reduce the heat to low and simmer the berries for 5 to 10 minutes, until they have released all their juices and are bubbling and fragrant.

Puree. Transfer the berries to a blender and let cool for 10 minutes. Blend on high speed until smooth. (If using blackberries or black raspberries, do not overblend or the seeds will break up too small to be removed with a sieve.)

Strain and store. Pass the puree through a fine-mesh sieve to catch as many seeds as possible. (Blueberry and huckleberry seeds are tiny and may be hard to catch; use the finest mesh strainer you have and push the puree through using a rubber spatula.) Store the berry puree in an airtight container in the refrigerator for 1 week, or in the freezer for 3 months.

Concord Grape Puree

MAKES ABOUT 2 CUPS

Concord grapes
450g | 1 pound

Clean and seed. Pick the grapes from the stems and place the grapes in a medium bowl. Cover with cold water and rinse thoroughly, then strain off the water. Carefully cut each grape in half and remove the seeds. (Alternatively, if you have a ricer or a food mill, you can cook the grapes whole and pass the cooked fruit through the ricer before you puree it. Do not puree the grapes with the seeds; the blades will break up the seeds and make your grape puree bitter and tannic.)

Cook. Place the grapes in a medium pot over medium heat. Cook, stirring with a spoon to help mash the grapes, until they start to bubble. Reduce the heat to low and simmer the grapes for 5 to 10 minutes, until they have released all their juices and are bubbling and fragrant.

Puree. Transfer the grapes to a blender and let them cool for 10 minutes. Blend on high speed until smooth and even.

Strain and store. Pass the puree through a fine-mesh sieve. Store in an airtight container in the refrigerator for 1 week, or in the freezer for 3 months.

Apricot, Plum, or Cherry Puree

MAKES ABOUT 2 CUPS

Apricots, plums, or cherries
600g | 1⅓ pounds (8 to 12 apricots or plums)

Clean and pit. For apricots or plums, rinse and cut each in half, and remove the pits. Cut the fruits into 1-inch pieces. For cherries, rinse and pit with a cherry pitter or cut in half and pit by hand.

Cook. Place the fruit in a medium heavy-bottomed saucepan. Cover and cook over medium heat, stirring every now and then with a spoon to help mash the fruit. When the fruit is bubbling, uncover the pot, reduce the heat to low, and simmer for 5 to 10 minutes, until the fruit has released its juices. Continue mashing the fruit with a spoon as necessary.

Puree. Transfer the fruit to a blender and let it cool for 10 minutes. Blend on high speed until smooth. Stop the blender occasionally to push the fruit down, if necessary.

Strain and store. Pass the puree through a fine-mesh sieve. Store in an airtight container in the refrigerator for 1 week, or in the freezer for 3 months.

Peach Puree

MAKES ABOUT 2 CUPS

Peaches
550g | 1¼ pounds (3 to 5 peaches)

Peel and pit the peaches. Bring 6 quarts of water to a boil. Fill a medium bowl with ice water. Cut small X's on the bottom of each peach. Carefully lower the peaches into the boiling water for 30 seconds, then immediately transfer to the ice bath. When the peaches have cooled, the skin should peel right off. (This only works with ripe peaches. If your peaches are still firm and not quite ripe, try peeling the skin with a sharp paring knife.) Cut each peach in half and remove the pit, then cut each peach half into four pieces. (For clingstone peaches, slice the peach off the pit with a knife.)

Cook. Place the peaches in a medium heavy-bottomed saucepan over medium heat. Cover and cook, stirring every now and then with a spoon to help mash the peaches, until the peaches are bubbling. Uncover the pot, reduce the heat to low, and simmer the peaches for 5 to 10 minutes, until they have released their juices. Continue mashing the fruit as necessary.

Puree. Transfer the peaches to a blender and let cool for 10 minutes. Blend the peaches on high speed until they are smooth.

Strain and store. Pass the puree through a fine-mesh sieve. Store in an airtight container in the refrigerator for 1 week, or in the freezer for 3 months.

Mango or Nectarine Puree

MAKES ABOUT 2 CUPS

Mangos
900g | 2 pounds (3 to 8 mangos)

or

Nectarines*
550g | 1¼ pounds (3 to 5 nectarines)

*Note: If the nectarines are anything less than fully ripe, cook them as you would peaches (page 217), but leave their skins intact.

Pit and prep. For mangos, peel and slice the fruit from the large flat pit in the center. For nectarines, rinse in cold water, cut in half, and remove the pits. Cut the nectarine halves into four pieces.

Puree. Transfer the fruit to a blender. Blend on medium speed until the fruit starts to break down, then increase the speed to high and liquefy. Stop the blender to press the fruit to the bottom, if necessary.

Strain and store. Pass the puree through a fine-mesh sieve. Store in an airtight container in the refrigerator for 1 week, or in the freezer for 3 months.

Roasted Pumpkin Puree

MAKES ABOUT 3 CUPS, DEPENDING ON THE SIZE OF YOUR PUMPKIN

1 small pumpkin
900g | 2 pounds

Vegetable oil
as needed

Prep and roast. Preheat the oven to 350°F. Cut the pumpkin in half and scoop out the seeds and strings; discard or save for another use. Lightly rub the pumpkin halves with a little vegetable oil, and place cut side down on a sheet pan. Roast for 1 hour, or until the flesh is very soft and yielding when a knife is inserted.

Peel and puree. Let the pumpkin cool completely. Separate the peel from the flesh, discarding the peel. Place the flesh in the bowl of a food processor (it will be too thick for a blender) and process for 5 minutes, until very smooth.

Strain and store. Use the curved bottom of a ladle to push the pumpkin puree through a basket strainer, catching any lumpy bits of pumpkin. Store the puree in an airtight container in the refrigerator for 2 days, or in the freezer for up to 3 months.

Rhubarb Puree

MAKES ABOUT 2 CUPS

Rhubarb
450g | 1 pound (4 to 8 stalks)

Clean and prep. Rinse the rhubarb stalks, using your hands to remove any dirt that remains. Chop the stems into 1-inch pieces.

Cook. Place the rhubarb in a medium heavy-bottomed saucepan over medium heat. Cover and cook, stirring occasionally with a spoon to help mash the rhubarb, until it is bubbling. Uncover the pot, reduce the heat to low, and simmer the fruit for 5 to 10 minutes, until it has released all its juices. Continue mashing the fruit, as necessary.

Puree. Transfer the rhubarb to a blender and let cool for 10 minutes. Blend on medium speed until it starts to break down, then increase the speed to high and liquefy it. Stop the blender to press the fruit to the bottom of the cup, if necessary.

Strain and store. Pass the puree through a fine-mesh sieve. Store in an airtight container in the refrigerator for 1 week, or in the freezer for 3 months.

Passion Fruit Juice

MAKES ABOUT 1/2 CUP

Passion fruits
8 large or 12 small

Collect and pulse the pulp. Cut the passion fruits in half and scoop out the seeds and pulp into a blender or food processor. Pulse in two or three quick bursts to break apart the fruit and flesh. Avoid breaking up the seeds too much.

Strain and store. Set a fine-mesh sieve over a bowl and pour the passion fruit into the sieve. Use the back of a spoon to press as much of the juice through the sieve as possible. Discard the seeds. Store the juice in a container in the refrigerator for 1 week, or in the freezer for 3 months.

APPENDIX

Ratios, or How Math Will Help You Make Your Own Ice Cream Recipes

Underneath every ice cream recipe—any recipe, really—is a ratio of ingredients. It's not the kind of thing you need to see on a regular basis, and likely it's something most home cooks will never look at or need. As a professional, it was years before I started looking under the hood of my recipes to examine the ratio of ingredients—looking beyond the *measurements* of each ingredient to examine how the percentage of each ingredient related it to the other ingredients, and the recipe as a whole. Understanding the ratio is crucial for those who want to start customizing ice cream recipes to suit their own flavor and textural desires.

The key to using ratios is to remember that the total always equals 100%, so if you increase the amount of one thing in your recipe, you have to decrease something else. The ingredients in an ice cream recipe directly interact with each other, so making adjustments to ingredients within the ratio protects you from throwing everything out of whack as you increase or decrease ingredients. For example, you can reduce the richness of an ice cream by lowering the quantity of cream, but a simple removal of a small amount of cream alters the ratio of every other ingredient. Instead, you might reduce the percentage of cream in the recipe, and increase the percentage of another single ingredient, like milk. Likewise, if you increase the ratio of an ingredient that contains sugar, like chocolate, you can reduce the ratio of the sugar in the recipe, keeping it within a workable range to maintain textural success. Learning to break down recipes into their ratios, and knowing the workable range for each ingredient, allows you to tinker with those recipes while ensuring textural success.

All that said, this is *math*, so put your thinking cap on, get your calculators out, and read on!

The Working and Functional Ratios

I'm going to discuss two different ratios in this section. One is what I call the *working ratio*, and buried deep within that, is what I call the *functional ratio*. The working ratio defines each real-world ingredient that you work with, like the cream and milk, as a percentage of the whole recipe. Within this ratio, we can make basic changes to the ingredients, like increasing cream for richness or exchanging granulated sugar for brown sugar. The working ratio also allows you to scale any recipe up and down precisely. And using the working ratio, we can easily compare different recipes to each other—for instance, if a recipe is giving you problems and you want to compare it to one that you know is successful to see where you need to troubleshoot it.

The *functional ratio* measures the components *within* each real-world ingredient that function to define the texture of the ice cream, like the butterfat in the cream, and the protein in the milk. If you remember "The Five Components of Ice Cream" (page 12), you have a good idea why balancing these components is so important. By understanding the functional ratio, we can tinker with the *structure* of the ice cream itself—and achieve a precise texture—further informing our choices in our ingredients, or troubleshooting a recipe that isn't working quite right.

Using the Working Ratio

The first rule of the working ratio is that you must work with a scale. Weight is the only truly consistent way to measure a variety of ingredients—try weighing a cup of water versus a cup of whipped cream—and since the point of a ratio is to measure ingredients against one another, consistency is necessary.

Also, we must break with standard measurements and work in the metric system—with grams. There is just no good way to use the ratio, which allows you to do math with regular numbers, with cups and tablespoons. Can you tell me, off the top of your head, how 6 egg yolks directly relates to ¾ of a cup of sugar? Don't bother; even I couldn't do that! But I'm sure you can tell me how 100g of egg yolks relates to 150g of sugar. Here's the good news: since all the recipes in this book are batched for a nice, round number of 1000g (we can ignore the ingredients that are strained out, or a few grams of salt here or there), the math will be pretty easy.

We will use our Blank Slate Philadelphia-Style Ice Cream (page 76) as an example. Those numbers followed by a percentage sign? They are the percentage of the ingredient as a part of the recipe as a whole, or the ratio.

MILK POWDER (2%)	20g | 3 tablespoons
SUGAR (15%)	150g | ¾ cup
CREAM (38%)	380g | 1¾ cups plus 2 tablespoons
MILK (40%)	400g | 2 cups
GLUCOSE (5%)	50g | ¼ cup

To find the working ratio, take the quantity of each ingredient and divide it by the batch size to find the percentage. The math is already done for you in the recipes in this book, but looking at our example, you'll see "Milk powder . . . 20g." To find its percentage in the ratio, take 20 (grams of this ingredient) and divide it by 1000 (total grams of the batch size); you get .02, or 2%.

Armed with the working ratio of your recipe, you can tune your recipe like a mixing board in a recording studio: more bass here, less treble there.

Since you must keep the total at 100%, the ratio will help guide you when you want to make ingredient substitutions.

When you make changes in a recipe purely to alter the flavor, you can simply swap like ingredients for like. For example, if you want to add honey to a recipe for its flavor, measure it and take out its weight in sugar so as to keep the ratio of sugar the same. Likewise, if you want to use buttermilk for some tang, exchange it for an equal amount of milk. If you want to use sour cream, decrease the same amount of the cream. If you remember to always substitute like ingredients for like, you should be able to adjust your recipes safely and maintain the textural success of your scoops.

But you can also intentionally alter the ratios to adjust the texture of your ice cream. In ice cream recipes, milk is what's known as the "balancing agent." That is, it is the ingredient that changes to accommodate the other ingredients. So, every time you want to change the ratio of a textural ingredient, you also adjust the milk to make up for it. If you want richer custards and add an additional 5% in egg yolks, you remove 5% in milk. If you want a lighter custard and decrease 5% in egg yolks, you add 5% in milk. If you want a denser ice cream and add 2% in milk solids, you remove 2% in milk. (There *are* limits on how much you can change the ratios, though, which we'll get to in the discussion on the functional ratio, page 226.)

How to Find the Working Ratio in Any Recipe

What if you want to look under the hood of one of your old tried-and-true recipes? First, convert the recipe into metric measurements. Here's a guide to common conversions.

METRIC CONVERSIONS	
Milk and cream	1 ounce = 28g
	Remember 3 teaspoons = 1 tablespoon = 1/16 cup
and other liquids	1 cup = 240g
	1/16 cup milk = 15g milk = 1 tablespoon milk (1 teaspoon = 5g)
Sugar	1 ounce = 28g
	1/16 cup sugar = 13g sugar = 1 tablespoon sugar
	(1 teaspoon = 4.3g)
	1 cup = 210g
Glucose	1 ounce = 28g
	1/16 cup glucose = 18g glucose = 1 tablespoon glucose
	(1 teaspoon = 6g)
	1 cup = 275g

Let's try it with the ingredients in a simple vanilla ice cream recipe; this is from the Cuisinart Instruction and Recipe Booklet. Use the Metric Conversions table to translate the standard measurements to grams. Then add them up to get your total batch weight.

Whole milk	1 1/2 cups	1.5 × 240 = 360g
Granulated sugar	1 1/8 cups	1.125 × 210 = 236g
Heavy cream	3 cups	3 × 240 = 720g
Vanilla extract	1 1/2 teaspoons	1.5 × 5g = 7g
TOTAL WEIGHT		1,323g

Now, you can find the percentage of the batch each ingredient represents, thus defining the ratio. To do this, divide each individual ingredient by the total weight of the recipe as you did above.

Whole milk	360/1,323 = 27%
Granulated sugar	236/1,323 = 18%
Heavy cream	720/1,323 = 54.5%
Vanilla extract	7/1,323 = .5%

Using the Working Ratio to Compare and Adjust Recipes

Now, let's look at that ice cream side by side with the Blank Slate Philadelphia-Style Ice Cream recipe (page 76), adjusted to include vanilla extract by exchanging 1% of the recipe's weight in milk for vanilla extract. If we just looked at the standard measurements, it would look like this:

	US	THEM
Whole milk	2 cups	1½ cups
Milk powder	2 tablespoons	n/a
Sugar	³/₄ cup	1⅛ cups
Glucose	¼ cup	n/a
Cream	1³/₄ cups + 2 tablespoons	3 cups
Vanilla extract	2 teaspoons	1½ teaspoons

I don't know about you, but it's really hard for me to tell exactly how much these recipes are alike, or are different. If you add our sugars together, you get 1 cup. Compared to the 1⅛ cups in their recipe, it would seem our recipe has less sugar.

Now, let's look at the ratios next to each other, and right away you can see how different the recipes are. We have more total sugar (sugar + glucose) than they do, after all!

	US	THEM
Whole milk	37%	27%
Milk powder	2%	0%
Sugar	15%	18%
Glucose	5%	0%
Cream	40%	54.5%
Vanilla extract	1%	.5%
TOTAL	100%	100%

What do you do with this information? You can use the ratio to create exactly the same recipe at any batch size. This is crucial for anyone making ice cream in a professional setting. Simply doubling and quadrupling recipes that have, say, rounded off to the nearest tablespoon can often lead to exaggerating imperfections in ingredient quantities; over time, you'll end up with inconsistencies in your results, the same way a game of telephone eventually distorts the truth. By designating a batch size, say 4,500g, then multiplying the ratio of each ingredient by the batch size, you ensure perfect results.

More important, you can draw on the ratio to help you troubleshoot and adjust a texturally unsuccessful ice cream. You can compare troublesome recipes with successful ones to get a sense of what might be the problem. And you can adjust the texture by dialing the ratio of specific ingredients up and down. As you reach the point in your ice-cream-making career that you desire ultimate control over the texture of your ice cream, the ratio will be your playground, and you can follow these guidelines:

- Increase the ratio of sugar for a softer ice cream. Decrease the ratio of sugar to help the ice cream firm up. (Remember that if you want to increase the sugar but not necessarily the sweetness, you can increase the glucose rather than the white sugar and vice versa.)
- Increase the ratio of fat for a richer, slower-melting ice cream. Decrease the ratio of fat for a leaner, faster-melting ice cream, or to make room for another high-fat ingredient.
- Increase the ratio of milk powder for a denser, chewier ice cream. Decrease the ratio of milk powder for a more lickable, refreshing ice cream.
- Increase the ratio of egg yolks for a richer, chewier custard. Decrease the ratio of egg yolks for a lighter, less rich custard.

The Functional Ratio

As mentioned earlier, within the working ratio is another ratio—the functional ratio. The functional ratio describes the quantity of four of the five components that create the texture of your ice cream. In order to understand the structure of your ice cream, you need to know not just how much cream or milk or glucose you have, but, going deeper, how much fat, milk-solids-non-fat (which is ice cream pro-speak for proteins), water (which will become ice), sugar, and total solids are in your recipe.

While the working ratio tells you the percentage of milk (40%) or cream (38%) used in the Blank Slate Philadelphia-Style recipe (page 76), the functional ratio tells you the percentage of butterfat the milk and cream provide in the recipe (17.5%).

If the working ratio is the bones of your recipe, the functional ratio is the marrow. To be honest, it's not necessary to read any further, unless you are very curious or very serious about making ice cream. In fact, I doubted whether to include this information in the book at all, because it's unlikely most readers will ever apply it in a home setting. But my mission in writing this book was to present all the information and let the readers decide when and how they wanted to use it. So, here it is— the functional ratio in all its glory. If you grasp the ratio of the functional components of ice cream, and at the very least can calculate for exact percentages of fat in your ice cream, you will have complete domination over all future ice creams and can rule the world!!!! Um, at least rule the world of ice cream.

How to Find the Functional Ratio

You need to understand a few numbers to find the ratio of the functional ingredients: water, fat, sugar, total solids, and milk-solids-non-fat. (Again, this is what I usually refer to as protein, but here we'll refer to it as the pros do—MSNF—as there technically are minerals, lactose, and a few other components to it as well.)

ASSUMED PERCENTAGES OF EACH INGREDIENT	
Heavy cream contains	40% butterfat, 9% MSNF, and 51% water
Milk contains	4% fat, 9% MSNF, and 87% water
Sugar contains	100% sugar
Glucose syrup contains	90% sugar and 10% water
Milk powder contains	100% MSNF

To find the percentages of the functional ratio in the ingredients listed in a recipe, you multiply the percentage in the working ratio by the percentage assumed from each ingredient. Let's use the Blank Slate Philadelphia-Style Ice Cream ratio again for this example.

CREAM	40%
MILK	38%
MILK POWDER	2%
SUGAR	15%
GLUCOSE	5%

TO CALCULATE FOR TOTAL WATER	
Water in the cream	51% water in cream by 40% cream in recipe = $.51 \times .40 = 20.5\%$ water
Water in the milk	87% water in milk by 38% milk in recipe = $.87 \times .38 = 33\%$ water
Water in the glucose	10% water in glucose by 5% glucose in recipe = $.10 \times .5 = .5\%$ water
Total water in our recipe	$20.5\% + 33\% + .5\% = 54\%$ water

TO CALCULATE FOR TOTAL BUTTERFAT

Butterfat in the cream	40% butterfat in heavy cream by 40% cream in recipe = .40 × .40 = 16% butterfat
Butterfat in the milk	4% butterfat in whole milk by 38% milk in recipe = .04 × .38 = 1.5% butterfat
Total butterfat in our recipe	16% + 1.5% = 17.5%

TO CALCULATE FOR TOTAL SUGARS

Sugar in the sugar	100% sugar in sugar by 15% sugar in recipe = 1 × .15 = 15% sugar
Sugar in the glucose	90% sugar in the glucose by 5% glucose in recipe = .9 × .05 = 4.5% sugar
Total sugar in our recipe	15% + 4.5% = 19.5% sugar

TO CALCULATE FOR TOTAL MSNF

MSNF in the cream	9% MSNF in cream by 40% cream in recipe = .09 × .40 = 3.5% MSNF
MSNF in the milk	9% MSNF in milk by 38% milk in recipe = .09 × .38 = 3.5% MSNF
MSNF in the milk powder	100% MSNF in milk powder by 2% milk powder in recipe = 1 × .02 = 2% MSNF
Total MSNF in our recipe	3.5% + 3.5% + 2% = 9% MSNF

The big reveal! Under the hood of our blank slate ice cream recipe, the functional ratio is:

9%	total MSNF
19.5%	total sugar
17.5%	total butterfat
54%	total water

How to Use the Functional Ratio

After all this math, the functional ratio really wouldn't be that helpful without some boundaries. That is, for each of these functional components, there are minimum, maximum, and ideal percentages to make what I consider the best textured ice cream around. "Ideal" is a matter of taste, but the minimums and maximums are key, as recipes that go outside these bounds usually produce obviously flawed ice creams. As you play with the functional ratios of recipes to adjust them, use this chart, as I do with my own recipes.

CUSTARD ICE CREAM

Butterfat	10% minimum	11–12% ideal	14% maximum
Sugar	15% minimum	17–19% ideal	22% maximum
Egg yolk	5% minimum	9–12% ideal	15% maximum
MSNF	5% minimum	6–8% ideal	10% maximum
Water	45% minimum	54–57% ideal	60% maximum

PHILADELPHIA-STYLE ICE CREAM

Butterfat	12% minimum	15–18% ideal	20% maximum
Sugar	15% minimum	17–19% ideal	22% maximum
MSNF	6% minimum	8–10% ideal	12% maximum
Water	50% minimum	54–57% ideal	60% maximum

SHERBET

Butterfat	2% minimum	3–4% ideal	6% maximum
Added* sugar	20% minimum	23–25% ideal	27% maximum
MSNF	2% minimum	3–4% ideal	5% maximum
Water	50% minimum	54–57% ideal	60% maximum

*This is "added" because the fruit purees in the recipes contain their own sugar as well.

FROZEN YOGURT

Butterfat	5% minimum	7–8% ideal	10% maximum
Sugar	20% minimum	23–25% ideal	27% maximum
MSNF	10% minimum	11–12% ideal	15% maximum
Water	50% minimum	54–57% ideal	60% maximum

The Last Thing about Ratios!

The very very last thing, I promise! If you add the milk solids and sugars, you get a number called "total-solids-non-fat." This number describes the density and relates to the chewiness of the ice cream (and it correlates to a legal requirement as well). Each manufacturer calculates the desired total solids for their ice creams, as well as total-solids-non-fat. If you are looking for an extra chew to your ice cream, or less of one, you'll need to look at your total-solids-non-fat.

So our blank slate ice cream would be described by a manufacturer as:

17.5%	butterfat	
19.5%	total sugars	} **28.5%** total-solids-non-fat
9%	total MSNF	
46%	total solids	
54%	water	

Now that I've got you into the marrow of our Philadelphia-Style Blank Slate ice cream recipe, let's look at the functional ratio in a premium ice cream from the "top shelf" of your grocery store freezer:

14%	butterfat	
16%	total sugars	} **25%** total-solids-non-fat
9%	total MSNF	
39%	total solids	
61%	water	

The water in a commercial ice cream is *way* higher than in the Blank Slate Philadelphia-Style recipe. At home, you are at a disadvantage mechanically. You simply can't freeze your ice cream fast enough to avoid the growth of large ice crystals. Instead, you tactically eliminate some of that water; by increasing the solid components in your recipe—like fat, sugar, and MSNF—you have less water to deal with. The remainder of the water is managed with a little help from grabby-handed proteins and sugars (see pages 16–19), but most of all, from additional ingredients called stabilizers. Flip to page 26 to read more about these helpful agents of water control!

It might not seem very sexy here, deep in the guts of our ice creams. But think of it as when a shrunken Dennis Quaid got to fly around inside Meg Ryan's body in the movie *Innerspace*. Sexy on the outside, yes, but it turns out she was cool to see on the inside, too. It was down here in the innerspace of ice cream that I started building the recipes included in this book, fine-tuned from the inside out for success in your home kitchen. And now, if you want, you can do the same.

Acknowledgments

This book wouldn't have been possible without the help of so many people. First, my family, who encouraged me to pursue a life of cooking, then bore the burden of my restaurant schedule along with me. My sisters, Libby and Sarah, who have let me drag them to every ice cream shop in every town we have traveled to, from San Francisco to Lake Como, where Libby orders chocolate every single time, and Sarah adventures into flavors unknown with me. My mom, Denise, who believed I could do anything and first placed cookbooks in my hands, supporting my growing passion for all things sweet, and who always ordered coffee ice cream. My dad, Bob, who introduced me to the joys of dining and gladly ate every one of my early attempts at cooking; he preferred to stir Hershey's syrup into vanilla ice cream, and I can still hear the sound of his spoon whipping against the bowl. My Grandma Eva, who began my baking lessons as soon as I could reach the counter. My Auntie Ellen, who first shared my love of deep, dark chocolate, and Uncle Dick, who loves hard-pack ice cream so much he carries a cooler to Husky Deli to keep his pints ultra-cold on the ride home. Aunt Mary, who shares my love of puckery lemon; Aunt Joanne, who always shares recipes and can be counted on to order vanilla; and Uncle Bill, who first introduced me to the black raspberry ice cream from Halo Farms. To Kelsey Crick, my dear friend, on-call scooper, and frequent taste tester. Becca Cressell, whose friendship and love have seen me through most of my life, and who's eaten almost every flavor of ice cream I've made. And to Dan Salls, my main squeeze, partner in crime, and all-around best guy, who supported me at every step of this book, despite his lack of a sweet tooth.

I'd like to thank my agent, Amy Collins, who fielded every question I had, who brought the idea of this book forth out of a conversation over pie, seeing it through until it was a reality, and who held meetings at her house just so I could play with her cats. To Judy Amster, cookbook collector and surrogate mother, who informed me one January it was my time to write a book, just a month before Amy appeared in my life. And the people who have supported my early attempts at writing: Hillel Cooperman, who invited me to write for Tasting Menu; Cassandra Landry, my editor at *Chefs Feed;* and Ryan Heely, my editor at *Lucky Peach.* To Francis Lam, my editor at Potter, who has guided me through this process with extensive support and a light but authoritative touch, who humored my obscure references and let me get away with things like *BFF* and *ride or die.* To Ian Dingman, the designer at Potter, who turned my writing and the artwork into a beautiful book.

To Anna Posey, my dear friend, who created the insanely beautiful illustrations for the entire book. To Andrea D'Agosto, the photographer, worked more professionally than anyone I've met and integrated Anna's illustrations into photography in a way none of us had ever seen. To Lauren Anderson, food stylist extraordinaire, who scooped and scooped ice cream for us, making it look more delicious than I could have. And to the prop stylist, Alicia Buszczek, whose extensive Surface Library prop collection and beautiful touch applying it helped the ice cream look like more than just a scoop.

Thank you to all the pastry cooks and sous chefs who have worked so hard in the kitchens I've managed, helping me refine ice cream after ice cream into what have ultimately become the recipes in this book: Lana, Beth, Allison, Janet, Stephanie, Ben, Craig, Kara, Molly, Krystal, Danielle, Harry, Crystal, Caroline, Roberto Mayonnaise, Amy D, Amy G, Dave, Ruth, Meredith, Lance, Aja, and Amelia. And to Jane Katte, who tested and tested these recipes in my house, with 4 machines churning at a time, washing every dish by hand. Special thanks to Donald Sutherland, who opened up his Guitard Studio to me to prepare for the photo shoot, and to Leah Choi, who spent three days with me making every recipe for the photo shoot.

To the chefs who let me run wild in their kitchens making any ice cream I could dream of: Scott Carsberg, Amy McCray, Johnny Zhu, Jerry Traunfeld, Nicolai Norregaard, Sherry Yard, David Posey, Perry Hendrix, and most of all, Paul Kahan, who has supported my ice cream endeavors wholeheartedly inside and outside his kitchens. To the people who have taught me about ice cream along the way, particularly Chris Young, who first opened up the can of worms that is ice cream science for me, and who offered so much early support in my understanding of it. To Jeni of house Splendid, who's been an open book regarding ice cream and business, and a constant inspiration as an artist and as an entrepreneur. And Dr. Bob Roberts and Dr. Arun Kilara, who put together the the Penn State Ice Cream short course.

And finally, I want to thank all the ice cream lovers out there who will pick up this book and use it to make ice cream. Without you, this book would have no need to exist. It is for you I wrote every word, designed every flavor, and carefully selected every piece of information in this book. Thank you for loving ice cream enough to make it yourself.

Index

Note: Page references in italics indicate photographs.

DON'T CRY
OVER SPILLED
ICE CREAM

Melted Ice Cream Cake

Makes one 9-inch double layer cake

Melted ice cream (any flavor)
800g | 1 quart

Eggs
100g | 2 large

Sugar
50g | ¼ cup

Flour
260g | 2 cups

Baking powder
10g | 2 teaspoons

Salt
2g | ¼ teaspoon

Fudge Ripple
250g | 1 cup (page 138)

Cream
500g | 1 pint, whipped
(can be sweetened with
50g | ¼ cup sugar)

Candied cherries
24

Bananas
2 medium, peeled and sliced

If our ice cream-making adventures only had happily-ever-afters, we'd live in an enchanted kingdom and get to ride Pegasus to work and eat all the ice cream we wanted and never get tummy aches. Sadly, no matter how long I wait with sugar cubes in hand for my winged chauffeur to arrive, I still live in a world where even my best attempts at ice cream don't always make the cut.

After a few years of hurriedly pouring buttered, soggy, bland, or icy ice creams down the drain before anyone could see my failures, I realized I could capitalize on my less than stellar scoops. With a couple eggs and a little flour, a melted ice cream can be baked into a cake! The texture is dense and moist, as if a cupcake and a muffin had a baby.

Melted ice cream cake can be baked with just about any flavor and come out A-okay. You can bake the batter as cupcakes or in rounds, and layer ice cream between them for a literal ice cream cake. One of my favorite ways to bake melted ice cream cake is inside ice cream cones. As a child my mother would make these for me to bring to school for my birthday, a treat to share with the kids in my class. Use the flat-bottomed cake cones, balanced carefully on a sheet pan, and reduce the bake time to 15-20 minutes.

After the melted ice cream cakes are baked and cooled, you can layer them with some of the components of a banana split for a truly spectacular, ice cream-inspired cake.

Preheat the oven and prepare the pans. Preheat the oven to 350°F. Lightly spray two 9-inch round cake pans with cooking spray or a light coating of oil. Line the pans with 9-inch circles of parchment paper.

Mix the cake batter. Place the melted ice cream in a large bowl and whisk until smooth. Add the eggs, and whisk until well combined. Sift the flour, baking powder, and salt into the bowl, and fold the cake batter together with a spatula until smooth.

Bake. Divide the batter between the two pans and use a spatula to spread evenly. Bake for 20 to 25 minutes, until a toothpick inserted in the center comes out clean or the cake springs back to the touch. Remove the cakes from the oven and let cool in the pans.

Make the layers. Carefully run a knife around the edge of each pan and invert the cakes onto a plate. Peel the parchment off the bottoms. Transfer one cake to a cake plate and top with half the Fudge Ripple, then the whipped cream. Distribute half the cherries and bananas across the whipped cream. Gently place the second layer on top, and cover with the ripple and whipped cream. Neatly arrange the remaining bananas and cherries in a ring around the top edge of the cake. Keep the cake chilled until you are ready to serve it.

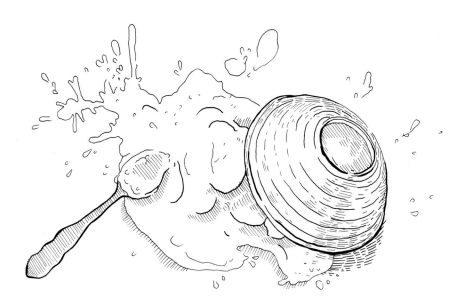

Library of Congress
Cataloging-in-Publication Data
Names: Cree, Dana, author.
Title: Hello, My Name is Ice Cream / Dana
Cree; photographs by Andrea D'Agosto ;
illustrations by Anna Posey.
Description: First edition. | New York:
Clarkson Potter, 2017.
Identifiers: LCCN 2016039388 (print)
| LCCN 2016041469 (ebook) | ISBN
9780451495372 (hardback) | ISBN
9780451495389 (Ebook)
Subjects: LCSH: Ice cream, ices, etc. |
Frozen desserts. | BISAC: COOKING /
Courses & Dishes / Desserts. | COOKING
/ Specific Ingredients / Dairy. | LCGFT:
Cookbooks.

Classification: LCC TX795 .C73 2017 (print)
| LCC TX795 (ebook) | DDC 641.86/2—dc23
LC record available at https://lccn.loc.
gov/2016039388.

ISBN 978-0-451-49537-2
Ebook ISBN 978-0-451-49538-9

Printed in China

Book and cover design by Ian Dingman
Cover photographs by Andrea D'Agosto
Cover illustrations by Anna Posey

3 5 7 9 10 8 6 4

First Edition